The

COOK BOOK
OF RARE AND
VALUABLE RECIPES

TO WHICH IS ADDED, THE
COMPLETE FAMILY DOCTOR

This facsimile edition of *The Cook Book of Rare and Valuable Recipes* was reproduced by permission from the volume in the collection of the American Antiquarian Society (AAS), Worcester, Massachusetts. Founded in 1812 by Isaiah Thomas, a Revolutionary War patriot and successful printer and publisher, the Society is a research library documenting the life of Americans from the colonial era through 1876. AAS aims to collect, preserve, and make available as complete a record as possible of the printed materials from the early American experience. The cookbook collection includes approximately 1,100 volumes.

OTHER BOOKS IN
THE AMERICAN ANTIQUARIAN SOCIETY
COOKBOOK COLLECTION

The Hygienic Cook Book, by John Harvey Kellogg

Jewish Cookery Book, by Esther Levy

The Kansas Home Cook-Book, by the Ladies of Leavenworth

Mackenzie's Five Thousand Receipts in All the Useful and Domestic Arts, by Colin Mackenzie

Miss Beecher's Domestic Receipt Book, by Catharine Beecher

Miss Leslie's New Cookery Book, by Eliza Leslie

Modern Cookery, In All Its Branches, by Eliza Acton and Sarah J. Hale

Modern Domestic Cookery, and *Useful Receipt Book*, by W. A. Henderson

The Modern Family Receipt Book, by Mrs. Mary Holland

Mrs. Hale's New Cook Book, by Mrs. Sarah J. Hale

Mrs. Owen's Illinois Cook Book, by Mrs. T.J.V. Owens

Mrs. Porter's New Southern Cookery Book, by Mrs. M.E. Porter

My Mother's Cook Book, by Ladies of St. Louis

The National Cook Book, by Eliza Leslie

New American Cookery, by An American Lady

The New Art of Cookery, by Richard Briggs

The New England Cook Book

The New England Economical Housekeeper, and Family Receipt Book, by Esther A. Howland

The New Housekeeper's Manual, by Catherine E. Beecher and Harriet Beecher Stowe

The New Hydropathic Cook Book, by Russell Thacher Trall

The New Whole Art of Confectionary, by W.Young

Nouvelle Cuisiniere Canadienne

One Thousand Valuable Secrets in the Elegant and Useful Arts

The Pantropheon, by Alexis Soyer

The People's Manual, by Perrin Bliss

The Philosophy of Eating, by Albert Bellows

The Physiology of Taste, by Jean A. Brillat-Savarin

The Picayune's Creole Cookbook, by The Picayune

The Practical Distiller, by John Wyeth

Presbyterian Cook Book

Science in the Kitchen, by Thomas Hopkins and Mrs. L.A. Hopkins

Seventy-Five Receipts for Pastry, Cakes, and Sweetmeats, by Eliza Leslie

The Times' Recipes, by The New York Times

Total Abstinence Cookery

A Treatise on Bread, by Sylvester Graham

Vegetable Diet, by William Alcott

The Virginia Housewife, by Mary Randolph

What to Do with the Cold Mutton

What to Eat and How to Cook It, by Joseph Cowan

The Young Housekeeper, by William Alcott

The

COOK BOOK
OF RARE AND
VALUABLE RECIPES

TO WHICH IS ADDED, THE
COMPLETE FAMILY DOCTOR

Andrews McMeel
Publishing, LLC
Kansas City • Sydney • London

Andrews McMeel Publishing, LLC
an Andrews McMeel Universal company
1130 Walnut Street, Kansas City, Missouri 64106

www.andrewsmcmeel.com

ISBN: 978-1-4494-5511-8

ATTENTION: SCHOOLS AND BUSINESSES
Andrews McMeel books are available at quantity discounts with
bulk purchase for educational, business, or sales promotional use. For
information, please e-mail the Andrews McMeel Publishing Special Sales
Department: specialsales@amuniversal.com

THE

COOK BOOK

OF

RARE AND VALUABLE RECIPES.

TO WHICH IS ADDED, THE

COMPLETE FAMILY DOCTOR

COMPILED BY AN EMINENT PHYSICIAN,

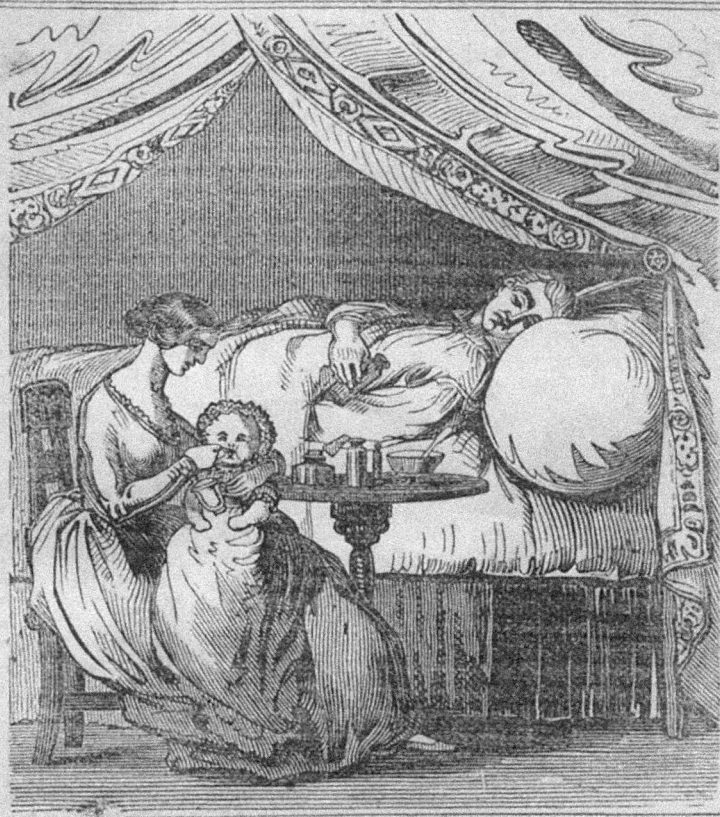

FISHER & BROTHER,
No 15 NORTH SIXTH STREET, PHILADELPHIA ;
74 CHATHAM STREET, NEW YORK ;
71 COURT STREET, BOSTON ;
62 BALTIMORE STREET, BALTIMORE.

REMARKS ON COOKING.

In every rank those deserve the greatest praise, who best acquit themselves of the duties which their station requires. Indeed, this line of conduct is not a matter of choice but of necessity, if we would maintain the dignity of our character as rational beings.

In the variety of female acquirements, though domestic occupations stand not so high in esteem as they formerly did, yet when neglected they produce much human misery. There was a time when ladies knew nothing *beyond* their own family concerns; but in the present day there are many who know nothing *about* them. Each of these extremes should be avoided; but there is no way to unite in the female character, cultivation of talents and habits of usefulness? Happily there are still great numbers in every situation, whose example proves that this is possible. Instances may be found of ladies in the higher walks of life, who condescend to examine the accounts of their house-steward; and, by overlooking and wisely directing the expenditure of that part of their husbands' income which falls under their own inspection, avoid the inconveniences of embarrassed circumstances.

The direction of the *table* is no inconsiderable branch of a lady's concern, as it involves judgment in expenditure, respectability of appearance, and the comfort of her husband and those who partake of their hospitality.

If a lady has never been accustomed while single, to think of family management, let her not upon that account fear that she cannot attain it; she may consult others who are more experienced, and acquaint herself with the necessary quantities of the several articles of family expenditure, in proportion to the number it consists of, the proper prices to pay, &c., &c.

A minute account of the annual income, and the times of payment, should be taken in writing; likewise an estimate of the supposed amount of each article of expence; and those who are early accustomed to calculations on domestic articles, will acquire so accurate a knowledge of what their establishment requires, as will give them the happy medium between prodigality and parsimony, without acquiring the character of meanness.

Many families have owed their prosperity full as much to the propriety of female management, as to the knowledge and activity of the father.

The following hints may be useful as well as economical :—

Every article should be kept in the place best suited to it, as much waste may be thereby avoided.

Vegetables will be kept best on a stone floor, if the air be excluded.—Meat in a cold dry place.—Sugar and sweetmeats require a dry place ; so does salt.—Candles, cold, but not damp,—Dried meats, hams, &c., the same. All sorts of seeds for puddings, saloop, rice, &c., should be close covered, to preserve from insects : but that will not prevent it, if long kept.

Bread is so heavy an article of expence, that all waste should be guarded against; and having it cut in a room will tend much to prevent it.—It should not be cut until a day old. Earthen pans and covers keep it best.

Straw to lay apples on should be quite dry, to prevent a musty taste.

Large pears should be tied up by the stalk.

Basil, savoury, or knotted marjoram, or thyme, to be used when herbs are ordered ; but with discretion, as they are very pungent.

The best means to preserve blankets from moths is to fold them and lay them under the feather-beds that are in use ; and they should be shaken occasionally. When soiled, they should be washed, not scoured.

Soda, by softening the water, saves a great deal of soap. It should be melted in a large jug of water, some of which pour into the tubs and boiler, and when the lather becomes weak, add more. The new improvement in soft soap, is, if properly used, a saving of near half in quantity.

A 2

BROILING.

Cleanliness is extremely essential in this mode of cookery.

Keep your gridiron quite clean between the bars, and bright on the top : when it is hot, wipe it well with a linen cloth: just before you use it, rub the bars with clean mutton suet, to prevent the meat being marked by the gridiron.

Take care to prepare your fire in time, so that it may burn quite clear : a brisk and clear fire is indispensible, or you cannot give your meat that browning which constitutes the perfection of this mode of cookery, and gives a relish to food it cannot receive any other way.

The chops or slices should be from half to three-quarters of an inch in thickness; if thicker, they will be done too much on the outside before the inside is done enough.

Be diligently attentive to watch the moment that any thing is done : never hasten any thing that is broiling, lest you make smoke and spoil it.

Let the bars of the gridiron be all hot through, but yet not burning hot upon the surface ; this is the perfect and fine condition of the gridiron.

Upright gridirons are the best, as they can be used at any fire without fear of smoke ; and the gravy is preserved in the trough under them.

N. B. Broils must be brought to table hot as possible; set a dish to heat when you put your chops on the gridirons, from whence to the mouth their progress must be as quick as possible.

When the fire is not clear, the business of the gridiron may be done by the Dutch oven or bonnet.

Take care to have a very clear, brisk fire ; throw a little salt on it ; make the gridiron hot, and set it slanting to prevent the fat from dropping into the fire, and making a smoke. It requires more practice and care than is generally supposed to do steaks to a nicety ; and for want of these little attentions, this very common dish, which every body is supposed capable of dressing, seldom comes to the table in perfection.

Ask those you cook for, if they like it under, or thoroughly done ; and what accompaniments they like best, it is usual to put a table-spoonful of ketchup, or a little minced eschalot into a dish before the fire ; while you are broiling, turn the steak, &c., with a pair of steak tongs, it will be done in about ten or fifteen minutes ; rub a bit of butter over it, and send it up garnished with pickles and finely-scraped horse-radish.

BAKING.

Baking is one of the cheapest and most convenient ways of dressing a dinner in small families ; and I may say, that the oven is often the only kitchen a poor man has, if he wishes to enjoy a joint of meat.

I do not mean to deny the superior excellence of roasting to baking ; but some joints when baked, so nearly approach to the same when roasted, that I have known them to be carried to the table, and eaten as such with great satisfaction.

Legs, and loins of pork, legs of mutton, fillets of veal, and many other joints, will bake to great advantage if the meat be good ; I mean well-fed, rather inclined to be fat ; if the meat be poor, no baker can give satisfaction.

When baking a poor joint of meat before it has been half baked, I have seen it start from the bone, and shrivel up scarcely to be believed.

Besides those joints above mentioned, I shall enumerate a few baked dishes which I can particularly recommend

A pig, when sent to the baker prepared for baking, should have its ears and tail covered with buttered paper properly fastened on, and a bit of butter tied up in a piece of linen to baste the back with, otherwise it will be apt to blister; with a proper share of attention from the baker, I consider this way equal to a roasted one.

A goose prepared the same as for roasting, taking care to have it on a stand, and when half done to turn the other side upwards. A duck the same.

A buttock of beef the following way is particularly fine. After it has been in salt about a week, to be well washed, and put into a brown earthen pan with

THE ART OF COOKING.

a pint of water; cover the pan tight with two or three thicknesses of cap or foolscap paper: never cover anything that is to be baked with brown paper, the pitch and tar that is in brown paper will give the meat a smoky, bad taste: give it four or five hours in a moderately heated oven.

A ham (if not too old) put in soak for an hour, taken out and wiped, crust made sufficient to cover it all over, and baked in a moderately heated oven, cuts fuller of gravy, and of a finer flavor, than a boiled one. I have been in the habit of baking small codfish, haddock, and mackerel, with a dust of flour, and some bits of butter put on them; eels, when large and stuffed; herrings and sprats, in a brown pan, with vinegar and a little spice, and tied over with paper. A rabbit, prepared the same way as for roasting, with a few pieces of butter, and a little drop of milk put into the dish, and basted several times, will be found nearly equal to roasting; or cut it up, season it properly, put it into a jar or pan, and cover it over and bake it in a moderate oven for about three hours. In the same manner, I have been in the habit of baking legs and shins of beef, ox cheeks, &c., prepared with a seasoning of onions, turnips, &c.; they will take about four hours; let them stand till cold, to skim off the fat, then warm it up all together, or part, as you may want it.

The time each of the above articles should take depends much upon the state of the oven, and I do consider the baker a sufficient judge, if they are sent to him in time, he must be very neglectful if they are not ready at the time they are ordered.

BOILING.

This most simple of culinary processes is not often performed in perfection. It does not require quite so much nicety and attention as roasting; to skim the pot well, and keep it really boiling (the slower the better) all the while, to know how long is required for doing the joint, &c., and to take it up at the critical moment when it is done enough, comprehends almost the whole art and mystery. This, however, demands a patient and perpetual vigilance, of which few persons are capable.

The cook must take especial care that the water really boils all the while she is cooking, or she will be deceived in the time; and make up a sufficient fire at first to last all the time, without much mending or stirring. A frugal cook will manage with much less fire for boiling than she uses for roasting.

When the pot is coming to the boil there will always, from the cleanest meat and the cleanest water, rise a scum to the top of it, proceeding partly from the water; this must be carefully taken off as soon as it rises.

On this depends the good appearance of all boiled things. When you have skimmed well, put in some cold water, which will throw up the rest of the scum.

The oftener it is skimmed, and the cleaner the top of the water is kept, the sweeter and the cleaner will be the meat.

If left alone, it soon boils down and sticks the meat, which instead of looking delicately white and nice, will have that coarse and filthy appearance we have too often to complain of, and the butcher and poulterer be blamed for the carelessness of the cook in not skimming her pot.

Many put in milk, to make what they boil look white: but this does more harm than good: others wrap it up in a cloth; but these are needless precautions; if the scum be attentively removed, meat will have much more delicate color and finer flavor than it has when muffled up. This may give rather more trouble, but those who wish to excel in their art must only consider how the processes of it can be most perfectly performed; a cook who has a proper pride and pleasure in her business, will make this her maxim on all occasions.

It is desirable that meat for boiling be of an equal thickness, or, before thicker parts are done enough, the thinner will be done too much.

Put your meat into cold water, in proportion of about a quart of water to a pound of meat; it should be covered

THE ART OF COOKING.

with water during the whole process of boiling but not drowned in it; the less water, provided the meat be covered with it, the more savory will be the meat, and the better will be the broth.

The water should be heated gradually, according to the thickness, &c. f the article boiled. For instance, a eg of mutton of ten pounds weight hould be placed over a moderate fire, which will gradually make the water hot, without causing it to boil for about forty minutes; if the water boils much sooner, the meat will be hardened, and shrink up as if it was scorched: by keeping the water a certain time heating without boiling, the fibres of the meat are dilated, and it yields a quantity of scum, which must be taken off as soon as it rises.

A thermometer having been placed in water in that state which cooks call gentle simmering, the heat was 212°, i. e. the same degree as the strongest boiling.

Two mutton chops were covered with cold water; one boiled a gallop, while the other simmered very gently for three-quarters of an hour: the chop which was slowly simmered was decidedly superior to that which was boiled; it was much tenderer, more juicy, and much higher flavored. The liquor which boiled fast was in like proportion more savory, and when cold had much more fat on its surface. This explains why quick boiling renders meat hard, &c., because its juices are extracted in a greater degree.

Reckon the time from its first coming to a boil.

The old rule of 15 minutes to a pound of meat, we think rather too little; the slower it boils, the tenderer, the plumper, and whiter it will be.

For those who choose their food thoroughly cooked (which all will who have any regard for their stomachs,) twenty minutes to a pound for fresh, and rather more for salted meat, will not be found too much for gentle simmering by the side of the fire, allowing more or less time according to the thickness of the joint, and the coldness of the weather; to know the state of which, let a thermometer be placed in the pantry; and when it falls below 40°, tell your cook to give rather more time in both roasting and boiling, always remembering the slower it boils the better.

Without some practice it is difficult to teach any art: and cooks seem to suppose they must be right, if they put meat into a pot, and set it over the fire for a certain time, making no allowance whether it simmers without a bubble or boils a gallop.

Fresh killed meat will take much longer time boiling than that which has been kept till it is what the butchers call ripe; and longer in cold than in warm weather; if it be frozen it must be thawed before boiling or before roasting; if it be fresh-killed it will be tough and hard, if you stew it ever so gently. In cold weather the night before the day you dress it bring it into a place of which the temperature is not less than 45 degrees of Fahrenheit's thermometer.

The size of the boiling-pots should be adapted to what they are to contain; the larger the saucepan the more room it takes upon the fire, and a larger quantity of water requires a proportionate increase of fire to boil it.

In small families we recommend block-tin saucepans, &c., as lightest and safest. If proper care be taken of them, and they are well cleaned, they are by far the cheapest; the purchase of a new tin saucepan being little more than the expense of tinning a copper one.

Let the covers of your boiling-pots fit close, not only to prevent unnecessary evaporation of the water, but to prevent the escape of the nutritive matter, which must then remain either in the meat or in the broth; and the smoke is prevented from insinuating itself under the edge of the lid, and so giving the meat a bad taste.

FRYING.

Frying is often a convenient mode of cookery; it may be performed by a fire which will not do for roasting or boiling; and by the introduction of a pan between the meat and the fire things get more equally dressed

THE ART OF COOKING.

The Dutch oven or bonnet is a very convenient utensil for small things, and a very useful substitute for the jack, the gridiron, or frying-pan.

A frying-pan should be about four inches deep, with a perfectly flat and thick bottom, twelve inches long and nine broad, with perpendicular sides, and must be half filled with fat ; good frying is, in fact, boiling in fat. To make sure that the pan is quite clean, rub a little fat over it, and then make it warm, and wipe it out with a clean cloth.

Be very particular in frying, never to use any oil, butter, lard, or drippings but what is quite clean, fresh, and free from salt. Any thing dirty spoils the look ; any thing bad-tasted or stale, spoils the flavor ; and salt prevents its browning.

For general purposes, and especially for fish, clean fresh lard is not near so expensive as oil or clarified butter, and does almost as well. Butter often burns before you are aware of it ; and what you fry will get a dark and dirty appearance.

To know when the fat is of a proper heat, according to what you are to fry, is the real secret in frying.

To fry fish, parsley, potatoes, or any thing that is watery, your fire must be very clear, and the fat quite hot ; which you may be pretty sure of, when it has done hissing, and is still. We cannot insist too strongly on this point : if the fat is not very hot, you cannot fry fish either to a good color, or firm and crisp.

ROASTING.

The first preparation for roasting is to take care that the spit be properly cleaned with sand and water ; nothing else. When it has been well scoured with this, dry it with a clean cloth. If spits are wiped clean as soon as the meat is drawn from them, and while they are hot, a very little cleaning will be required.

Make up the fire in time ; let it be proportioned to the dinner to be dressed, and about three or four inches longer at each end than the thing to be roasted, or the ends of the meat cannot be done nice and brown

A cook must be as particular to proportion her fire to the business she has to do, as a chemist : the degree of heat most desirable for dressing the different sorts of food ought to be attended to with the utmost precision.

Never put meat down to a burned-up fire, if you can possibly avoid it ; but should the fire become fierce, place the spit at a considerable distance, and allow a little more time.

Preserve the fat, by covering it with paper, for this purpose called " kitchen paper," and tie it on with a fine twine ; pins and skewers can by no means be allowed : there are so many taps to let out the gravy ; besides, the paper often starts from them and catches fire, to the great injury of the meat.

If the thing to be roasted be thin and tender, the fire should be little and brisk ; when you have a large joint to roast, make up a sound, strong fire, equally good in every part, or your meat cannot be equally roasted, nor have that uniform color which constitues the beauty of good roasting.

Half an hour before your meat is done, make some gravy, and just before you take it up, put it nearer the fire to brown it. If you wish to froth it, baste it, and dredge it with flour carefully, you cannot do this delicacy nice without a very good light. The common fault seems to be using too much flour. The meat should have a fine light varnish of froth, not the appearance of being covered with a paste. Those who are particular about the froth use butter instead of drippings.

SOUPS.

To extract the strength from the meat, long and slow boiling is necessary, but care must be taken that the pot is never off the boil. All soups are better for being made the day before they are to be used, and they should then be strained into earthen pans. When soup has jellied in the pan, it should not be removed into another, as breaking it will occasion its becoming sour sooner than it would otherwise do : when in danger of not keeping, it should be boiled up.

To Roast Wild Fowl.—The flavor is best preserved without stuffing. Put pepper, salt, and a piece of butter into each.

Wild fowl require much less dressing than tame: they should be served of a fine colour, and well frothed up. A rich brown gravy should be sent in the dish; and when the breast is cut into slices, before taking off the bone; a squeeze of lemon, with pepper and salt, is a great improvement to the flavour.

To take off the fishy taste which wild fowl sometimes have, put an onion, salt, and hot water into the dripping pan, and baste them with the first ten minutes with this; then take away the pan, and baste constantly with butter.

Ruffs and Reeves.—Are skewered as quails; put bars of bacon over them, and roast them about ten minutes. Serve with a good gravy in the dish.

Wild Ducks, Teal, Widgeon, Dunbirds, &c., should be taken up with the gravy in Baste them with butter, sprinkle a little salt before they are taken up, put a good gravy upon them, and serve with shallot-sauce, in a boat.

Woodcocks, Snipes, and Quails, keep good for several days. Roast them without drawing, and serve on toast. Butter only should be eaten with them, gravy takes off the fine flavour. The thigh and back are esteemed the most

To dress Plovers.—Roast the green ones in the same way as woodcocks and quails, without drawing; and serve on a toast. Gray Plovers may either roasted, or stewed, with gravy, herbs, and spice.

To Roast Ortolans. — Pick and singe, but do not draw them. Tie on a bird-spit and roast them. Some persons like bacon in slices tied between them, but the taste of it spoils the flavour of the Ortolan. Cover them with crumbs of bread.

Breast of Mutton. — Cut off the superfluous fat, and roast and serve as meat with stewed cucumbers; or eat cold, covered with chopped parsley. Or half broil, and then grill before the fire, in which case cover with crumbs and herbs, and serve with caper sauce. Or, if boned, take off a good deal of the fat, and cover it with bread, herbs, and seasoning, then roll and boil, and serve with chopped walnuts, or capers and butter.

To Roast a Hog's Head.—Choose a fine young head, clean it well, and put bread and sage as for a pig; sew it up tight, and on a string or hanging jack, roast it as a pig, and serve with the same sauce.

To Roast a Leg of Pork.—Choose a small leg of fine young pork; cut a slit in the knuckle with a sharp knife and fill the space with sage and onion chopped, and a little pepper and salt. When half done, score the skin in slices, but do not cut deeper than the outer rind.

Apple sauce and potatoes should be served to eat with it.

Sweetbreads Roasted.—Parboil two large ones; when cold, lard them with bacon, and roast them in a Dutch oven. For sauce, plain butter, and mushroom catsup.

Breast of Veal.—Before roasted, if large, the two ends may be taken off and fried to stew, or the whole may be roasted. Butter should be poured over it.

Serve the sweetbread whole upon it, which may be stewed or parboiled, and then covered with crumbs, herbs, pepper and salt, and browned in a Dutch oven.

Shoulder of Veal.—Cut off the knuckle, for a stew or gravy. Roast the other part for stuffing—you may lard it. Serve with melted butter.

To Boil a Ham.—To every pound allow a quarter of an hour, boiling slowly all the time. When dished, put spots of pepper at equal distances over it; garnish the dish with sprigs of parsley and boiled eggs, cut into thin slices.

To Boil Fowls.—Fill with oysters seasoned, bread and butter; boil in water, just sufficient to cover it; when done tender, put in in a deep dish, and pour over it a pint of stewed oysters well buttered and peppered; garnish the dish with sprigs of parsley or celery. Celery sauce may be substituted where oysters cannot be obtained, which is made by boiling the celery, (chopped fine,) in a little water, salt, and pepper, and thickened with butter and flour.

To Boil a Shoulder of Mutton with Oysters.—Hang it some days, then salt it well for two days, bone it, and sprinkle it with pepper, and a bit of mace pounded; lay some oysters over it, and roll the meat up tight and tie it. Stew it in a small quantity of water, with an onion and a few pepper corns, till quite tender. Have ready a little good gravy, and some oysters stewed in it, thicken this with flour and butter, and pour over the mutton when the tape is taken off. The stew-pan should be kept close covered.

To Boil a Calf's Head.—Clean it very nicely, and soak it in water, till it may look very white, take out the tongue to salt, and the brains to make a little dish. Boil the head extremely tender; then stew it over with crumbs and chopped parsley, and brown them; or if liked better, leave one side plain. Bacon and greens are to be served to eat with it.

The brains must be boiled; and mixed with melted butter, scalded sage chopped; pepper and salt.

If any of the head is left, it may be hashed next day, and a few slices of bacon just warmed and put round. Cold calf's head eats well if grilled.

Neck of Veal.—Cut off the scrag to boil, and cover it with onion sauce. It should be boiled in milk and water. Parsley and butter may be served with it, instead of onion-sauce.

To Fry Tripe.—Boil the tripe the day before, till it is quite tender, which it will not be in less than four or five hours. Then cover it and set it away. Next day cut it into long slips, and dip each piece into beaten yolk of egg, and afterwards roll them in grated bread crumbs. Have ready in a frying pan over the fire, some good beef dripping. When it is boiling hot put in the tripe, and fry it about ten minutes, till of a light brown.

To Fry Oysters.—Season them, dip them in egg, and then in grated cracker; let the fat be hot as you drop them in.

Veal is fried in the same way; it takes a half an hour to cool, but must be watched or it will burn. When the veal is taken out, brown some flour in the vessel, and pour in some boiling water, for gravy.

Beef Steaks.—Should be cut from a rump that has hung a few days. Broil them over a very clear or charcoal fire; put into the dish a little minced shallot, and a table-spoonful of catsup, and rub a bit of butter on the steak the moment of serving. It should be turned often, that the gravy may not be drawn out on either side.

This dish requires to be eaten so hot and fresh done, that it is not in perfection if served with any thing else. Pepper and salt should be added when taken off the fire.

To Broil Chickens.—Take those that are young and tender, break the breast bone, and lay it flat, season high with pepper and salt, broil half an hour on hot coals. Stew the giblets in as much water as will cover them; when done add flour and butter mixed, and some parsley chopped fine, and let them come to the boil.

Dish the chickens and pour the gravy over.

To Broil Pigeons.—After cleaning, split the backs, pepper and salt them, and broil them very nicely; pour over them either stewed or pickled mushrooms in melted butter, and serve as hot as possible.

Mutton Steaks.—Should be cut from a loin or neck that has hung; if a neck, the bones should not be long. They should be broiled on a clear fire, seasoned when half done, and often turned: take them up into a very hot dish, rub a bit of butter on each, and serve hot the moment they are done.

Steaks of Mutton, or Lamb, and Cucumbers.—Quarter cucumbers, and lay them into a deep dish, sprinkle them with salt, and pour vinegar over them. Fry the chops of a fine brown, and put them into stew-pan; drain the cucumbers, and put over the steaks; add some sliced onions, pepper, and salt; pour hot water or weak broth on them: stew and skim well.

Calf's Liver.—Slice it, season with pepper and salt, and broil nicely; rub a bit of cold butter on it, and serve hot.

Pork Steaks.—Cut them from a loin or neck, and of middling thickness pepper and broil them, turning them often; when nearly done, put on salt, rub a bit of butter over, and serve the moment they are taken off the fire, a few at a time.

To Stew Oysters.—Put your oysters with all their liquor into a sauce pan; no water; to every dozen add a lump of butter size of a walnut, salt, black pepper, a blade of mace, two bay leaves; bubble for five minutes, add a little cream, shake all well together, and turn them out, grating a little nutmeg on each oyster as it lies in the sauce.

To Stew Giblets.—Do them as will be directed for giblet-pie (under the head *Pies;*) season them with salt and pepper, and a very small piece of mace. Before serving, give them one boil with a cup of cream, and a piece of butter rubbed in a tea-spoonful of flour.

Pigeon Pie.—Take four pigeons, and pick and clean them very nicely. Season them with pepper and salt, and put inside of every one a large piece of butter and the yolk of a hard-boiled egg. Have ready a good paste, allowing a pound of butter to two pounds of sifted flour. Roll it out rather thick, and line with it the bottom and sides of a large deep dish. Put in the pigeons, and lay on the top some bits of butter rolled in flour. Pour in nearly enough of water to fill the dish. Cover the pie with a lid of paste rolled out thick, and nicely notched, and ornamented with paste leaves and flowers.

Giblet Pie.—Clean well, and half stew two or three sets of goose giblets; cut the leg in two, the wing and neck into three, and the gizzard into four pieces; preserve the liquor, and set the giblets by till cold, otherwise the the heat of the giblets will spoil the paste you cover the pie with; then season the whole with black pepper and salt, and put them into a deep dish rub it over with yolk of egg, ornament and bake it an hour and a half in a moderate oven; in the mean time take the liquor the giblets were stewed in, skim it free from fat, put it over a fire in a clean stew-pan, thicken it a little with flour and butter, or

flour and water, season it with pepper and salt, and the juice of half a lemon, strain it through a fine sive, and when you take the pie from the oven, pour some of this into it through a funnel. Some lay in the bottom of the dish a moderately thick rump steak;—if you have any cold game or poultry, cut it in pieces, and add it to the above.

Pig's Feet Soused.—Having cleaned them properly, and removed the skin, boil them slowly till they are quite tender, and then split the feet and put them with the ears into salt and vinegar, flavored with a little mace. Cover the jar closely, and set it away. When you use them, dry each piece well with a cloth; dip them first in beaten yolk of egg, and then in bread-crumbs, and fry them nicely in butter and lard. Or you may eat them cold, just out of the vinegar.

Ham Sandwitches.—Cut some thin slices of bread very neatly, having slightly buttered them; and if you choose, spread on a very little mustard. Have ready some very thin slices of cold boiled ham, and lay one between two slices of bread. You may either roll them up, or lay them flat on the plates. They are used at supper, or at luncheon.

To Corn Beef or Pork.—Wash the beef well, after it has lain awhile in cold water. Then drain and examine it, take out all the kernels, and rub it plentifully with salt. It will imbibe the salt more readily after being washed. In cold weather warm the salt by placing it before the fire. This will cause it to penetrate the meat more thoroughly.

In summer do not attempt to corn any beef that has not been fresh killed, and even then it will not keep more than a day and a half or two days. Wash and dry it, and rub a great deal of salt well into it. Cover it carefully, and keep it in a cold dry cellar.

To Fricassee Chickens.—Boil rather more than half, in a small quantity of water; let them cool, then cut up, and put to simmer in a little gravy made of the liquor they are boiled in, and a bit of veal or mutton, onion, mace, and lemon peel, some white pepper, and a bunch of sweet herbs. When quite

B

tender, keep them hot while you thicken the sauce in the following manner; strain it off, and put it back into the sauce-pan with a little salt, a scrape of nutmeg, and a bit of flour and butter; give it one boil; and when you are going to serve, beat up the yolk of an egg, and add half a pint of cream, and stir them over the fire, but do not let it boil. It will be quite as good without the egg.

The gravy may be made (without any other meat) of the necks, feet, small wing-bones, gizzards, and livers; which are called the trimmings of the fowl.

Pheasants and Partridges.—Roast them as turkey, and serve with a fine gravy (into which put a very small bit of garlic,) and bread sauce. When cold, they may be made into excellent patties, but their flavor should not be overpowered by lemon.

A very cheap way of Potting Birds. —When baked and grown cold, cut them into proper pieces for helping, pack them close into a large potting pan, and (if possible,) leave no spaces to receive the butter. Cover them with butter, and one third part less will be wanted than when the birds are done whole. The butter that has covered potted things will serve for basting, or for paste or meat pies.

Guinea and Pea Fowl.—Eat much like pheasants. Dress them in the same way.

Rabbits.—May be eaten various ways, as follows:

Roasted with stuffing and gravy, or without stuffing; with sauce of the liver and parsley chopped in melted butter, pepper, and salt; or larded.

Boiled and smothered with onion sauce; the butter to be melted with milk instead of water.

Fried in joints, with dried or fried parsley. The same liver-sauce, this way also.

Fricasseed, as before directed, for chickens.

In pie, as chickens, with forcemeat, &c. In this way they are excellent when young.

Jelly of Pig's Feet and Ears.— Clean and prepare, then boil them in a very small quantity of water, till

every bone can be taken out; throw in half a handful of chopped sage, the same of parsley, and a seasoning of pepper, salt, and mace in fine powder; simmer till the herbs are scalded then pour the whole in a melon form

Sausages.—Chop fat and lean pork together; season it with sage, pepper and salt, and you may add two or three berries of alspice; *half fill* hog's guts that have been soaked and made extremely clean; or the meat may be kept in a very small pan closely covered; and so rolled and dusted with a very little flour before it is fried. Serve on stewed red cabbage, or mash potatoes put in a form, brown with salamander, and garnish with the above; they must be pricked with a fork before they are dressed, or they will burst.

Sweetbreads.—Half boil them, and stew them in a white gravy, add cream, flour, butter, nutmeg, salt, and white pepper.

Or do them in white sauce seasoned

Or parboil them, and then cover them with crumbs, herbs, and seasoning: and brown them in a Dutch oven. Serve with butter, and mushroom catsup, or gravy.

Kidney.—Chop veal-kidney, and some of the fat—likewise a little leak or onion, pepper and salt—roll it up with an egg into balls, and fry them.

To roll a Breast of Veal.—Bone it, take off the thick skin and gristle, and beat the meat with a rolling-pin. Season it with herbs chopped very fine, mixed with salt, pepper, and mace. Lay some thick slices of fine ham—or roll it into two or three calves' tongues of a fine red, boiled first an hour or two, and skinned. Bind it up tight in a cloth, and tape it. Set it over the fire to simmer in a small quantity of water, till it is quite tender—this will take some hours. Lay it on the dresser, with a board and a weight on it till quite cold.

Pigs, or calves' feet boiled and taken from the bones, may be put in or round it. The different colors laid in layers look well when cut—and you may put in yolks of eggs boiled, beef-root, grated ham, and chopped parsley in different parts.

To Dress a Calf's Head.—Take a calf's head with the skin on, and scald off all the hair and clean it very well, cut it in two, take out the brains, boil the head very white and tender, take one part quite off the bone, and cut it into nice pieces with the tongue; dredge it with a little flour, and let it stew on a slow fire for about half an hour in rich white gravy made of veal, mutton, and a piece of bacon, seasoned with pepper, salt, onion and a very little mace; it must be strained off before the hash is put in it, thicken it with a little butter rolled in flour; the other part of the head must be taken off in one whole piece, stuff it with nice forcemeat, and roll it like a collar, and stew it tender in gravy, then put it in the middle of the dish, and the hash all round, garnish it with forcemeat balls, fried oysters, and the brains made into little cakes dipped in rich butter and fried. You may add, morels, truffles, or what you please to make it good and rich

To A-la-mode Beef.—Take the bone out of a rump of beef, lard the top with bacon, then make a forcemeat of four ounces of marrow, two heads of garlick, the crumbs of a penny loaf, a few sweet herbs shred small, nutmeg, pepper and salt to your taste; add the yolks of four eggs well beat, mix it up, and stuff your beef where the bone came out, and in several places in the lean part, skewer it round and bind it about with a fillet, put it in a pot and tie it down with strong paper, bake it in the oven for three hours; when it comes out, if you want to eat it hot, skim the fat off the gravy, and add half an ounce of morels, a spoonful of pickled mushrooms, thicken it with flour and butter; dish up your beef and pour on the gravy; lay round it forcemeat balls, and send it up.

An excellent way of doing Tongues to eat Cold.—Season with common salt and saltpetre, brown sugar, a little bay-salt, pepper, cloves, mace and allspice, in fine powder for a fortnight; then take away the pickle, put the tongue into a small pan, and lay some butter on it; cover it with brown crust, and bake slowly till so tender that a straw would go through it

The thin part of the tongues, when hung up to dry, grates like hung beef, and also makes a fine addition to the flavor of omlets.

To Dress Venison.—A haunch of buck will take three hours and a half, or three quarters, roasting; doe, only three hours and a quarter. Venison should be rather under than over done.

Spread a sheet of white paper with butter, and put it over the fat, first sprinkle it with a little salt: then lay coarse paste on strong paper, and cover the haunch; tie it with fine packthread, and set it at a distance from the fire, which must be a good one. Baste it often; ten minutes before serving take off the paste, draw the meat nearer the fire, and baste it with butter and a good deal of flour, to make it froth up well.

To Pickle Pork.—Cut your pork in such pieces as will be most convenient to lie in your powdering tub, rub every piece all over with saltpetre, then take one part bay salt, and two parts common salt, and rub every piece well, lay the pieces as close as possible in your tub, and throw a little salt over.

To Souse Tripe.—When your tripe is boiled, put it into salt and water, change the salt and water every day till you use it, dip it in a batter and fry it as pig's feet and ears, or boil it in fresh salt and water, with an onion sliced, and a few sprigs of parsley, and send melted butter for sauce.

To Boil French Beans.—Cut the ends of your beans off, then cut them slant ways, put them in a strong salt and water as you do them, let them stand an hour, boil them in a large quantity of water with a handful of salt in it, they will be a fine green; when you dish them up, pour on them melted butter, and send them up.

To Boil Parsnips.—Wash your parsnips very well, boil them till they are soft, then take off the skin, beat them in a bowl with a little salt, put to them a little cream and a lump of butter, put them in a tossing pan, and let them boil till they are like a light custard pudding, put them on a plate and send them to the table.

MACKEREL.—Choose as whitings. Their season is May, June, and July. They are so tender a fish, that they carry and keep worse than any other.

TROUT.—They are a fine-flavoured fresh-water fish, and should be killed and dressed as soon as caught. When they are to be bought, examine whether the gills are red and hard to open, the eyes bright, and the body stiff. The season is July, August, and September.

EELS.—There is a greater difference in the goodness of eels than of any other fish. The true silver-eel (so called from the bright colour of the belly, is caught in all our rivers; those taken in great floods are generally good; but in ponds they have generally a strong rank flavour. Except the middle of summer, they are always in season.

FLOUNDERS.—They should be thick, firm, and have their eyes bright. They very soon become flabby and bad.

LOBSTERS.—If they have not been long taken, the claws will have a strong motion when you put your finger on the eyes and press them. The heaviest are the best. The cock-lobster is known by the narrow back part of his tail, and the uppermost fins within are stiff and hard; but those of the hen are soft, and the tail broader. The male, though generally smaller, has the highest flavour, the flesh is firmer, and the colour, when boiled, is a deeper red.

TO DRESS FISH.—In frying fish, always observe to dry it well in a clean cloth. Beat up the yolks of two or three eggs, according to the quantity of fish. Take a small pastry-brush, and put the egg on: shake crumbs of bread and flour (mixed) over the fish, and fry it. Fry quick, and let it be of a fine light brown. Some like fish in batter: for this, beat an egg fine, and dip the fish in, just as you are going to put it in the pan. As good a batter as any, is a little ale and flour beaten up, just as you are ready for it, and dip the fish before frying. With all boiled fish, you should put a good deal of salt and horse-radish in the water, except mackerel, with which put salt and mint, parsley and fennel, which chop to put in the butter. Be sure to boil the fish well; but take great care they do not break.

AN EXCELLENT WAY OF DO-ING TONGUES TO EAT COLD. Season with common salt and saltpetre brown sugar, a little bay-salt, pepper cloves, mace, and alspice, in fine powder, for a fortnight; then take away the pickle, put the tongue in a small pan, lay some butter on it; cover it with brown crust, and bake slowly till so tender that a straw would go through it. The thin part of tongues, when hung up to dry, grates like hung beef, and makes a fine addition to the flavour of omlets.

TRIPE may be served in a tureen, stewed with milk and onion till tender. Melted butter for sauce. Or fry it in small bits dipped in batter. Or stew the thin part, cut into bits, in gravy, thicken with flour and butter, and add a little catsup. Or fricasee it with white sauce.

TO POT BEEF.—Take two pounds of lean beef, rub it with saltpetre, and let it remain so one night; then salt with common salt, and cover it with water four days in a small pan. Dry it with a cloth, and season with black pepper; lay it into as small a pan as will hold it, cover it with coarse paste, and bake it five hours in a very cool oven. Put no liquor in. When cold, pick out the strings and fat: beat the meat very fine, at the same time put on a quarter of a pound of good butter, just warmed but not oiled, and as much of the gravy as will make it into a paste; put it into small pots, and cover them with melted butter.

TO POT VEAL.—Cold fillet make the best potted veal; or you may do it in this way:—Season a large slice of the fillet before it is dressed, with some mace, pepper-corns, and two or three cloves, lay it close into a pot, in a pan that will but just hold it; fill it up with water, and bake it three hours, then pound it quite small in a mortar, and add salt to taste; put a little gravy that was baked to it in pounding, if to be eaten soon, otherwise, only a little butter just melted. When done, cover it over with butter.

SOUSED TRIPE.—Boil the tripe, but not quite tender; then put it into salt and water, which must be changed every day till it is all used. When you dress the tripe, dip it into batter of flour and eggs, and fry it to a good brown.

VEGETABLES.

To Stew Red Cabbage.—Slice a small, or half a large, red cabbage; wash and put it into a sauce-pan with pepper, salt, no water but what hangs about it, and a piece of butter. Stew till quite tender, and when going to serve, add two or thee spoons full of vinegar, and give one boil over the fire. Serve it for cold meat, or with sausages on it.

Another way.—Shred the cabbage, wash it; and put over a slow fire, with slices of onion, pepper and salt, and a little plain gravy. When quite tender and a few minutes before serving, add a bit of butter rubbed with flour, and two or three spoons full of vinegar, and boil up.

To Stew Mushrooms—The large buttons are best, and the small flaps while the fur is still red. Rub the large buttons with salt and a bit of flannel; cut out the fur, and take off the skin from the others. Sprinkle them with salt, and put into a stew-pan with some pepper-corns; simmer slowly till done: then put a small bit of butter and flour and two spoons full of cream; give them one boil, and serve them with sippets of bread.

To Stew Onions.—Peel six large onions, fry gently of a fine brown, but do not blacken them; then put them into a small stew-pan, with a little weak gravy, pepper and salt; cover and stew two hours gently. They should be lightly floured at first.

To Stew Cucumbers.—First slice them thick; then cut in half or divide them into two lengths; stew some salt and pepper, and sliced onions, add a little broth, or a bit of butter. Simmer very slowly; and before serving, if no butter was in before, put some, and a little flour, or if there was butter in, only a little flour; unless it was richness.

To Dress Beans.—Boil tender with a bunch of parsley, which must be chopped to serve with them. Bacon or pickled pork must be served to eat with, but not boiled with them.

To Boil Vegetables Green.—Be sure the water boils when you put them in. Make them boil very fast. Do not cover, but wash them; and if the water has not slackened, you may be sure they are done when they begin to sink. Then take them out immediately, or the colour will change. Hard water, especially if chalybeate spoils the color of such vegetables as should be green.

To boil them green in hard water.—Put a teaspoonful of salt of wormwood into the water when it boils, before the vegetables are put in.

To Mash Potatoes.—Boil the potatoes, peel them, and break them to paste; then to two pounds of them, add a quarter of a pint of milk, a little salt, and two ounces of butter, and stir it all well over the fire. Either serve them in this manner, or place them on the dish in a form, and then brown the top with a salamander, or in scallops.

To Fry Potatoes.—Take the skin off raw potatoes, slice and fry them, either in butter or thin batter.

To Roast Potatoes.—Half-boil, take off the thin peel, and roast them of a beautiful brown.

To Boil Cauliflowers—Choose those that are close and white. Cut off the green leaves, and look carefully that there are no caterpillars about the stalk. Soak an hour in cold water; and take care to skim the sauce-pan, that not the least foulness may fall on the flower. It must be served very white and rather crimp.

French Beans—String and cut them into four or eight; the last looks best. Lay them in salt and water; and when the sauce-pan boils, put them in with some salt. As soon as they are done, sever them immediately, to preserve the green color.

Or when half done, drain the water off, and put them into two spoonsful of broth, strained; and add a little cream, butter, and flour, to finish doing them.

SOUPS.

Calf's Head, or Mock-Turtle Soup. —Parboil a calf's head, take off the skin and cut it in bits about an inch and a half square, cut the fleshy part in bits, take out the black part of the eyes, and cut the rest in rings, skin the tongue, and cut it in slices, add it all to three quarts of good stock, and season it with cayenne, two or three blades of mace, salt, the peel of half a lemon, with about a dozen forcemeat balls; stew all this an hour and a half, rub down with a little cold water, two table-spoons full of flour, mix well amongst it half a pint of the soup, and then stir it into the pot; put in the juice of half a large lemon, and the hard-boiled yolks of eight eggs; let it boil a few minutes.

Thick Beef Soup. —In eight quarts of water boil gently seven or eight hours, skimming it well, a shin or a leg of beef, and a bunch of sweet herbs, strain it the next day, take off the fat, and cut all the gristly and sinewy parts from the banes, add them to the soup, with some leeks, onions, celery, pepper, salt, and ten or twelve ounces of Scotch barley parboiled; boil it gently for two or three hours. This stock or jelly will keep good for weeks in cold weather.

Beef or Mutton Soup. —Boil very gently in a closely covered sauce-pan, four quarts of water, with two table-spoons full of sifted bread raspings, three pounds of beef cut in small pieces or the same quantity of mutton chops taken from the middle of the neck; season with pepper and salt, and two turnips, two carrots, two onions, and two heads of celery, all cut small; let it stew with these ingredient for four hours, when it will be ready to serve.

Giblet Soup. —Clean very nicely two sets of giblets, parboil them. Take the skin off the feet; cut the gizzards in quarters the necks in three bits, the feet, pinions, and livers, in two, the head in two also, first taking off the bill; boil them till nearly done enough in a quart of weak gravy soup with an onion. Have ready boiling some rich highly-seasoned brown gravy soup; add the giblets and the liquor they have been boiled in, with some rolled in flour

chopped parsley; take out the onion and thicken the soup with a bit of butter kneeded in flour. If the giblets are not perfectly sweet and fresh, do not add the weak soup they were boiled in.

Green Pea Soup, without meat. — Take a quart of green peas, (keep out half a pint of the youngest; boil them separately, and put them in the soup when it is finished;) put them on in boiling water; boil them tender, and then pour off the water, and set it by to make the soup with; put the peas into a mortar, and pound them to a mash; then put them into two quarts of the water you boiled the peas in; stir all well together; let it boil up for about five minutes, and then rub it through a hair sieve or tamis. If the peas are good, it will be as thick and fine a vegetable soup as need be sent to table.

Herb Soup. —Wash and cut small twelve cabbage lettuces, a handful of chervil, one of purslane, one of parsley, eight large green onions, and three handfuls of sorrel; when peas are in season omit half the quantity of sorrel, and put in a quart of young green peas; put them all into a sauce-pan, with half a pound of butter and three carrots cut small, some salt and pepper; let them stew closely covered for half an hour, shaking them occasionally to prevent their adhering to the pan; fry in butter six cucumbers cut longways in four pieces; add them with four quarts of hot water, half a French roll, and a crust of bread toasted upon both sides and let the whole boil till reduced to three quarts, then strain it through a sieve; beat up the yolks of four eggs with half a pint of cream and stir it gently into the soup just before serving.

Beet Root Soup. —Boil till tender two roots of beet, and rub off the skin with a coarse towel, mince them finely as also two or three onions; add this to five pints of rich gravy soup, so as to make it rather thick, then stir in three or four table-spoons full of vinegar and one of brown sugar; let it boil and throw in some fricandellans made up in the form of corks and

BREAD SAUCE. — Take four oz. of grated stale bread; pour over it sufficient milk to cover it, and let it soak about three quarters of an hour, or till it becomes incorporated with the milk. Then add a dozen corns of black pepper, a little salt, and a piece of butter the size of a walnut. Pour on a little more milk, and give it a boil. Serve it up in a sauce-boat, and eat it with roast wild fowl, or roast pig. Instead of the pepper, you may boil in it a handful of dried currants, well picked, washed, and floured.

CUCUMBER SAUCE.—Put into a sauce-pan a piece of butter rolled in flour, some salt, pepper, and one or two pickled cucumbers minced fine. Moisten it with boiling water. Let it stew gently a few minutes and serve it up.

LOBSTER SAUCE.—The lobster being boiled, extract the meat from the shell, and beat it in a mortar. Rub it through a cullender or sieve, and put it into a sauce-pan with a spoonful of velouté (or velvet essence), if you have it, and one of broth. Mix it well, and add a piece of butter, some salt, and cayenne pepper. Stew it ten minutes, and serve it up, with boiled fresh fish.

SOUPS.

The best soup is made of the lean of fine fresh beef. The proportion is four pounds of meat to a gallon of water. It should boil at least six hours. Mutton soup may be made in the same manner.

Put the meat into cold water, with a little salt; set it over a good fire; let it boil slowly but constantly, and skim it well. When no more fat rises to the top, put in what quantity you please of carrots, turnips, leeks, celery, and parsley, all cut into small pieces; add, if you choose, a laurel-leaf, or two or three peach-leaves, a few cloves, and a large burnt onion to heighten the colour of the soup. Grate a large red carrot and strew it over the top. Then continue to let it boil, gently but steadily, till dinner time.

Have ready in the tureen some toasted bread, cut into small squares; pour the soup over the bread, passing it through a sieve so as to strain it thoroughly. Some, however, prefer serving it up with all the vegetables in it.

Soups made of veal, chickens, &c., are only fit for invalids.

After you have strained out the vegetables, you may put into the soup some vermicelli (allowing two ounces to each quart), and then boil it ten minutes longer.

PEASE SOUP.—Take four pounds of lean beef, cut it in small pieces, and a pound of lean bacon, or pickled pork, set it on the fire with two gallons of water, let it boil, and skim it well Then put in six onions, two turnips one carrot, and four heads of celery cut small, twelve corns of allspice, and put in a quart of split pease, boil it gently for three hours, strain them through a sieve, and rub the pease well through. Now put the soup in a clean pot, and put in dried mint rubbed to powder; cut the white of four heads of celery, and two turnips in slices, and boil them in a quart of water for fifteen minutes; strain them off, and put them in the soup: then take a dozen of small rashers of bacon fried, and put them in the soup, and season with pepper and salt. Boil the whole for fifteen minutes, then put it in a tureen, with slices of bread fried crisp. The liquor of the boiled leg of pork makes excellent pease soup.

BEEF BROTH. — Take a leg of beef, crack the bone in two or three parts, wash it clean, put it in a pot with a gallon of water, skim it, put in two or three blades of mace, a bundle of parsley, and a crust of bread; boil it till the beef is tender, and likewise the sinews. Toast bread, and cut it in slices, put it in a tureen; lay in the meat, and pour on the soup.

MUTTON BROTH.—Cut a neck of mutton of six pounds in two, boil the scrag in a gallon of water, skim it, put in a bundle of sweet herbs, an onion, and a crust of bread. Let it boil an hour, then put in the other part of the mutton, a turnip or two, a few chives chopped fine, and a little parsley chopped small. Put these in a quarter of an hour before the broth is done. Season it with salt, or put in a quarter of a pound of barley or rice at first. Some like it thickened with oat meal, and others with bread, others season with mace, instead of sweet herbs and onion.

MUTTON OR VEAL GRAVY.— Cut and hack veal, set it on the fire with water, sweet herbs, mace and pepper Boil till it is as required—strain it off.

PUDDINGS. PIES, &c.

Quince Pudding.—Take six large ripe quinces; pare them, and cut out all the blemishes. Then, scrape them to a pulp, and mix the pulp with half a pint of cream, and a half a pound of powdered sugar, stirring them together very hard. Beat the yolks of seven eggs, (omitting all the whites except two,) and stir them gradually into the mixture, adding two wine glasses of rose water. Stir the whole well together, and bake it in a buttered dish three quarters of an hour. Grate sugar over it when cold.

Rice Milk.—Pick and wash half a pint of rice, and boil it in a quart of water till it is quite soft. Then drain it, and mix it with a quart of rich milk. You may add half a pound of whole raisins. Set it over hot coals, and stir it frequently till it boils. When it boils hard, stir in alternately two beaten eggs, and four large table-spoonsful of brown sugar.

Plain Rice Pudding.—Boil three cups of rice in two quarts of milk till soft, then add two quarts of cold milk, eight eggs beat light, a quarter pound of butter, two nutmegs, and sugar to the taste.

Another.—Boil in water one pound ground rice till soft, add four quarts of milk, sixteen eggs, twelve ounces butter, two pounds raisins; bake two hours.

Bread Pudding.—Cut one loaf of bread in fine pieces, sprinkle with a little salt, boil two quarts of milk and pour over, cover close until well soaked, mash it well, add six eggs, one pound butter; some cinnamon or nutmeg, sweeten it, bake it in a quick oven one hour and a half.

Flour Pudding.—Beat one dozen eggs light, add two quarts of milk, a little salt, mix with wheat flour to a batter, beat it well, pour into a bag and boil four hours; two pounds of currants added to it is a great improvement, but it is very good without.

Plum Pudding, (boiled.)—Three quarts of flour, a little salt, twelve eggs, two pounds of raisins, one pound of beef suet chopped fine, one quart of milk; put into a strong cloth floured boil three hours. Eat with sauce.

Apple Pudding.—Pare and stew three pints of apples, mash them, add eight eggs, half a pound of butter, sugar and nutmeg, or grated lemon peel; bake on short crust.

Boiled Apple Pudding.—Pare, core and quarter as many fine juicy apples as will weigh two pounds when done. Strew among them a quarter of a pound of brown sugar, and add a grated nutmeg, and the juice and yellow peel of a large lemon. Prepare a paste of suet and flour, in the proper tion of a pound of chopped suet to two pounds of flour. Roll it out of moderate thickness; lay the apples in the centre, and close the paste nicely over them in the form of a large dumpling; tie it in a cloth and boil it three hours. Send it to the table hot, and eat it with cream sauce, or with butter and sugar.

Indian Pudding.—Three quarts of scalded milk, fourteen spoonsful fine Indian meal, stir well; when cool add eight eggs, one pound butter, spice and sugar; bake four hours.

Another.—(*A cheap one.*)—Scald four cups of Indian meal with boiling water, add two cups molasses and milk, (each,) half pound raisins, a little suet chopped fine, four eggs, and some ground cinnamon.

A Suet Pudding.—Mince very fine as much beef suet as will make two large table spoonsful. Grate two handsful of bread-crumbs; boil a quart of milk and pour it hot on the bread. Cover it, and set it aside to steep for half an hour; then put it to cool. Beat eight eggs very light; stir the suet, and three table spoonsful of flour alternately into the bread and milk, and add by degrees, the eggs. Lastly stir in a table spoonful of powdered nutmeg and cinnamon mixed. Pour it into a bag that has been dipped in hot water and floured; tie it firmly put it into a pot of boiling water and boil it two hours. Do not take it up till immediately before it is wanted, and send it to the table hot.

Eat it with sauce, or with molasses.

Plain Suet Dumplings.—Sift two pounds of flour into a pan, and add a salt-spoon of salt. Mince very fine one pound of beef suet, and rub it into a stiff dough with a little cold water. Then roll it out an inch thick or rather more. Cut it into dumplings with the edge of a tumbler. Put them into a pot of boiling water, and let them boil an hour and a half. Send them to the table hot, to eat with boiled loin of mutton, or with molasses after the meat is removed.

Boiled Milk Pudding.—Pour a pint of new milk, boiling hot, on three spoonsful of fine flour, beat the flour and milk for half an hour, then put in three eggs and beat it a little longer, grate in half a tea-spoonful of ginger, dip the cloth in boiling water, butter it well, and flour it, put it in the pudding, tie it close up, and boil it an hour. It requires great care when you turn it out. Pour over it thick melted butter.

Plain Pudding.—Boil half a pint of milk with a bit of cinnamon, four eggs with the whites well beaten, the rind of a lemon grated, half a pound of suet chopped fine, as much bread as will do—pour your milk on the bread and suet, keep mixing it till cold, then put in the lemon peel, eggs, a little sugar, and some nutmeg grated fine. It may be either baked or boiled.

Ground Rice Pudding.—Boil four ounces of ground rice in water, till it be soft, then beat the yolks of four eggs and put to them a pint of cream, four ounces of sugar, and a quarter of a pound of butter mix them all well together, you may either boil or bake it.

Little Citron Puddings.—Take half a pint of cream, one spoonful of fine flour, two ounces of sugar, a little nutmeg, mix them all well together, with the yolks of three eggs, put it in tea-cups, and stick in it two ounces of citron cut very thin, bake them in a pretty quick oven.

Raspberry Dumplings.—Make a good cold paste, roll it a quarter of an inch thick, and spread over it raspberry jam to your own liking, roll it up, and boil it in a cloth one hour at

least, take it up, and cut it in five slices, and lay one in the middle and the other four round it, pour a little good melted butter in the dish, and grate fine sugar round the edge of the dish.

Puff Paste.—Rub two pounds of butter into four pounds of flour, beat four whites of egg light, and add with cold water, make it into paste—roll in six or seven times two pounds more of butter, flouring it each roll—do not knead it—work it with your knife and rolling pin.

Boiled Custard.—Take two hands-ful of peach-leaves, let them come to the boil in a quart of milk, strain and let it it cool, beat twenty yolks of eggs, add two quarts of cream and loaf sugar, mix them altogether and stir them until they come to the boil, but do not let them boil; take them off, and let it cool, stirring all the time put in jelly or wine-glasses around a "Floating Island." For a dessert for dinner.

Baked Custards.—Two quarts of milk, twelve eggs, twelve ounces sugar, four spoonsfull of rose-water, one nutmeg.

Another.—Eight eggs beat and put into two quarts of cream, sweetened to the taste, a nutmeg, a little cinnamon.

Mince Pies.—Two pounds of meat, one pound suet, half of a peck apples, one pound raisins, one pound currants, four ounces citron, two nutmegs, four spoonsful ground cinnamon, two dozen ground cloves, the juice of two lemons, the rinds of two grated, a little ground alspice, sugar to the taste, moisten with tamarind water.

Floating Island.—Put four quarts of cream or milk in your glass, sweeten and add rose-water and grated lemon peel, to your taste, beat the whites of twenty eggs until stiff, color it with currant or quince jelly, beating all the time, until it will stand alone, then put it with a table-spoon on top of the milk. To be eaten immediately.

Lard Paste.—Take half a pound of nice lard, and half a pound of fresh butter; rub them together into two pounds and a quarter of flour, and mix it with a little cold water to a stiff dough.

PUDDINGS, PIES, &c

A Baked Bread Pudding.—Take a stale five cent loaf of bread; cut off all the crust, and grate or rub the crumb as fine as possible. Boil a quart of rich milk, and pour it hot yver the bread; then stir in a quarter of a pound of butter, and the same quantity of sugar, a glass of rose-water. Or you may omit the latter and substitute the grated peel of a large lemon. Add a table-spoonful of mixed cinnamon and nutmeg powdered. Stir the whole very well, cover it, and set it away for half an hour. Then let it cool. Beat seven or eight eggs very light, and stir them gradually into the mixture after it it is cold. Then butter a deep dish, and bake the pudding an hour.

Quince Pies.—Peel twelve apples and two quinces, stew and sweeten them; bake in a rich crust.

Cranberry Tarts.—Put two pounds of sugar into two quarts of cranberries, wet with water, and stew them until done. When wanted for use, put them on puff-paste crusts.

Apple Pies.—Peel and stew the apples, mash them fine with sugar, a little butter, and grated nutmeg, or lemon peel: bake in a rich crust and quick oven, but not hot enough to scorch.

Peach Pot-Pie.—Put your crust into a pot, fill with peaches and cover them with sugar-house molasses, put a crust on the top, and let it boil until the peaches are done. Plums, apples, and berries of all kinds, may be made the same way.

Cherry Pies.—A rich crust. The cherries must be well sweetened, and the pie well baked.

Plum Pies.—Make a rich crust, put in one pound of sugar to two pound of plums, and a little molasses—it must be well baked.

Peach Pies.—Do not require a great deal of sweetening; the crust must be rich, and the pie well baked.

Cheese Cakes.—Take half a pint of good curds, beat them with four eggs, three spoonsful of rich cream, half a nutmeg grated, one spoonful of ratifia, rose or orange water, put to them a quarter of a pound of sugar, half a pound of currants well washed and dried before the fire, mix them all well together, and bake in patty pans, with a good crust under them.

Rhubarb Pies.—Take the green stalks of the rhubarb plant, having peeled the thin skin off, cut the stalks into small pieces about an inch long, put in a great deal of brown sugar and put it in the crust raw, and bake it about three quarters of an hour.

Seed Cake.—Take two pounds of flour, rub it into half a pound of powdered sugar, one ounce of carraway seed beaten, have ready a pint of milk, with half a pound of butter melted in it, and two spoonsful of new barm, make it up into a paste, set it to the fire to rise, flour your tin, and bake it in a quick oven.

Syllabub.—Sweeten two quarts of cream with loaf sugar grate nutmeg into it, milk your cow into the mixture very fast, that it may be very frothy. This is very good for evening entertainments, &c.

Another.—Take a quart of cream, grate in the skin of a lemon, beat the whites of six eggs, sweeted, until light, put it into your syllabub glasses, &c.

Curds-and-whey.—Take a piece of rennet about two inches square, and wash it in two or three cold waters to get off the salt; wipe it dry, and fasten a string to one corner of it. Have ready in a deep dish or pan, a quart of unskimed milk that has been warmed but not boiled. Put the rennet into it, leaving the string hanging out over the side, that you may know where to find it. Cover the pan, and set it by the fire-side or in some other place. When the milk becomes a firm mass of curd, and the whey looks clear and greenish, remove the rennet as gently as possible, pulling it out by the string; and set the pan in ice, or in a very cold place. Send to the table with a bowl of sweetened cream, with nutmeg grated over it.

Trifle.—Break some rusk, spiced cake, or any cake you may have in the house into a dish, pour a good boiled custard over it, and put a syllabub over that. Garnished with jelly and flowers, it makes a handsome dessert for dinner.

DAMSONS FOR WINTER PIES. —Put them in small stone jars, or wide-mouthed bottles; set them up to their necks in a boiler of cold water; and lighting a fire under, scald them. Next day, when perfectly cold, fill up with spring water: cover them.

OBSERVATIONS ON MAKING PUDDINGS AND PANCAKES. —The outside of a boiled pudding often tastes disagreeably; which arises by the cloth not being nicely washed, and kept in a dry place. It should be dipped in boiling water, squeezed dry, and floured when to be used. If bread, it should be tied loose; if batter, tight over. The water should boil quick when the pudding is put in; and it should be moved about for a minute, lest the ingredients should not mix. Batter pudding should be strained through a coarse sieve, when all is mixed; in others, the eggs separately. The pans and basins must be always buttered. A pan of cold water should be ready, and the pudding dipped in as soon as it comes out of the pot, and then it will not adhere to the cloth. Very good puddings may be made without eggs, but they must have as little milk as will mix, and must boil three or four hours. A few spoonfuls of fresh small beer, or one of yeast, will answer instead of eggs, either in puddings or pancakes. Two large spoonfuls will supply the place of one egg, and the article it is used in will be equally good. The yolks and whites beaten long and separately, make the article they are put into much lighter.

SAGO PUDDING. —Boil a pint and a half of new milk, with four spoonfuls of sago, nicely washed and picked, lemon-peel, cinnamon, and nutmeg; sweeten to taste; then mix four eggs, put a paste round the dish, and bake slowly.

PUDDINGS IN HASTE. —Shred suet, and put, with grated bread, a few currants, the yolks of four eggs and the whites of two, some grated lemon-peel and ginger. Mix, and make into little balls about the size and shape of an egg, with a little flour. Have ready a skillet of boiling water, and throw them in. Twenty minutes will boil them; but they will rise to the top when done. Pudding-sauce.

BREAD AND BUTTER PUDDING. —Slice bread spread with butter, and lay it in a dish with currants between each layer; add sliced citron orange, or lemon; if to be very nice. Pour over an unboiled custard of milk, two or three eggs, a few pimentos, and a very little ratafia, two hours at least before it is to be baked; and lard it over to soak the bread. A paste round the edge makes all puddings look better, but is not necessary.

BAKED APPLE PUDDING. —Pare and quarter four large apples; boil them tender, with the rind of a lemon, in so little water that, when done, none may remain; beat them quite fine in a mortar; add the crumb of a small roll, four ounces of butter, melted; the yolks of five and whites of three eggs, juice of half a lemon, and sugar to taste; beat all together, and lay it in a dish with paste to turn out.

PLUM PUDDING. —Mix a pound of suet, ditto flour, half a pound of currants, ditto raisins, stoned and a little cut, with spice, lemon, a glass of wine or not, and one egg, and milk, will make an excellent pudding, if long boiled.

RICH PUFF PASTE. —Puffs may be made of any sort of fruit, but it should be prepared first with sugar. Weigh an equal quantity of butter with as much fine flour as you judge necessary; mix a little of the former with the latter, and wet it with as little water as will make it into a stiff paste. Roll it out, and put all the butter over it in slices, turn in the ends, and roll it thin: do this twice, and touch it no more than can be avoided. The butter may be added at twice, and to those who are not accustomed to make paste it may be better to do so. A quicker oven than for short crust is necessary.

MINCE PIE. —Of scraped beef free from the skin and strings, weigh 2 pounds, 4 pounds of suet, picked and chopped, then add 6 pounds of currants, nicely cleaned and perfectly dry, 3 pounds of chopped apples, the peel and juice of two lemons, a pint of sweet wine, a nutmeg, a quarter of an ounce of cloves, ditto mace, ditto pimento, in finest powder: press the whole into a deep pan when well mixed, and keep it in a cool dry place.—Half the quantity is enough, unless for a very large family.

POTATO PASTE.—Pound boiled potatoes very fine, and add, while warm, a sufficiency of butter to make the mash hold together, or you may mix with it an egg; then before it gets cold, flour the board pretty well to prevent it from sticking, and roll it to the thickness wanted. If it become quite cold before it is put on the dish, it will be apt to crack.

APPLE PIE.—Pare and core the fruit, having wiped the outside; which with the cores, boil with a little water till it taste well: strain and put a little sugar, and a bit of bruised cinnamon, and simmer again. In the mean time place the apples in a dish, a paste being put round the edge; when one layer is in, sprinkle half the sugar, and shred the lemon-peel, and squeeze some juice, or a glass of cider. If the apples have lost their spirit, put in the rest of the apples, sugar, and the liquor that you have boiled. Cover with paste. You may add some butter when cut, if eaten hot; or put quince-marmalade, orange-paste, or cloves, to flavour.

SWEET PATTIES.—Chop the meat of a boiled calf's foot, of which you use the liquor for jelly, two apples, one ounce of orange and lemon-peel candied, and some fresh peel and juice; mix with them half a nutmeg grated, the yolk of an egg, a spoonful of brandy, and four ounces of currants washed and dried. Bake in small pattypans.

APPLE PUFFS.—Pare the fruit, and either stew them in a stone jar on a hot hearth, or bake them. When cold, mix the pulp of the apple with sugar, and lemon-peel shred fine, taking as little of the apple-juice as you can. Bake them in a thin paste, in a quick oven: a quarter of an hour will do them, if small. Orange or quince marmalade is a great improvement. Cinnamon pounded, or orange-flower water, in change.

RICH CUSTARDS.—Boil a pint of milk with lemon-peel and cinnamon—mix a pint of cream and the yolks of five eggs well beaten; when the milk tastes of the seasoning, sweeten it enough for the whole; pour it into the cream, stirring it well: then give the custard a simmer till of a proper thickness. Do not let it boil; stir the whole time one way; season as above. If to be extremely rich, put no milk, but a quart of cream to the egg.

POULTRY AND GAME.—Poultry should be very carefully picked every plug removed, and the hair nicely singed—be careful in drawing poultry not to break the gall bag, for no washing will take off the bitter where it has touched. In dressing wild fowl, be careful to keep a clear brisk fire. Let them be done of a fine yellow-brown, but leave the gravy in: the fine flavour is lost if done too much. Tame fowls require more roasting, and are longer in heating through than others. All sorts should be continually basted, that they may be served with a froth, and appear of a fine colour. A large fowl will take three-quarters of an hour; a middling one half an hour, and a very small one or a chicken, twenty minutes. A capon will take from half an hour to thirty-five minutes; a goose, an hour wild ducks, a quarter of an hour; pheasants, twenty minutes; a small turkey stuffed, an hour and a quarter; turkey-poults, twenty minutes: grouse, a quarter of an hour; quails, ten minutes, and partridges from twenty to twenty-five minutes. Pigs and geese require a brisk fire, and quick turning.

TO CHOOSE COMMON FOWLS.—If young, the rooster's spurs are short and dubbed · take particular notice that they are not pared or scraped; if old, they will have an open vent; if young, a close and hard vent. And so of a hen, if old, her legs and comb are rough; if young, smooth.

GEESE.—If the bill be yellow, and she has but a few hairs, she is young; but if full of hairs, and the bill and foot red, she is old; if new, limber-footed if stale, dry-footed. And so of a wild bran-goose.

TURKEYS.—If the cock be young his legs will be black and smooth, and his spurs short: if stale, his eyes will be sunk in his head, and the feet dry; if new, the eyes lively, and the feet pliable. Observe the same by the hens and, moreover, if the hen be with egg, she will have a soft open vent; if not, a hard close vent. Turkey-poults are known in the same way, their age can not deceive you.

WILD AND TAME DUCKS.—When fat, are hard and thick on the belly; if not, thin and lean; if new limber-footed; if stale, dry-footed. A true wild duck has a red foot, smaller than the tame one.

EPICUREAN STEWS, SWEETMEATS, JAMS, &c.

TO STEW ONIONS. — Peel six large onions; fry gently to a fine brown, but do not blacken them; then put them into a small stew-pan, with a little weak gravy, pepper, and salt; cover and stew two hours gently. They should be lightly floured at first.

TO STEW RED CABBAGE. — Slice a small, or halve a large red cabbage; wash and put it into a sauce-pan, with pepper, salt, no water but what hangs about it, and a piece of butter. Stew till quite tender; and when going to serve, add two or three spoonfulls of vinegar, and give one boil over the fire. Serve it for cold meat, or with sausages on it.

TO MASH PARSNIPS. — Boil them tender; scrape, then mash them into a stew-pan, with a little cream, a good piece of butter, and pepper and salt.

TO BROIL POTATOES. — Parboil, then slice and broil them. Or parboil, then set them whole on the gridiron over a very slow fire; and when thoroughly done, send them up with their skins on.

TO STEW CELERY.—Wash six heads; strip off the outer leaves; cut into lengths of four inches; put into a stew-pan, with a little broth or weak gravy; stew till tender, then add cream, flour and butter; season with pepper, salt and nutmeg, and simmer all together.

SWEETMEATS — should be kept carefully from the air, and in a very dry place, unless they have a very small proportion of sugar, a warm one does not hurt; but when not properly boiled (that is, long enough, but not quick), heat makes them ferment, and damp causes them to grow mouldy. They should be looked at two or three times in the first two months, that they may be gently boiled again, if not likely to keep. Jellies of fruit, made with equal quantity of sugar, (that is, a pound to a pint,) requires no very long boiling. Sweetmeats keep best in drawers that are not connected with a wall. If there be the least damp, cover them only with paper dipped in brandy, laid quite close: putting a little fresh over in spring, to prevent insects or mould.

WHITE GOOSEBERRY JAM.— Gather the finest white gooseberries, or green if you choose, when just ripe; top and tail them. To each pound put three-quarters of a pound of fine sugar and half a pint of water. Boil and clarify the sugar in the water as before directed, then add the fruit, simmer gently till clear; then break it, and in a few minutes put the jam into small pots.

RASPBERRY JAM.—Weigh equal quantities of fruit and sugar, put the former into a preserving-pan, boil and break it; stir constantly, and let it boil very quickly. When most of the juice is wasted, add sugar, and simmer half an hour. This way the jam is greatly superior in colour and flavour to that which is made by putting the sugar in at first.

PEARS.—Pare them very thin, and simmer in a thin syrup; let them lie a day or two. Make the syrup richer, and simmer again, and repeat this till they are clear, then drain and dry them in the sun or a cool oven a very little time. They may be kept in syrup, and dried as wanted, which makes them more moist and rich.

GOOSEBERRY JAM FOR TARTS. —Put twelve pounds of red hairy gooseberries, when ripe and gathered in dry weather, into a preserving-pan, with a pint of currant-juice, drawn as for jelly: let them boil pretty quick, and beat them with the spoon; when they begin to break, put to them six pounds of pure white sugar, and simmer slowly . . . a . . . requires long boiling, or it will not keep; but is an excellent thing for tarts or puffs. Look at it in two or three days, and if the syrup and fruit separate, the whole must be boiled longer. Be careful it does not burn at the bottom.

CURRANT JAM, BLACK, RED, OR WHITE.—Let the fruit be ripe, pick it clean, bruise it, and to every pound put three-quarters of a pound of loaf-sugar; stir it well, and boil half an hour.

GOOSEBERRIES.—Pick full grown, but not ripe gooseberries, strip them, and put them into wide-mouthed bottles: cork them gently with new soft corks, and put them in an oven, from which the bread has been drawn, and let them stand till quarter shrunk; then take them out, and beat the corks in tight, cut them off level with the bottle, and rosin them down close. them in a dry place to k

C

CAKES:

POUND, OR BRIDE CAKE.

One pound of butter, one pound of sugar, one pound of flour, ten eggs, two nutmegs, one wine-glass of rose-water, one table-spoon full of powdered cinnamon, and a tea-spoon full of powdered mace.

Beat the butter to a cream, after squeezing all the buttermilk out of it; separate the white from the yolk of the eggs, beat the latter and add to the butter, then beat in the sugar. Beat the whites of the eggs light, and add them, and the flour—when beaten half an hour, grate the nutmeg and other spices into it, and add the rose-water.

SPONGE CAKE.

Sift one pound of flour and one pound of loaf sugar—take the juice of one lemon—beat ten eggs very light, mix them well with the sugar, then add the lemon and flour. If baked in a pan, two hours is necessary.

SWEET CAKES.

Half a pound of butter, three quarters of a pound of sugar, a little mace, five eggs beat light, put this into one pound of flour, and cut into small cakes.

CUP CAKES.

Take one pound of sugar, the same of butter, four pounds of flour, two glasses of rose-water, two nut-megs, some currants and a little yeast.

DOUGHNUTS.

Six pounds of flour, one pound of butter, two pounds of sugar, two nutmegs, six ounces of ground cinnamon, some orange-peel, and a little yeast; knead it well, let it rise; when light, cut into shapes and boil in lard.

SAUSAGE ROLLS.

Make small balls of sausage meat, envelope each one with light bread dough, and bake them.

HONEY CAKES.

Twelve pounds of flour, four pounds of honey, two pounds of sugar, four ounces of cinnamon, a little orange peel, twelve eggs, pearlash dissolved in milk; mix it up with milk, and bake less than half an hour.

INDIAN CAKES.

Beat four eggs, add two quarts of milk, two hands full of flour, and Indian meal enough to bake thin cakes on the griddle—they must be made small in size.

PAN CAKES.

Mix two quarts of milk with flour enough to make a thin batter, a little salt, beat twelve eggs light, mix it well together an hour before you fry them.

SWEET POTATOE CAKES.

Grate boiled sweet potatoes and mix with an equal quantity of flour, four ounces of butter, add salt and milk; cut out and bake in a hot oven; slice and butter for tea.

SCOTCH CAKES.

Four pounds of flour, one pound of butter, two nutmegs, two table-spoons full of rose-water, three pounds of sugar, and ten eggs.

DUTCH CAKE.

Two and a half pounds of flour, one pound of butter, one pound of sugar, a little yeast, cinnamon, nutmegs, two glasses of rose-water, some currants or raisins.

CREAM PANCAKES.

Take the yolk of two eggs, mix them with half a pint of good cream, two ounces of sugar, rub your pan with lard, and fry them as thin as possible, grate sugar over them, and serve them up hot.

POOR MAN'S POUND CAKE.

Two cups of bread dough, one cup of sugar, one cup of butter, one egg, a tea-spoon full of pearlash, with rose water according to taste.

APEES.

Take one pound of butter, two pounds of flour, one pound of powdered loaf sugar, a grated nutmeg, a table-spoon full of powdered cinnamon, and four large table-spoons full of carraway seeds, add a wine glass full of rose water, mix the whole with sufficient cold water to make it a stiff dough.

CAKES.

WAFERS.

Two pounds of flour, one pound of butter, eight eggs well beaten, rose water and nutmeg; heat the wafer iron moderately when you put them into bake; grate sugar over them when they are done.

BUNNS.

One pound of butter cut fine into two and a half pobnds of flour, six table-spoons of yeast, two pints of milk, two glasses of rose water, two tea-spoons of spice; set them to rise until you can beat ten eggs, add one pound of sugar, half a pound of flour, both sifted; put them in your pans, and let them rise for the space of three or four hours.

FRUIT CAKE.

Two pounds of sugar, two pounds of flour, two pounds of butter, twenty eggs, four pounds of raisins stoned and chopped fine, four pounds of dried currants, two pounds of citron.

Beat the butter to a cream, beat the yolks light, mix them and add the sugar, flour and whites, beaten stiff, spice to the taste, dust some flour on the dried fruit, squeeze the juice of a lemon, and grate in the peel, one glass of rose water; add the fruit last. Black cake is made the same way, with the addition of two tea-spoons full of pounded nutmegs, two dozen cloves pounded, mace, and cinnamon.

GINGER NUTS.

Two quarts of molasses, twelve ounces of ground cloves, one pound of sugar, two ounces of ground ginger, two ounces alspice, as much flour as will make a batter with two pounds of butter.

MACAROONS.

Blanche eight ounces of almonds, with eight spoons full of orange flower water, beat the whites of eight eggs, then mix it with two pounds of sugar sifted with the almonds to a paste, lay a sheet of paper on a tin, put it on with a spoon.

SOFT GINGER BREAD.

Four cups of molasses, two of butter, two cups of milk, eight eggs, two tea-spoons full of pearlash, ginger, and sufficient flour to make it stiff as pound cake.

SOFT CAKES FOR TEA.

Beat ten eggs light, and one and a half pounds of sugar, add a half pound of butter, and two pounds of flour, a glass of rose water, and half a nutmeg.

MILK BISCUIT.

Take one half pound of butter, one pint of milk, half a pint of yeast, two tea-spoons full of salt, and flour sufficient to knead it stiff.

FLANNEL CAKES.

Put a table-spoon full of butter into a quart of milk, and warm them together till the butter has melted; then stir it well, and set it away to cool. Beat five eggs as light as possible, and set them into the milk in turn with half a pound of flour; add a small tea-spoon full of salt, and a large table-spoon full and a half of the best fresh yeast. Set the pan of batter near the fire to rise; and if the yeast is good, it will be light in three hours Then bake it on a griddle in the manner of buckwheat cakes.

SHORT CAKES.

Rub three quarters of a pound of fresh butter into a pound and a half of sifted flour; and make it into a dough with a little cold water. Roll it out into a sheet half an inch thick, and cut it into round cakes with the edge of a tumbler. Prick them with a fork; lay them in a shallow iron pan sprinkled with flour, and bake them in a moderate oven till they are brown.

CRULLERS.

Eight eggs, one pound of sugar, six ounces of butter, two gills of thick cream, cinnamon, and sufficient flour to make it stiff enough to roll out— boil in lard, like doughnuts.

BUCKWHEAT CAKES.

Take a quart of buckwheat meal, mix with a tea-spoon full of salt, and add a hand full of Indian meal. Pou. a large table-spoon full of the best brewer's yeast into the centre of the meal. Then mix it gradually with cold water till it becomes a batter Cover it, put it in a warm place and set it to rise; it will take about three hours. When it is quite light, and covered with bubbles, it is fit to bake

PRESERVES. &c:

Preserved Peaches.—Take ripe free-stone peaches; pare, stone, and quarter them. To six pounds of the cut peaches allow three pounds of the best brown sugar. Strew the sugar among the peaches, and set them away in a covered vessel. Next morning put the whole into a preserving kettle, and boil it slowly about an hour and three quarters, or two hours, skimming it well.

Preserved Raspberries.—Choose raspberries not too ripe, take the weight of them in sugar, wet the sugar with a little water, and put in the berries, let them boil softly, take care not to break them; when clear take them up, boil the syrup until it be thick enough, then put them in again: do not put them away until cold.

Preserved Quinces.—Pare and core your quince, put them into a kpttle, cover them with the parings and cores, fill up with spring water, and let them boil until they are a pink color; take out the quinces, strain the liquor through a bag, and set it away for quince jelly; make a syrup of loaf sugar, pound for pound, boil the quinces in it two hours, slowly, frequently putting them under the liquor; after taking them out let the liquor boil until it is reduced to a syrup.

Preserved Tomatoes—Take of small ripe tomatoes one peck, stick them full of holes, make a syrup of eight pounds of sugar, and put them in it, with eight lemons sliced, and two ounces of race ginger chopped fine, boil slowly three hours; take the tomatoes out, and boil the liquor to a syrup.

Preserved Pears.—Take six pounds of pears to four pounds of sugar, boil the parings in as much water as will cover them, strain it through a culender, lay some pears in the bottom of your kettle, put in some sugar, and so on, alternately; then pour the liquor off the pear skins over, boil them until they begin to look transparent, then take them out, let the juice cool, and clarify it, put the pears in again, with a great deal of race ginger chopped

fine, boil till done; let the liquor boil after taking them out until it is reduced to a syrup

Preserved Currants for Tarts.—Get your currants when they are dry, and pick them; to every pound and a quarter of currants put a pound of sugar into a preserving pan with as much juice of currants as will dissolve it, when it boils skim it, and put in your currants and boil them till they are clear; put them into a jar, lay paper over, tie them down, and keep them in a dry place.

Raspberry Jam.—Take fine raspberries that are perfectly ripe. Weigh them, and to each pound of fruit, allow three quarters of a pound of fine loaf sugar. Mash the raspberries, and break up the sugar. Then mix them together, and put them into a preserving kettle over a good fire. Stir them frequently and skim them. The jam will be done in half an hour

Preserved Pumpkins.—Cut the pumpkin into leaves, &c., according to taste, sprinkle them with white sugar grated, let them lay all night; make a syrup pound for pound, cut some lemons in thin slices, add a little race ginger, and boil slowly until done.

Black Currant Jam.—Get your black currants when they are full ripe, pick them clear from the stalks, and bruise them in a bowl with a wooden mallet, to every two pounds of currants put a pound and a half of loaf sugar beat fine, but them into a preserving pan, boil them full half an hour, skim it and stir it all the time, then put it in the pots, and keep it for use.

Preserve Red Gooseberries.—To every quart of rough red gooseberries, put a pound of loaf sugar put your sugar into a preserving pan with much water as will dissolve it, and skim it well, then put in your gooseberries, let them boil a little, and set them by till the next day, then boil them till they look clear, and the syrup thick, then put them into pots or glasses, cover them with papers, and keep them for use

Red Strawberry Jam.—Gather the scarlet strawberries very ripe, bruise them very fine, and put to them a little juice of strawberries, beat and sift their weight in sugar, strew it among them, and put them in the preserving pan, set them over a clear slow fire, skim them, and boil them twenty minutes, then put them in pots and glasses for use.

Ice Cream.—Pare, stone, and scald twelve ripe apricots, beat them fine in a marble mortar, put to them six ounces of double refined sugar, a pint of scalding cream, work it through a hair sieve, put it into a tin that has a close cover, set it in a tub of ice broken small, and a large quantity of salt put amongst it, when you see the cream grow thick round the edge of your tin, stir it, and set it in again till it grows quite thick; when your cream is all froze up, take it out of your tin, and put it into the mould you intend it to be turned out of, then put on the lid, and have ready another tub with ice and salt in as before; put your mould in the middle, and lay your ice under and over it, let it stand four or five hours, dip your tin in warm water when you turn it out; if it be summer, you must not turn it out till the moment you want it; you may use any sort of fruit if you have not apricots, only observe to work it in fine.

A Good Cream.—Take a quart of cream, sweeten it to the taste, grate a little nutmeg, add two spoons full of rose and orange-flower water, beat eight eggs and four white; stir it altogether one way until it thickens, have cups ready, and pour it in.

Whipt Cream.—Take two quarts of cream and the whites of sixteen eggs, beaten, sweeten, and perfume it to the taste, whip it with a piece of lemon peel tied in the middle of the whist, take off the froth with a spoon, and put into glasses.

Raspberry Cream.—Boil two quarts of thick cream; when it is nearly cold strain some juice of raspberries into it and sweeten it to your taste; stir it a quarter of an hour, and when cold you may send it up.

Quince Jelly.—To every quart of the liquor off the quinces take two
G2

pounds of loaf sugar, cut up a few sour apples in it, when they are boiled sufficiently, take them out and mash them, put them back and boil altogether till done.

Calve's Foot Jelly.—Boil eight feet in eight quarts of water; when boiled to pieces strain the liquor, next day take off the grease from the top, and scrape the sediments from beneath—there should be four quarts of jelly. Put it in a clean vessel with two pounds of loaf sugar, one ounce of cinnamon broken in small pieces, orange peel, lemons, (or two spoons full of cream of tartar,) whip up the whites of ten eggs to a froth, and put all together over the fire, stirring occasionally till melted; when it has boiled until it looks clear, skim it, take it off and strain through a flannel bag.

Damson Plums.—Make a syrup, pound for pound, strain and skim it, boil your plums in it slowly an hour for every pound.

Watermellon Rinds.—Cut all the green off the rind, cut the inner part of the rind into shapes, and green them with cabbage leaves; make a syrup, pound for pound, boil slowly till done, with lemon peel and race ginger.

Currant Jelly.—Put the currants into a pitcher, cover it close, and set the pitcher in warm water over the fire, this will extract the juice; squeeze them through a flannel bag, and to one quart of juice add two pounds loaf-sugar—boil it twenty minutes, but no longer.

Apple Marmalade.—Pare twenty pounds of pippin apples, make a syrup of ten pounds of sugar, boil the apples in it until done sufficiently to mash, take them out, beat fine, and put them back, cut six oranges into small slices and boil all together, stirring all the time until done.

Blamange—Boil four ounces of ising-glass in six pints of water, boil it half an hour, strain and add to it one pint of cream, sweeten, and put some bitter almonds in it, let it boil up, let it settle before pouring it into your forms.

Lemon Tuffy.—Grate a fresh lemon peel into a pint of molasses, and boil it until, when cool, it will be crisp

A SEED CAKE.— Mix a quarter of a peck of flour with half a pound of sugar, a quarter of an ounce of allspice, and a little ginger; melt three quarters of a pound of butter, with half a pint of milk: when warm, put to it a quarter of a pint of yeast, and work up to a good dough. Let it stand before the fire a few minutes before it goes to the oven; add seeds, or currants, and bake an hour and a half.

SPONGE CAKE. — Weigh ten eggs, and their weight in very fine sugar, and that of six in flour; beat the yolks with the flour; and the whites alone, to a very stiff froth; then by degrees mix the whites and the flour with the other ingredients, and beat them well half an hour. Bake in a quick oven an hour.

HOAR-HOUND CAKE.—— Boil three pounds of raw sugar in one pint of water, till candied; then rub a little dried hoar-hound into the pan while boiling. Pour it on buttered paper.

CANDIED LEMON.— Boil three pounds of loaf sugar in a pint of water, till candied; then drop sixteen drops of the essence of lemon therein, stir it well, and then pour it out immediately into little round hoops made of tin; or butter a large piece of paper, and lay it on your stove with a square frame on your paper; pour your sugar on the paper, and it will become all over beautifully spotted, and you may, with a knife, cut it into what size or shape you please.

CANDIED GINGER. — Boil three pounds of raw sugar in a pint of water, till candied, then grate some ginger into it, stir it well, and then pour it out immediately. Make up as above.

CANDIED LOAF SUGAR.—Boil three pounds of loaf sugar in one pint of water, till candied; pour it out on paper, previously rubbed with butter, and it will be very clear. You may either use oil of peppermint, or essence of lemons.

QUINCE CREAM.—Take quinces when full ripe, cut them into quarters, scald them till they are soft, pare them, and mash the clear part of them and the pulp, and put it through a sieve; take an equal weight of quince and double refined sugar beaten and sifted, and the whites of eggs, beat till it is as white as snow, then put it into dishes. You may do apple cream the same way.

SWEETMEAT FOR TARTS.. Cut four pounds of ripe plums, and take out the stones, blanch the kernels and put them to the fruit, add six pounds of green gages, and five pounds of lump-sugar. Let the whole simmer till the fruit be a clear jam. Remember it must not boil, and it must be well skimmed. When done, pour it into small pots.

CHERRIES.—Take as much clarified sugar as will cover the cherries to be preserved; boil till it blows, then put in the cherries, let them boil briskly two minutes, take the scum off them, let them stand till the next day, and drain them. Boil the syrup till it blows; then put in the cherries, and as soon as they boil, take them off. When cold, put them into jars.

DAMSONS.—Boil three pounds of sugar with six pounds of damsons, over a slow fire, till the juice adheres to the fruit. Pour it into small jars, and when cold, cover with paper and leather.

TO CANDY ANY SORT OF FRUIT.—When finished in the syrup, put a layer into a new sieve, and dip it suddenly into hot water, to take off the syrup that hangs about it; put it on a napkin before the fire to drain, and then do some more in a sieve. Have ready sifted double refined sugar, which sift over the fruit on all sides till quite white. Set it on the shallow end of sieves in a lightly warmed oven, and turn it two or three times. It must not be cold till dry. Watch it carefully, and it will be beautiful.

PEACHES IN BRANDY.—Wipe, weigh, and pick the fruit, and have ready a quarter of the weight of fine sugar in fine powder. Put the fruit into a pot that shuts very close; throw the sugar over it, and then cover the fruit with brandy. Between the top and the cover of the pot, put a piece of double cap-paper. Set the pot into a sauce-pan of water till the brandy be as hot as you can possibly bear to put your finger in, but it must not boil. Put the fruit into a jar, and pour the brandy on it. When cold, put a bladder over, and tie it down tight.

TO PRESERVE STRAWBERRIES IN WINE.—Put a quantity of the finest large strawberries into a large gooseberry bottle, and strew in three large spoonfuls of fine sugar; fill up with Madeira wine, or fine sherry.

ON CARVING.

In carving, your knife should not be too heavy, but of a sufficient size, and keen edge. In using it, no great personal strength is required, as constant practice will render it an easy task to carve the most difficult articles; more depending on address than force.

The dish should be sufficiently near to enable the carver to reach it without rising, and the seat should be elevated so as to give command over the joint.

Show no partiality in serving, but let each person at table have a share of such articles as are considered best, for however you conciliate the one you favour, you must bear in mind that you make enemies of the other guests.

SECTION I.

FISH

Requires very little carving; it should be carefully helped with a fish-slice, which not being sharp, prevents the flakes from being broken, and in Salmon and Cod, these are large and add much to their beauty; a portion of the roe, milt, or liver, should be given to each person.

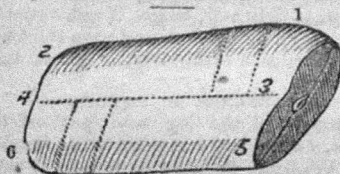

SALMON

Is rarely sent to table whole, but a piece cut from the middle of a large fish, which is the best flavoured part of it. Make an incison along the line, at 2, and another from 5 to 6; then divide the side about the middle, in the line 3, 4, cut the thickest part, between 1, 3, 2, 4, for the lean, the remainder for the fat, ask which is preferred, and help as the fancy of your guests may demand. When the fish is very thick, do not venture too near the bone, as there it has an ill-flavour, and is discoloured.

In paying your respects to a whole Salmon, you will find the choice parts next the head, the thin part next, the tail is considered less savoury.

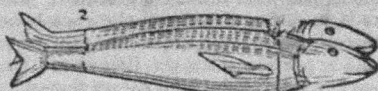

MACKEREL

In helping, first cut the head, at 1, as that part is very inferior, and unsavoury, then divide own the back, and give a side to each; if less is asked for, the thickest end, which is the most choice, should be served. Enquire if the roe is liked; it may be found between 1, and 2; that of the female is hard, of the male, soft.

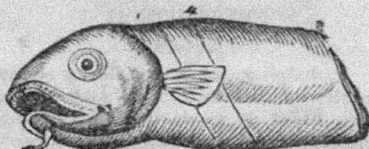

COD'S HEAD AND SHOULDERS.

Introduce the fish-slice at 1, and cut quite through the back, as far as 2, then help pieces from between 3 and 4, and with each slice give a portion of the sound, which lines the under side of the back bone. It is thin and of a darker colour than the other part of the fish, and is esteemed a delicacy.

Some persons are very partial to the tongue and palate, for which you must insert a spoon into the mouth. The jelly part is about the jaw, the firm part within the head, on which are some other delicate pickings; the finest portions may be found about the shoulders.

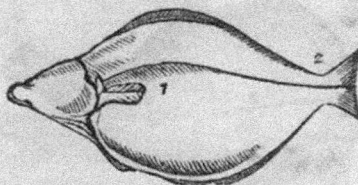

TURBOT.

The under side of this fish is the most esteemed, and is placed uppermost on the dish, the fish slice must be introduced at 1, and an incision made as far as 2; then cut from the middle, which is the primest part. After helping the whole of that side, the upper part must be attacked, and as it is difficult to divide the back bone, raise it with the fork, while you separate a portion with the fish slice; this part is more solid and is preferred by some, though it is less delicate than the under side. The fins are esteemed a nicety, and should be attended to accordingly.

CARP, PERCH, HADDOCK, ETC.

Will be easily helped by attending to the foregoing directions. The head of the Carp is esteemed a delicacy, which should be born in mind.

SECTION II.

JOINTS.

In helping the more fleshy joints, such as a Sirloin of Beef, Leg of Mutton, Fillet of Veal, cut thin smooth slices, and let the knife pass through to the bones of Mutton and Beef.

It would prevent much trouble, if the joints of the loin, neck, and breast, were cut through by the butcher, previous to the cooking, so that when sent to the table they may easily be severed. Should the whole of the meat belonging to each bone be too thick, one or more slices may be taken off from between every two bones.

In some boiled joints, round and aitch-bone of beef for instance, the water renders the outsides vapid, and of course unfit to be eaten, you will therefore be particular to cut off, and lay aside a thick slice from the top, before you begin to serve.

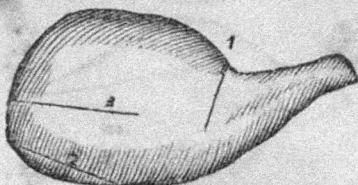

SHOULDER OF MUTTON.

Cut into the bone, at the line 1, and help thin slices of lean from each side of the incision; the prime part of the fat lies at the outer edge, at 2.

Should more meat be required than can be got from that part, cut on either side of the line 3, which represents the blade bone, and some good and delicate slices may be procured. By cutting horizontally from the under side, many "nice bits" will be obtained.

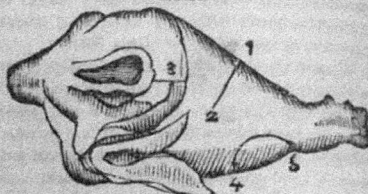

LEG OF MUTTON.

The finest part is situated in the centre, at 1, between the knuckle and farther end: insert the knife there and cut thin deep slices each way, as far in as 2. The outside rarely being very fat, some neat cuts may be obtained off the broad end, at 3. The knuckle of a fine leg is tender, though dry, and many prefer it, although the other is the most juicy. There are some good cuts on the broad end of the back of the leg, from which slices may be procured lengthways.

The cramp bone is by some esteemed a great delicacy, to get it cut down to the thigh bone, at 4, and pass the knife under it in a semi-circular course to 5.

HAUNCH OF MUTTON

Consists of the leg and part of the loin, cut so as to resemble a haunch of Venison. It must be helped at table in a similar manner.

SADDLE OF MUTTON.

This is an excellent joint, and produces many nice bits. Cut the whole length of it close to the back bone, and take off some long thin slices in that direction. The upper division consists of lean, the fat may be easily got at by cutting from the left side.

LOIN OF MUTTON.

As the bones of this joint are divided it is very easily managed; begin at the narrow end and take off the chops when the joints are cut through, some slices may be obtained between the bones.

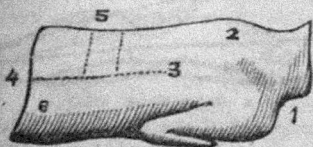

FORE QUARTER OF LAMB.

First divide the shoulder from the scoven, which consists of the breast, and ribs, by passing the knife under the knuckle, in the direction of 1, 2, 3 and cutting so as to leave a fair portion of meat on the ribs, lay it on a separate dish, and squeeze the juice of half a Seville orange over the other part, which after being sprinkled with pepper and salt, should be divided in the line, 3, 4. This will separate the ribs from the gristly part, and you may help from either as may be chosen, cutting as directed by the lines, 5, 6.

SHOULDER OF LAMB

Must be carved like a shoulder of mutton, of which it is a miniature edition.

LEG OF LAMB.

Follow the directions given for a leg of mutton.

LOIN OF LAMB.

May be helped similar to a loin of mutton. This, and the two foregoing, being small joints, should be helped sparingly, as there is very little meat on them, especially when first in season.

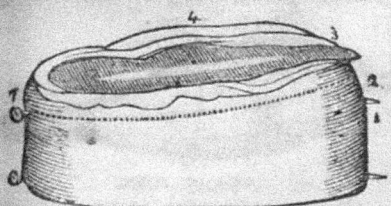

AITCH-BONE OF BEEF.

Cut off and lay aside a thick slice from the entire surface, as marked 1, 2, then help. There are two sorts of fat to this joint, and as tastes differ, it is necessary to learn which is preferred;

the solid fat will be found at 3; and must be cut horizontally, the softer which resembles marrow at the back of the bone below 4.

A silver skewer should be substituted for the one which keeps the meat properly together while boiling, and it may be withdrawn when you cut down to it.

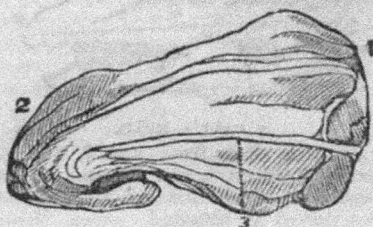

SIRLOIN OF BEEF.

There are two modes of helping this joint, the better way is by carving long thin slices from 1 to 2; the other way is by cutting it across, which however spoils it. The most tender and prime part is in the direction of the line 3 there will also be found some delicate fat, part of which should be given with each piece.

ROUND OF BEEF.

This joint is so very easy to attend to, that we have not deemed it necessary to give a drawing of it; it only requires a steady hand and a sharp knife. The upper surface being removed, as directed for the aitch-bone of beef, carve thin slices and give a portion of fat with each.

You must cut the meat as even as possible, as it is of consequence to preserve the beauty of its appearance.

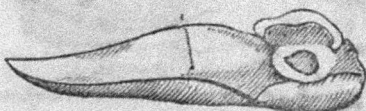

A TONGUE.

Cut nearly through the middle at the line 1, and take thin slices from each side. The fat is situated underneath, at the root of the tongue.

RIBS OF BEEF.

May be carved similar to the Sirloin, always commencing at the thin end of the joint, and cutting long slices so as to give fat and lean together.

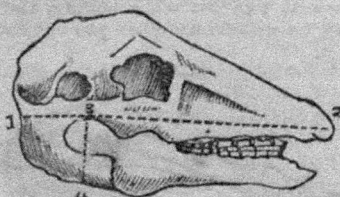

A CALF'S HEAD.

Cut thin slices from 1 to 2, and let the knife penetrate to the bone; at the thick part of the neck end 3, the throat sweetbread is situated, carve slices from 3 to 4 and help with the other part. Should the eye be asked for, it must be extracted with the point of the knife, and a portion given. The palate, esteemed a delicacy, is situated under the head, and some fine lean will be found by removing the jaw-bone; portions of each of these should be helped round.

A LOIN OF VEAL.

Should be jointed previous to being sent to table, when each division may be easily cut through with a knife The fat surrounds the kidney, and portions of each should be given with the other parts.

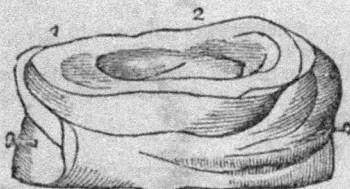

FILLET OF VEAL

Resembles a round of beef, and should be carved similar to it, in thin and very smooth slices, off the top; cut deep into the flap, between 1 and 2, for the stuffing, and help a portion of it to each person.

Slices of lemon should always be served with this dish.

A BREAST OF VEAL

Is composed of the ribs and brisket, which must be separated by cutting through the line, 1, 2; the latter is the thickest and has gristles. Divide each portion into convenient pieces and proceed to help.

HAND OF PORK.

Cut thin slices from this delicate joint, either across from the knuckle, or from the blade bone, as directed for a shoulder of mutton. This forms a nice dish for a tête-à-tête dinner, then is not sufficient for a third person.

ROAST PIG.

As this is usually divided as above before sent to table, little remains to be done by the carver. First separate a shoulder from the body, and then the leg; divide the ribs into convenient portions, and send round with a sufficiency of the stuffing and gravy Many prefer the neck end between the shoulders, although the ribs are considered the finest part, but as this all depends on taste, the questions should be put. The ear is reckoned a delicacy.

Should the head not be divided, it must be done, and the brains taken out, and mixed with gravy and stuffing

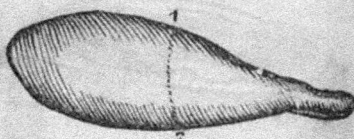

LEG OF PORK.

Commence carving about midway between the knuckle and farther end, and cut thin deep slices from either side of the line 1. For the seasoning in a roast leg, lift it up, and it will be found under the skin at the large end.

A LOIN OF PORK

Is cut up in the same manner as a loin of Mutton.

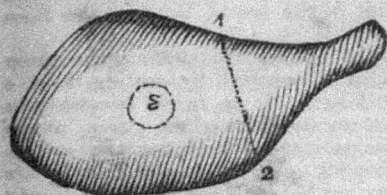

HAM.

The usual mode of carving this joint, is by long delicate slices, through the thick fat in the direction 1, 2, laying open the bone at each cut, which brings you to the prime part at once. A more saving way is to commence at the knuckle and proceed onwards.

Some persons take out a round piece at 3, and enlarge the hole, by cutting thin circular slices with a sharp knife, this keeps the meat moist, and preserves the gravy, but seldom looks handsome.

SECTION III.

POULTRY, GAME, ETC.

The carving knife for poultry is smaller and lighter than the meat carver; the point is more peaked and the handle longer.

In cutting up a Turkey, Goose, Duck, or Wild Fowl, more prime pieces may be obtained by carving slices from pinion to pinion, without making wings; this is an advantage when your party is large, as it makes the bird go farther.

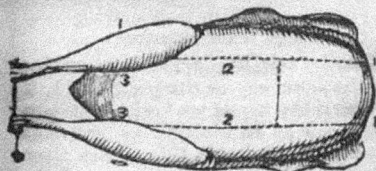

A FOWL.

It will be more convenient in carving this to take it on your plate, and lay the joints as divided, neatly on the dish. Fix your fork in the middle of the breast, and take the wing off in the direction of 1, 2; divide the joint at 1, lift up the pinion with your fork, and draw the wing towards the leg, which will separate the fleshy part more naturally than by the knife; cut between the leg and body at 3 to the bone, 2, give the blade a sudden turn, and the joint will break if the fowl is not old. When a similar operation is performed on the other side, take off the merrythought, by cutting into the bone at 4, and turning it back, which will detach it; next remove the neck bones, and divide the breast from the back, by cutting through the whole of the ribs, close to the breast. Turn up the back, press the point of the knife about half way between the neck and rump, and on raising the lower end it will separate easily. Turn the rump from you, take off the sidesmen, and the operation is complete.

The breast and wings are the most delicate parts, but the leg is more juicy in a young bird. Great care should be taken to cut the wings as handsome as possible.

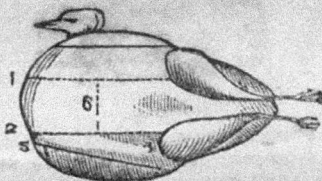

A PHEASANT.

Fix your fork in the centre of the breast, and make an incision to the bone at 1, 2, then take off the leg in the line 3, 4, and the wing at 3, 5; serve the other side in the same manner, and separate the slices you had previously divided on the breast. In taking off the wings, be careful not to venture too near the neck, or you will hit on the neck bone, from which the wing should be divided. Pass the knife through the line 6, and under the merrythought towards the neck, which will detach it. The other parts may be served as directed for a fowl.

The breast, wings, and merrytho are the most delicate parts altho the leg has a higher flavour.

A TURKEY.

The finest parts of this bird are the breast and wings: the latter will bear some delicate slices being taken off After the four quarters are severed, the thighs must be divided from the drumsticks, which being tough, should be reserved till last. In other respects a turkey must be dealt with exactly as recommended for a fowl, except that it has no merrythought.

Give a portion of the stuffing or forced-meat, which is inside the breast, to each person.

A PARTRIDGE

Is cut up in the same manner as a fowl, only on account of the smallness of the bird, the merrythought is seldom divided from the breast. The wings, breast, and merrythought, are the finest parts of it, but the wing is considered the best, and the tip of it is reckoned the most delicious morsel of the whole

PIGEONS.

The usual way of carving these birds is to insert the knife at 1, and cut to 2 and 3, when each portion may be divided into two pieces and helped; sometimes they are cut in halves, either across or down the middle, but as the lower part is thought the best, the first mode is the fairest.

Should they be very large and fine, they may be served like fowls.

A GOOSE.

Take off the wing by putting the fork into the small end of the pinion and press it close to the body, divide the joint at 1 with the knife, carrying it along as far as 2. Remove the leg by cutting in the direction of 2, 3, and divide the thigh from the drumstick, then sever the limbs on the other side, and cut some long slices from each side of the breast between the lines a and b.

To get at the stuffing, the apron must be removed, by cutting from 4 to 5 by 3. It is rarely necessary to cut up the whole of the goose, unless the company is large, but the merrythought may be taken off: there are two sidebones by the wing which may be cut off, likewise the back, and lower sidebones. The best pieces are the breast and thighs.

A DUCK.

Remove the legs and wings as directed above for a goose, and cut some slices from each side of the breast, the seasoning will be found under the flap, as in the other bird. Should it be necessary, the merrythought, side bones, &c., can be detached in the same manner as recommended for a fowl.

WOODCOCKS, GROUSE, ETC.

Are carved similar to a fowl, if not too small, when they may be cut into quarters and helped.

Snipes and Reed birds, being smaller, should be divided in halves.

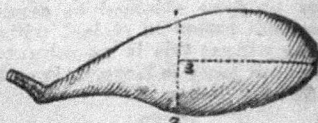

HAUNCH OF VENISON.

First let out the gravy by cutting into the bone across the joint at 1, 2 then turn the broad end towards you make as deep an incision as you can from 3 to 4, and help thin slices from each side. The greater part of the fat, which is much esteemed, will be found on the left side, and those who carve must take care to proportion both it and the gravy to the number of the company.

THE ART OF CARVING.

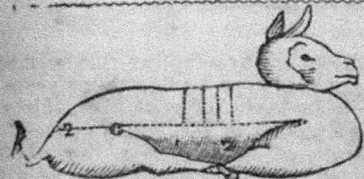

HARE.

Insert the point of the knife inside the shoulder at 1, and divide all the way down to the rump, at 2; do the same on the other side, and you will have the hare in three pieces. Pass the knife under the rise of the shoulder at 2, 1, to take it off; the leg must be severed in a similar manner: then *ahead it*—cut off the ears close to the roots, and divide the upper from the lower jaw. Next place the former flat on a plate, put the point of the knife into the forehead, and divide it through the centre down to the nose. Cut the back into convenient portions, lay the pieces neatly on the dish, and proceed to serve the company, giving some stuffing (which will be found in the inside) and gravy to each person.

The prime parts are the back and legs; the ears are considered a luxury by some, as are the head and brains: they may be distributed to those that like them.

Should the hare not be very tender, it will be difficult to divide the sides from the back, but take off the legs by cutting through the joints, which you must endeavour to hit, you will then be able to cut a few slices from each sides of the back. Next dissever the shoulders, which are called the sportsman's joints, and are preferred by many. The back, &c. may then be carved as directed above.

RABBIT.

The directions for cutting up a hare will be amply sufficient to enable the carver to dispose of the rabbit. The best part is the shoulders and back, which must be divided into three or four pieces according to its size. The head, and legs are generally considered the poorest parts about a rabbit, and unless asked for, should never be helped; a portion of gravy should be given each person.

ON DINING OUT.

To dine out it is usually understood that you must receive an invitation, which you accept or decline in plain terms.—If you accept, be there at the time appointed. It is inconvenient on many accounts to yourself and to your friends, either to be too late or too early.

You will probably have to wait a little time before dinner is announced During this short period render yourself as agreeable as possible to the assembled company.

Your host will doubtless point out to you the lady he wishes you to escort to the dining room. You will be in readiness to attend upon her the moment you are summoned to adjourn. Offer her your right arm and follow in order. Should you have to pass down stairs give the lady the wall. You will take your seat at the table on the right hand of the lady you conducted.

When seated, you will doubtless be asked whether you have a preference for any dish, or any particular part of a dish, answer plainly and distinctly as you wish.

Pay as much attention to your companion on your left as politeness requires, but do not be unnecessarily officious. People do not like to be stared at when eating.

When you are helped to any thing do not wait until the rest of the company are provided.

Do not allow your plate to be overloaded with a multifarious assortment of vegetables, but rather confine yourself to one kind. When you take another sort of meat, or a dish not properly a vegetable, you must change your plate.

Finally do all these things well, and to be *au fait* at a dinner party, be perfectly at your ease. To be at ease is a great step towards enjoying your own dinner, and making yourself agreeable to the company. Fancy yourself at home; performing all the ceremonies without any apparent effort, For the rest, observation and your own judgment will be the best guide, and render you perfect in the etiquette of the dinner table.

D

RARE AND VALUABLE RECEIPTS.

For a Burn or Scald.—If on the hand, tie it up in a bag of flour, or on the face or neck, shake flour from a dredge, and continue to do so till all the heat is drawn out. By this method all the fire may be drawn out without breaking the skin.

To cure Ringworms.—Get the comb of a church bell, that is, the grease which is applied to make it work easy, which with the metal forms a kind of verdigris, mix it with unsalted lard, and apply a fresh plaster twice a day. It is a certain cure.

Varnish for Boots and Shoes, by which they are rendered Water-proof.—Take a pint of linseed oil, with half a pound of mutton suet, six or eight ounces of bees-wax, and a small piece of rosin Boil all these in a pipkin, and let the liquid cool till milk-warm—then with a brush lay it on boots or shoes. The leather must be perfectly dry.

To Remove Mildew from Linen.—Moisten a piece of soap, and rub it thickly into the part effected; then scrape fine whitening, and rub that in also. Lay the linen on the grass, and from time to time, as it becomes dry, wet it a little. If the spots are not quite removed, repeat the process.

To Remove Ink Spots.—Wet the place immediately with sorrel or lemon juice, and rub on it hard white soap. Ink or iron mould may be removed by holding over a vessel of boiling water, and squeezing on the spot juice of sorrel, then rubbing with dry salt.

To Remove Grease from Woollen or Silk.—Clay is never injurious. It should be moistened with boiling water, and when cold laid on the spot damp; it will draw out oil, and when brushed off, leaves the garment uninjured. For solid grease, such as tallow, it will be necessary to pass a hot iron over without touching.

Preserving Eggs—There is a new patent in England for preserving eggs; the composition used is as follows, and by adopting this method eggs have been kept good two years:—"One bushel of quick lime, thirty two ounces of salt, eight ounces of cream of tartar. Mix the whole together, with as much water as will reduce the composition to such a consistency that an egg, when put into it, will swim."

To cure Bots in Horses.—Pour down the horse's throat a quarter of a pound of alum dissolved in a pint of water, milk warm; in ten minutes after administer a pint of linseed oil—in ten minutes the horse will rise and eat.

To prevent a cough coming on.—According to the writer in Le Gazette Medicale, persons coughing may be prevented by rubbing pretty smartly with the point of the finger the edge of the lips, the eye-lids, or the tip of the nose, when the first desire to cough is felt.

How to boil Eggs.—The Hartford Times recommends boiling eggs 30 minutes. It says, on the authority of the late Dr. Remington, of that city, who was an invalid, and very careful of his health, that they are better thus boiled than when boiled 5 minutes—that they become tender and mealy. We prefer ours after being boiled about one minute.

Very Superior Bread—A lady in Duchess county, N. Y., has furnished the following recipe for making superior bread:—Melt 2 oz. of butter in a pint of warm water, then add a tea-spoonful of salt. 1½ lbs. of flour and two table-spoonsful of yeast. Now beat well the yolks of three eggs and stir them in; then beat the whites to a stiff froth and stir them in also. They must be the last things put in. Beat the whole well together from 8 to 10 minutes, or until the mixture will not adhere to the spoon. Fill the pans about three quarters full and set it to rise, which will take from 3 to 4 hours. It must be baked in the pans in which it is set to rise, and is to be eaten moderately warm.

RARE AND VALUABLE RECIPES.

Soap Suds.—Instead of suffering your washerwoman to throw out the soap suds about the kitchen door, make her pour them in a barrel in your garden, and water your plants of all kinds with them.

Whooping Cough.—Equal parts of lamp oil and molasses is an excellent remedy; or a tea-spoonful of castor oil to a table-spoonful of molasses: a tea-spoonful of the mixture to be given whenever the cough is troublesome. It will afford relief at once, and in a few days it effects a cure. The same remedy relieves the croup, however violent the attack.

To prepare Pure Lard.—Get good white lard. Wash it in cold water, then put it into warm water and shake them well together, to wash out the salt; let them cool, then collect the lard from the top of the water, drain it, melt it again in a water bath, let it remain so for half an hour, and then pour off the clearest portion and preserve it from the air.

Worms.—A farmer recommends a good remedy for the worms which annually make such havoc among the noble shade trees of our public promenades. He says—apply a sponge tied on the end of a pole and saturated with sperm oil, to the nests or clusters of worms, which may be found in the branches early in the morning after a dew or rain.

A Good Tooth-ache Tincture.—Kreosote, 1 part; spirit of wine, 10 parts. Mix, and apply by means of a small piece of lint.

Dry Rot.—Dry rot may oftentimes be prevented in living trees, if the wounds are carefully covered with a composition made of rosin, tallow, beeswax and ochre, melted and mixed well together.

A good Wash Ball.—Take white soap 7 pounds; pearlash 6 ounces; orris powder 8 ounces; bergamot 1 ounce; oil of lavender half an ounce; cassia oil quarter of an ounce; oil of cloves 1 drachm; caraway half a drachm; mix with water to a paste, and finish to fancy.

Grease for Leather.—The common oil termed *dubbing*, usually applied to fire hose, is said by curriers to be very unsuitable for such a purpose, as it contains a portion of salt; the neats foot oil, to be had of butchers, is commended as far preferable, and should be applied to the hose when it is in a damp state, as it is then absorbed by the leather with facility.

An excellent Liquid Japan, for Harness, Shoes, and Boots, &c.—Take molasses, 8 parts; lampblack, 1 part; sweet oil, 1 part; gum arabic, 1 part; isinglass, 1 part. Mix well in 32 parts of water. Apply heat; when cool, add one ounce of spirits of wine. You may add an ox's gall. Place the bottle by the side of the fire before use, and apply it with a sponge, or the tip of the finger.

Dysentery.—As all classes of citizens are liable to be afflicted with Dysentery, Diarrhœa, &c., (says the Farmer's Gazette) we deem it our duty to make public the following simple and efficacious remedy, which has been known to us for several years, and which we have repeatedly used with complete success. It is simply to take a tumbler of cold water, thicken it with wheat flower to about the consistency of thick cream, and drink it. This is to be repeated several times in the course of the day, or as often as you are thirsty; and it is not very likely you will need to try it on the second day. We have not only used it in our case, but we have recommended it to our friends in many instances, and we never knew it to fail of effecting a speedy cure, even in the worst stages of dysentery. It is a simple remedy, and costs nothing.

Simple Method of Perforating Glass.—Place a drop of spirits of turpentine on the spot where the perforation is to be made, and in the centre of this put a small piece of camphor. The perforation can then be made with a well tempered borer or file.

To clean Metals.—Take oxalic acid, 1 part; rotten stone, 6 parts. Mix with equal parts of train oil and spirits of turpentine to a paste.

To make rose water.—Gather roses on a dry day, when they are full blown pick off the leaves, and to a peck put a quart of water, then put them into a cold still, make a slow fire under it; the slower you distil it the better it will be; then bottle it, and in two or three days you may cork it.

To make milk of roses.—To one pint of rose water, add one ounce of oil of almonds, and a ten drops of the oil of tartar.

N. B.—Let the oil of tartar be poured in last.

Wash for skin.—Four ounces of potash, four ounces of rose water, two ounces of pure brandy, and two ounces of lemon juice; put all these into two quarts of water, and when you wash, put a table spoonful or two of the mixture into the basin of water you intend washing in.

Lavender water—Put two pounds of lavender pips into two quarts of water, put them into a cold still, and make a slow fire under it; distil it off very slowly, and put it into a pot till you have distilled all your water, then clean your still well out, put your lavender water into it, and distill it off slowly again; put it into bottles and cork it well.

To make Hungary water.—Take a quantity of the flowers of rosemary, put them into a glass retort, and pour in as much spirits of wine as the flowers can imbibe; dilute the retort well, and let the flowers macerate for six days, then distill it in a sand heat.

Furniture Varnish.—White wax, eight ounces; oil of turpentine, one pint; melt the wax, and gradually mix in the turpentine.

To take stains out of mahogany.—Mix six ounces of spirits of salts, and a half an ounce of rock salt of lemons, powdered, together. Drop a little on the stains, and rub it with a cork till it disappear. Wash off with cold water.

To clean paint.—Paint should never be wiped with a cloth, but the dust loosened with bellows, and then removed with a dusting brush. If soiled, remove it with a spunge or flannel dipped in soda water, or pearl ash and water, and wring out dry; then immediately rinse it with a flannel and clean water, and dry as quickly as possible. When it is scoured all over, do it in the same manner, from the top downwards, and to ensure its being quickly dried one person should follow and dry with an old rag as fast as another has scoured off the dirt and washed away the soda.

To revive guilt frames.—Beat up the white of eggs with chloride of potasse or soda, in the proportion of three ounces of egg to one ounce of chloride. Blow off the dust from the frames, then do them over with a soft brush dipped in this mixture, and they will immediately become bright and fresh.

To remove mildew from linen.—Moisten a piece of soap, and rub it thickly into the part affected, Then scrape fine chalk, or rather whitening and rub that also in. Lay the linen on the grass, and from time to time, as it becomes dry, wet it a little. If the spots are not quite removed, repeat the process.

To remove spots of grease from paper.—Take equal parts of rock alum burnt, and flower of sulpher finely powdered together; moisten the paper with cold water; lay a small quantity of powder on the spot, rub gently with the finger, and the grease will disappear.

To remove ink spots.—Wet the place immediately with sorrel or lemon juice and rub on it hard white soap. Ink or iron mould may be removed by holding over a silver or pewter vessel of boiling water, and squeezing in the spot juice of sorrel, then rubbing with dry salt.

To remove grease from woollen or silk.—Potter's earth is never injurious. It should be moistened with boiling water and when cold laid on the spot damp, it will draw out oil, and when brushed off leave the garment uninjured—for solid grease, as tallow, it will be necessary to pass a hot iron over without touching.

To preserve feathers.—When poultry is picked, the feathers should be carefully preserved from damp and dirt, and all hard bits of quill cut out; then put them in paper bags, and hang them about a kitchen or dry laundry to season. When enough are collected to be of use they had better be dried in a cool oven. Fresh feathers must not be put in a bag with those that are partly dry.

To destroy rats.—Equal parts of ox-gall and oil of amber made into a paste with oatmeal; make it up into little balls; lay them about, and set plenty of vessels of water close at hand. The rats will eagerly eat the balls, which will make them very thirsty, and then they will drink till they kill themselves.

To get rid of beetles or cockroaches.—Lay about the floor, and stuff into the chinks and holes, unslacked lime, or common red wafers made of red lead, *not vermilion*

To get rid of bed and other bugs,—Gather a handful of the weed called assmart: boil in a pint of water, and when cold, rub the liquid where they frequent, and they will disappear.

To clean plate.—Let it be always washed in boiling water as soon as possible after using, and wiped dry with a soft cloth. Salt should never be suffered to remain in silver. Attention to these particulars will greatly lighten the labour of plate cleaning. The best whitening, which is sold in balls, wet with water or spirits of wine, applied wet, and then rubbed with the hand or with a soft cloth, till dry. Then brush off the remains of whitening, and polish with soft leather; or with a bit of flannel rub the plate over with salad oil, and then rub with the hand till quite bright.

N. B.—Leather, brushes, and rag must never be used in cleaning plate after they have been used on any other kind of metal.

To clean tin covers, sauce-pans, &c.—Keep them perfectly free from grease, and clean them with rotten stone and rape oil.

D 2

Britannia metal.—Having well scaled and dried, rub over every part with flannel, moistened with rape oil. Then rub briskly with a soft linen rag till quite clean, and polish with soft wash leather and fine whitening.

To clean carpets—Having well beaten and brushed, scour with ox gall, which will both extract grease and refresh the colors. A pint of gall, in three gallons of soft water, warm, will do a large carpet. It had better not all be mixed at once, but a third or a fourth part at a time; and when that is cold and dirty, throw it away and mix more.

Table baizes may be washed in the same mixture as above: then well rinsed in several waters, to take out the smell. Hang up to dry, without wringing, and while yet damp, fold smooth; they should remain a day or two.

To preserve polished steel from rusting.—Wrap the article in coarse brown paper and keep them in a dry place.

To preserve cheese from mites.—Paste r it coarse brown paper to cover every part.

Potato glue.—Take a pound of potatoes, peel them, and boil them, pound them while they are hot in three or four pounds of boiling water; then pass them through a hair sieve; afterwards add to them two pounds of good chalk, very finely powdered, previously mixed with four pounds of water, and stir them both together.—The result will be a species of glue or starch, capable of receiving every sort of coloring matter, even of powdered charcoal of brick, or lampblack, which may be employed as an economical means of painting door-posts walls, pailings, and other parts of buildings exposed to the action of the air.

Substitute for salt of sorrel for removing ink-spots or iron moulds—Take six parts of crystals of tartar in powder, three parts of alum, likewise pulversed, and use them in the same manner as salt of sorrel.

Varnish for boots and shoes, by which they are rendered impervious to water.—Take a pint of linseed oil, with a pound of mutton suet, six or eight ounces of bees' wax, and a small piece of rosin. Boil all these in a pipkin, and let the liquid cool till milk warm. Then with a hair brush lay it on new boots and shoes.

If old boots or shoes are to be varnished, the mixture is to be laid on when the leather is perfectly dry.

Cure for the black tongue.—A handful of fine salt rubbed upon the tongue of a horse that has the black tongue, will cure it, in at the most two applications. It is infallible, and simple and cheap enough.

Gapes in chickens.—It is said that if you keep iron standing in vinegar, or what is the same thing we suppose, vinegar standing in an iron vessel, and put a little of the liquid in the food every few days, it will cure or prevent the gapes in chickens. So simple a remedy for a fatal disease, may be worth trying.

Summer complaint.—The leaf of ße *bene plant* is highly efficacious in this disease, so prevalant among young children. A single leaf of this plant put into a glass of water immediately produces a beautiful thick mucilage, which is rendered pleasant by the addition of a small quantity of loaf sugar and is readily taken by children.

Protection of Vines—Plaister sprinkled over squashes, and cucumbers, when they first come out of the ground, will protect them from that little destroyer, the stripped bug.

Cure for corns.—Corns may be cured by binding on them at night a piece or spunge, moistened in a weak solution of pearl-ash. The skin may be brushed off in the morning, having been dissloved by the action of the caustic,

Expeditious method of taking out stains from scarlet, or velvet of any other color.—Take soap wort, bruise it, strain out its juice, and add to it a small quantity of black soap. Wash the stain with this liquor suffering it to dry between whiles, and by that method the spots will in a day or two entirely disappear.

To take spots out of silk.—Rub the spots with spirits of turpentine ; this spirit exhaling, carries off with it the oil that causes the spot.

Frost bitten.—Spirits of turpentine applied at once is a cure for freezing

To take iron moulds out of linen.—Hold the iron mould on the cover of a tankard of boiling water, and rub on the spot a little juice of sorrel and a little salt, and when the cloth has thoroughly imbibed the juice, wash it in lye.

To clean cotten gowns.—Make a solution of soap, put in the articles, and wash them in the usual way. If greens, reds, &c, run: add lemon juice, vinegar, or oil of vitriol, to the rinsing water.

To clean black veils.—Pass them through a warm liquor of bullock's gall and water ; rinse in cold water ; then take a small piece of glue, pour boiling water on it, and pass the veil through it ; clap it, and frame it to dry.

Cloths' ball.—Mix two pounds of pipe-clay, four ounces of Potter's clay, four ounces of whiting, and a quater of a pint of ox gall.

Chapped hands.—After washing, drop a few drops of honey and rub the hands together till the stickiness is entirely removed.

Slugs may be prevented from getting into fruit trees, by tightly tying a bit of hair-cloth round the stem of the tree. They can never get over it.

To clean all sorts of metal.—Mix half a pint of refined neat's foot oil, and half a gill of spirits of turpentine. Scrape a little kernel or rotten stone; wet a woollen rag therewith, dip it into the scraped kernel, and rub the metal well. Wipe it off with a soft cloth, polish it with dry leather, and use more of the kernel. In respect to steel, if it is very rusty, use a little powder of pumice with the liquid, on a separate woollen rag.

How to get a tight ring off a finger.
—Thread a needle, flat in the eye,
with a strong thread; pass the head
of the needle, with care, under the
ring, and pull the thread through a
few inches towards the hand; wrap
the long end of the thread thickly
round the finger regularly, all down
to the nail, to reduce its size. Then
lay hold of the short end of the
thread, and unwind it. The thread
pressing against the ring will
gradually remove it from the finger.
This never failing method will
remove the tightest ring without
difficulty, however much swolen the
finger may be.

To revive faded black cloth.—
Having cleaned it well, boil two or
three ounces of logwood for half an
hour. Dip it in warm water and
squeeze it dry, then put it into the
copper, and boil half an hour. Take
it out and add a small piece of green
copperass, and boil it another half
hour. Hang it in the air for an hour
or two, then rinse it in two or three
cold waters, dry it and let it be
regulary brushed with a soft brush,
over which a drop or two of oil of
olives has been rubbed.

To take stains out of silver plate.
—Steep the plate in soap leys for the
space of four hours; then cover it
over with whiting, wet with vinegar,
so that it may stick thick upon it,
and dry it by a fire; after which, rub
off the whiting, and pass it off with
bran, and the spots will not only disappear, but the plate will look exceedingly bright.

Sick Head-ache.—It is said that
three or four drops of nitre acid
dissolved in cold water and drank, is
a sure remedy for sick head ache,
when it arises from a want of acid in
the stomac.

Those who make candles, will find
it a great improvement to steep the
wicks in lime. The light will be
clear and the tallow will not run.
Britannia-ware should at be first
rubbed gently with a woollen cloth
and sweet oil; then washed in warm
suds and rubbed with soft leather

and whiting. Thus treated it will
retain its beauty to the last.

New iron should be very gradually
heated at first; after it has become
inured to the heat it is not likely
to crack.

It is a good plan to put new
earthenware into cold water, and let
it heat gradually until it boils, then
cool again.

The oftener carpets are shaken
the longer they will wear; the dirt
that collects under them grinds out
the thread.

Do not wrap knives and forks in
woollens—wrap them in a good
strong brown paper. Steel is
injured by lying in woolen.

Brass andirons should be cleansed,
done up in papers, and put in dry
places during the summer.

It is easy to have a supply of horse
raddish all winter. Have a quantity
grated while the root is in perfection,
put it into bottles, fill it with vinegar,
and keep it corked tight.

Nails are prevented from rusting,
by heating them, and dropping them
while hot in oil

Flies, wasps, and ear-wigs, may
be instantly killed by the application
of a drop of sweet oil to their backs.

To clean mahogany furniture.—
Dust it well; wash off spots and
dirt with vinegar. Apply cold drawn
linseed oil with a woolen cloth. Let
this remain an hour; then rub with
soft linen cloths till quite dry and
pollished. Bees' wax and turpentine
should never be used but for the
very commonest furniture, and then
in very small quantities.

To clean floor cloths.—Use no
soap or scrubbing brush; but wash
off the dirt with water and flannel.
Then do over with milk, and rub
with a soft brush till dry and shiny.
A flannel with a little bees' wax
gives them a good polish, but is apt
to make them slippery.

To clean looking glasses.—Remove
all fly stains and other dirt, by breathing on them and rubbing with a soft
rag. Then polish with a bit of flannel
in which is tied up powder blue.

To clean glass vessels, bird fountains, &c. A little sand and a very few small shot are useful to get off fur; but they sometimes scratch the glass and even break that which is very slight. The shells of raw eggs should always be saved for the purpose, they give the glass a beautiful polish: crush them, and shake about in the glass with cold water.

To scour boards.—Mix in a saucer three parts of common sand and one part of lime; lay a little of this on a scrubbing-brush. It is very useful in removing grease, and in getting rid of vermin. It is also a considerable saving, as no soap is required. Rinse the boards well, and they will look nice and bright.

To remove grease from boards.—Moisten Potter's clay with boiling water, and spread a thick plaster of it over the grease; let it remain all night before scouring; scour with hot water. If necessary repeat this process.

A strong cement for glass and wood—Steep isinglass twenty-four hours in common white brandy, then gently boil and keep stirring, until the composition is well mixed, and a drop, if cooled will become a strong jelly. Then strain it through a clean linen cloth into a vessel to be kept closely stopped. A gentle heat will dissolve this glue into colorless fluid. Dishes of wood, glass, or earthen, if united with this cement, will break elsewhere rather than separate in the old break. In applying the cement, rub the edges which are to be united then place them together, and hold them for two minutes, and the work is done. This is very easily done, and incomparably better than anything else for the purpose.

A cure for epileptic fits.—Take the roots of comfrey, sassafras, burdock, elecampane, and horse-radish, of each a large handfull, and the tops and buds of horehound and raspberry, each one handful; put these ingredients into a new earthen pot which

holds two gallons, fill it with soft water, let it simmer over hot ashes for eight hours; strain the decoction and put it in bottles for use; dose for an adult, a gill four times a day for a week before both the full and change of the moon. This preparation has been tried and proved effectual, when all other means have failed.

Insects taken into the stomach may generally be destroyed by a small quantity of vinegar, to which salt may be added. For insects that may get into the ear, use a little salad oil.

To clean paper hangings.—First blow off all the dust with the bellows Then take a very stale loaf of wheat bread; cut it in eight parts, so that each shall be of a size that the hand can grasp, and leave a crust by way of handle. Begin at the top of the room, and lightly wipe downwards in one direction half a yard at a stroke Thus go round and round the room till you get to the bottom. The dirt of the paper will fall with the crumbs.

To cure ring worms.—Get the comb of a church bell, that is, the grease which is applied to make it work easy, and which with the metal forms a kind of verdigris; mix it with unsalted lard, and apply a fresh plaster twice a day. It is not superstition that dictates the use of a church bell above any other, but the peculiar combination of metal employed for that purpose produces a different kind of verdigris. this remedy was long kept a profound secret, and many cures effected at an enormous charge. It has been equally efficacious as freely and openly communicated.

For a burn or scald.—If on the hand, tie it up in a bag of flour, or on the face or neck, shake flour from a dredge, and continue to do so till all the heat is drawn out. By this method the fire may be extracted without breaking the skin, and the sore will be quite healed and the skin drop off dry.

For a wasp sting.—Bind on the place a plaster of common salt just moistened; it will soon extract the venom. In case of swallowing a wasp, which is a most dangerous accident, it should be instantly attempted to get down a spoonful or more of salt with just water enough to make it liquid. This is a remedy always at hand. Salt and oil would be very useful in such a case, or salt, oil, honey, and vinegar, but there is not a moment to be lost in fetching a mixing what may not be close at hand.

To cure the bots in horses.—Pour down the horse a quarter of a pound of alum dissolved in a pint of water, (milk warm;) in five or ten minutes after pour down him a pint of linseed oil or other mild active purgative; in ten minutes the horse will rise and eat.

Ring worms, may be in most cases simply cured by scratching around the outer surface with the point of a sharp pin The disease will not, pass the line, if the skin is thus cut.

To choose Water for Brewing—Use soft water, or if it cannot be procured, expose hard water in the coolers to the air for two or three days, and throw a handful of soda into each hogshead.

Wainscot Varnish.—Gum anime, 32 parts; pale oil, 100 parts; litharge (in powder), 1 part; sugar of lead (in powder), 1 part; boil, until stringy, then cool a little, and add spirits of turpentine, 170 parts. Mix well and strain.

How to clean silks.—A quater of a pound of soft soap, a teaspoonful of brandy, a pint of gin; mix all well together. With a sponge or flannel spread the mixture on each side of the silk without creasing it; wash it in two or three waters, and iron it on the wrong side; it will look as good as new.

German method of making flowers grow in the winter.—We saw off such a branch of any shrub as will answer our purpose, and lay it for an hour or two in a running stream, if we can find one. The object of this is to get the ice from the bark, and soften the buds. It is afterward carried into our warm rooms and fixed upright in a wooden box or tub containing water. Fresh burnt lime is then added to the water and allowed to remain in it about twelve hours, when it is removed, and water added, with which a small quantity of vitriol is mixed to prevent its putrifying. In the course of some hours the blossoms begin to make their appearance, and afterwards the leaves. If more lime be added, the process is quickened, while if it be not used at all, the process is retarded and the leaves appear before the blossom.

A discovery for Housekeepers.—A correspondent of the Boston Transcript says, that a small quantity of green sage, placed in the closet, will cause red ants to disappear.

Cholera cure:—Drink plentifully of rice water, made very strong, with much sugar and a little laudanum in it. The effect is quick and certain. Out of 140 of the crew of the French frigate Arethusa, afflicted with Cholera, by taking the above, all but one recovered.

Cure for Hydrophobia.—3 pints of vinegar, one morning,—one noon, and one at night.

Typhus fever.—It cannot be too widely known that nitrous acid gas possesses the property of destroying the contagion of the typhus fever, and certainly preventing its spread. By the following simple method, the gas may be procured at a trifling expense: Place a little saltpetre in a saucer, and pour on it as much oil of vitriol as will just cover it; a copious discharge of acid gas will instantly take place, the quantity of which may be regulated by lessening or increasing the quantity of the ingredients.

For the Scarlet Fever.—Bath the patient with lye water with a sponge all over, and it will have the most salutary effect.

Musquitoe Bites.—We copy the following cure for a musquito bite from the New York Advertiser. It may be of use to some of our friends in the vicinity of the Capes: " Dissolve sal soda (bleaching powder) in water, and with the tip of your finger apply it to the bite, letting it dry—the cure is complete. A teaspoon full of the solution is sufficient for a hundred of bites."

To cure Rheumatism.—Col. J. O. Craig, or Readfield, says he has cured himself and several others of Rheumatism, by an external application of the following liniment. Take one pint of brandy, 1½ oz. saltpetre, 1 oz. camphor, 1 gill spirits turpentine, mix together, and when about to use it, shake it up well. Apply it by wetting a flannel with it, and dry it in by a flat or other iron as hot as it can be borne.

Eggs—as a remedy.—The white of an egg is said to be a specific for fish bones sticking in the throat. It is to be swallowed raw, and will carry down a bone very easily and certainly. There is another fact touching eggs which it will do very well to remember. When, as sometimes by accident, corrosive sublimate is swallowed, the white of one or two eggs, taken immediately, will neutralize the poison. and change the effect to that of a dose of calomel.

Pesimmons unripe, are said to have the effect of arresting cholera infantum and common diarrhæ. A simple infusion suffices to be administered when astringent remedies are indicated. Dr. Mettaircr, of Virginia, says it acts like a charm, when other astringents fail. A syrup of the same, or a tincture, can, of coarse be easily prepared, and would answer the same purpose.

Remedy for sea-sickness.—Take as much Cayenne pepper as you can rightly bear, in a basin of hot soup, and, it is said, all sickness, nausea, and squeamishness will disappear.

Who has the Tooth Ache?—Pulverized alum, mixed with salt moistened with water, and placed on cotten in the hollow tooth, stops the pain.

Alum and Children vs. Fire—We commend the following to the attention of parents just now, when we scarcely open a paper but a melancholy statement of " a child burnt" attracts our observation ;

" The danger and difficulty can very easily be avoided by the use of alum.

" When clothing are washed they should be rinsed out of alum water—the solution should be tolerably strong. If the clothing, which has been newly washed, should require starch, the alum may be put in the starch water.

" Alum should be used on all occasions; it renders the clothing fireproof. All clothing about a house or steamboat made of cotton should be impregnated with alum. For instance, bed and window curtains &c. Such articles generally having much fringing about them.

" This hint, if intended to, will prove a perfect safety to clothing from fire."

An excellent way of improving the hair.—Once in three days take some rich *unskimmed* milk that has been turned sour by setting in the sun.—Stir it up, to mix through it the cream that has collected on the surface.—Wash the hair with it, rubbing it well into the roots Let it remain on about a quarter of an hour ; then wash it off with while soap and warm water ; rinsing it afterwards with fresh water either warm or cold, according to the season —This is an Asiatic process: and if continued every third day, never fails to render the hair thick, soft and glossy.

Warner's Cordial.—12½ cts. worth of Cordial Seed, (burst the pods;) 12½ cts. of Lump Rhubarb, (cut in small pieces;) 12½ cts. of English Saffron, (broke a little;) one large Nutmeg. (cut in small pieces;) one quart of the best Brandy ; all to be put into a bottle and stand a day and a night in a vessel of warm water —not *too* warm.

Effectual cure for Rheumatism.—The following recipe, given by an Englishman to a respectable tradesman of Limerick (Ireland,) who had for a considerable time labored under the most violent rheumatic pains in all his limbs and joints, having been used by him as directed but five or six times, as he states, eradicated the disease completely. Anxious that so effectual a remedy should be made publicly known, we publish the recipe:

"Take 1 oz. of sulpher, 1½ oz. of saltpetre, ½ oz. of gum guscum, 2 nutmegs, the whole to be finely pounded in a mortar; add 12 oz. of treacle. A teaspoonful to be taken every night on going to bed. Should it operate too much of the bowels, a smaller quantity is to be taken."

Receipt for making Blackberry Syrup.—The following recipe for making the above medicine, which has been used in many families with great success for several years. It is said to be almost a specific cure for the summer complaint, and in 1832 was used with success in the cholera. In all kinds of complaints usual in warm weather, it has been proved to be useful; and every family should supply themselves with it. To two quarts of juice of blackberries, add the following ingredients: —1 lb. loaf sugar, ½ oz. nutmegs, ½ oz. cinnamon, ¼ oz. cloves, ¼ oz. allspice. Boil altogether for a short time, and when cold, add a pint of fourth proof brandy. From a teaspoonful to a wine glass, according to the age of the patient, is to be given at proper intervals, until relieved.

To Eradicate Corns.—Every one knows that the surface of the body is covered, above the true skin, by the cuticle or scarf skin. This is a thin membrane, save when it is exposed to pressure and rubbing, (friction) In this case it becomes much thickened and hardened, as on the soles of feet, and on the palms of the hands. And it is not unworthy of remark, that the indura tion is in direct proportion to the exigency of nature; but there is a morbid induration when the pressure exceeds, or is applied where it is not necessary. In this case, the distinguished name of corns has been applied to the diseased parts.

Every one who has seen a poultice applied, may remark, that it has the effect of softening — generally, of detaching the cuticle. Now, let a poultice, of such size and consistency as will preserve its moisture around the part, be applied to the offending corn at bed time; on the following morning the greater part of the indurated cuticle (the corn) may be removed by the fingers. A little spermaceti ointment may be used during the following day, or the part may be entirely neglected. I may, in some cases, be necessary to repeat this process once or twice, and the cure will be safe, easy and certain.

Recipe for Rheumatism.— One gill of whiskey, one gill sweet oil, one tablespoonful of garlic juice, one teaspoonful of turpentine, 6 cts. of camphor, 6 cts. laudanum, 12½ cts. oil of sassafrass; let stand on the stove for one hour, and simmer very gently.

To wash Chintz.— Take two pounds of rice, boil it in two gallons of water till soft; then pour the whole into a tub; let it stand till about the warmth in general used for coloring linens; then put the chintz in, and use the rice instead of soap; wash it in this till the dirt appears to be out, then boil the same quantity as above, but strain the rice from the water, and mix it in warm clear water. Wash in this till quite clean; afterwards rinse it in the water which the rice has been boiled in, and this will answer the end of starch, and no dew will affect it. If a gown, it must be taken to pieces, and when dried be careful to hang it as smooth as possible;—after it is dry, rub it with it a sleek stone, but use no iron.

To clean white satin and flowered silks.—Mix sifted stale bread crumbs with powder glue, and rub it thoroughly all over, then shake it well, and dust it with clean soft cloths. Afterwards, where there are any gold or silver flowers, take a piece of crimson ingrain velvet, rub the flowers with it, which will restore them to their original lustre.

To clean colored silks of all kinds.—Put some soft soap into boiling water, and beat it till dissolved in a strong lather. At a hand heat put in the article. If strong, it may be rubbed as in washing; rinse it quickly in warm water, and add oil of vitriol, sufficient to give another water a sourish taste, if for bright yellows, crimson, maroons, and scarlet; but for oranges, fawns, browns, or their shades, use no acid. For bright scarlet, use a solution of tin. Gently squeeze and then roll it in a coarse sheet, and wring it. Hang it in a warm room to dry, and finish it by calendering or mangling.

For pink, rose colours, and thin shades, &c. instead of oil of vitriol, or solution of tin, prefer lemon juice, or white tartar, or vinegar.

For blues, purples, and their shades, add a small quantity of American pearl-ash; it will restore the colors. Wash the articles like a linen garment, but instead of wringing, gently squeeze and sheet them, and when dry, finish them with fine gum water, or dissolved isinglass, to which add some pearl ash, rubbed on the wrong side; then pin them out.

Blues of all shades are dyed with archil, and afterwards dipped in a vat: twice cleaning with pearl-ash, restores the color. For olive greens, a small quantity of verdigris dissolved in water, or a solution of copper, mixed with the water, will revive the color again.

To dip rusty black silks.—If it requires to be red dyed, boil logwood, and in half an hour, put in the silk, and let it simmer half an hour. Take it out, and dissolve a little blue vitriol and green copperas, cool the copper, let it simmer half an hour, then dry it over a stick in the air. If not red dyed, pin it out, and rinse it in spring water, in which half a tea-spoonful of oil of vitriol has been put. Work it about five minutes, rinse it in cold water, and finish it by pinning and rubbing it with gum water.

To clean silk stockings.—Wash with soap and water; and simmer them in the same for ten minutes, rinsing in cold water. For a blue cast, put one drop of liquid blue into a pan of cold spring water, run the stockings through this a minute or two, and dry them. For a pink cast, put one or two drops of saturated pink dye in cold water, and rinse them through this. For a flesh color, add a little rose pink in a thin soap liquor, rub them with clean flannel, and calender or mangle them.

To clean cotton gowns.—Make a solution of soap, put in the articles, and wash them in the usual way. If greens, reds, &c. run, add lemon juice, vinegar, or oil of vitrol, to the rinsing water.

To clean gloves without wetting.—Lay the gloves upon a clean board, make a mixture of dried fulling-earth, and powdered alum, and pass them over on each side with a common stiff brush; then sweep it off, and sprinkle them well with dry bran and whiting, and dust them well; this, if they be not exceedingly greasy, will render them quite clean; but if they are much soiled, take out the grease with crumbs of toasted bread, and powder of burnt bone; then pass them over with a woolen cloth dipped in fulling-earth or alum powder: and in this manner they can be cleaned without wetting, which frequently shrinks and spoils them.

To make plate look like new.—Take of unslaked lime and alum, a pound each; of aqua-vitæ and vinegar each a pint, and of beer grounds two quarts; boil the plate in the, and they will set a beautiful gloss upon it.

To take stains out of silver plate.—Steep the plate in soap leys for the space of four hours; then cover it over with whiting, wet with vinegar, so that it may stick thick upon it, and dry it by a fire; after which, rub off the whiting, and pass it over with dry bran, and the spots will not only disappear, but the plate will look exceedingly bright.

To clean all sorts of metal.—Mix half a pint of refined neat s-foot oil, and half a gill of spirits of turpentine. Scrape a little kernel or rotten stone, wet a woolen rag therewith, dip it into the scraped kernel, and rub the metal well. Wipe it off with a soft cloth, polish with dry leather, and use more of the kernel. In respect to steel, if it is very rusty, use a little powder of pumice with the liquid, on a separate woolen rag first.

To prevent the tooth-ache.—Rub well the teeth and gums with a hard tooth brush, using the flowers of sulphur as a tooth powder, every night on going to bed; and if it is done after dinner it will be best; this is an excellent preservation to the teeth, and void of any unpleasant smell.

A radical cure for the tooth-ache.—Use as a tooth powder the Spanish snuff called Sibella, and it will clean the teeth as well as any other powder, and totally prevent the tooth-ache; and make a regular practice of washing behind the ears with cold water every morning. The remedy is infallible.

To clean the teeth.—Take of good soft water, 1 quart; juice of lemon, 2 oz.; burnt alum, 6 grains; common salt, 6 grains; mix. Boil them a minute in a cup, then strain and bottle for use; rub the teeth with a small bit of sponge tied to a stick, once a week.

To make the teeth white.—A mixture of honey with the purest charcoal will prove an admirable cleanser.

To sweeten the breath.—Take two ounces of terra japonica; half an ounce of sugar-candy, both in powder. Grind one drachm of the best ambergris with ten grains of pure musk, and dissolve a quarter of an ounce of clean gum tragacanth in two ounces of orange-flower water. Mix all together, so as to form a paste, which roll into pieces of the thickness of a straw. Cut these into pieces, and lay them in clean paper. This is an excellent perfume for those whose breath is in any way, disagreeable.

To preserve flour.—Attach a number of lofts to every mill, so that the flour, in place of being thrust into sacks, the moment it escapes from the friction of the stones, may be taken up by the machinery, and spread out to cool in the most careful manner. The violent friction of the stones necessarily creates a great heat and steam; and if flour is thrust into sacks in this state, a chemical action will make it moist, soft, and clammy.

To extinguish a chimney on fire.—Shut the doors and windows, throw water on the fire in the grate, and then stop up the bottom of the chimney.

Another method.—The mephitic vapour produced by throwing a handful of flour of sulphur on the burning coals, where a chimney is on fire, will immediately extinguish the flames.

To remove stains from mourning dresses.—Boil a good handful of fig leaves in two quarts of water, till reduced to a pint. Bombazine, crape, cloth, &c. need only be rubbed with a sponge dipped in the liquor, and the effect will be instantly produced.

To keep up sash windows.—This is performed by means of cork, in the simplest manner, and with scarcely any expense. Bore three or four holes in the sides of the sash, into which insert common bottle corks, projecting about the sixteenth part of an inch. These will press against the window frames, along the usual groove, and by their elasticity support the sash at any height which may be required   E

To warm a carriage, or small apartment.—Convey into it a stone bottle of boiling water, or for the feet, a single glass bottle of boiling water wrapped in flannel.

To preserve furs.—When laying up muffs and tippets for the summer, if a tallow candle be placed on or near them, all danger of caterpillars will be obviated.

To choose a carpet.—Always select one the figures of which are small; for in this case the two webs in which the carpeting consists, are always much closer interwoven than in carpets where large figures upon ample grounds are represented.

To prevent cold feet at night.—Draw off the stocking, just before undressing, and rub the ancles and feet with the hand as hard as can be borne for five or ten minutes. This will diffuse a pleasurable glow, and those who do so, will never have to complain of cold feet in bed. Frequent washing, and rubbing them thoroughly dry, with a linen cloth or flannel, is useful for the same purpose. In removing from the feet the accumulating dirt that obstructs the pores, we promote health, by facilitating that perspiration which nature intended.

Prescription to make the Medicine called "Brown's Mixture."—Take 3 cents worth of liquorice, 2 cents worth of rock candy, and 3 cents worth of gum arabic, put them in a vessel, with a pint of water; simmer them till nearly dissolved, then add three cents worth of paregoric, and a like quantity of antimonial wine. Let it cool and sip whenever the cough is troublesome. It is pleasant and infallible.

To clean water casks.—Scour the inside well out with water and sand, and afterwards, apply a quantity of charcoal dust; another and better method is, to rinse them with a pretty strong solution of oil of vitriol and water, which will entirely deprive them of their foulness.

To remove flies from rooms.—Take half a tea-spoonful of black pepper, in powder, one tea-spoonful of brown sugar, and one table-spoonful of cream; mix them well together, and place them in the room, on a plate, where the flies are troublesome, and they will soon disappear.

Easy method of preserving Animal Food sweet for several days.—Veal, mutton, beef, or venison may be kept for nine or ten days perfectly sweet and good, in the of summer, by lightly covering the same with bran, and hanging it in a high and windy room; therefore, a cupboard full of small holes, or a wire safe, so as the wind may have a passage through, is recommended to be placed in such a room, to keep away the flies.

To purify fly blown Meat. It has been successfully proved, by many experiments, that meat entirely fly-blown has been sufficiently purified to make good broth, and had not a disagreeable taste, by being previously put into a vessel containing a certain quantity of beer. The liquor will become tainted, and have a putrid smell.

To loosen the glass stoppers of Smelling Bottles and Decanters.—With a feather rub a drop or two of olive oil round the stopple, close to the mouth of the bottle or decanter, which must be then placed before the fire, at the distance of a foot or eighteen inches; in which position the heat will cause the oil to spread downward between the stopple and the neck. when the bottle or decanter has grown warm, gently strike the stopple on one side, and on the other, with any light wooden instrument; then try it with the hand, if it will not yet move, place it again before the fire, adding, if you choose, another drop of oil, after a while strike again as before; and by persevering in this process, however tightly the stopple may be fastened in, you will at length succeed in loosening it.

To revive a dull fire.—Powdered nitre strewed on the fire, is the best bellows that can be used.

To prevent Children from eating their Food too quickly.—Children, when very young, get into the habit of eating their food too quickly, particularly fruit, other substances of which they are fond. To prevent their acquiring this habit, amusing devices might be employed, as cutting an apple, a pear, a piece of cake, or any other article of the same sort, into a number of pieces, arranging them in lines like an army, with one as an officer in the centre, and telling them that the whole army must be devoured piece by piece, and in a regular manner! This interests little children so much, that they soon prefer it to a more speedy mode of consumption

To clean Marble—Take a bullock's gall, a gill of soap less, half a gill of turpentine, and make it into a paste with pipe clay; then apply it to the marble, and let it dry a day or two; then rub it off; and, if not clean, apply it a second or third time until it is clean.

To clean White Veils.—Put the veil in a solution of white soap, and let it simmer a quarter of an hour. Squeeze it in some warm water and soap, till quite clean. Rinse it from soap, and then in clean cold water, in which is a drop of liquid blue. Then pour boiling water on a tea-spoonful of starch, run the veil through this, and clear it well by clapping it. Afterwards pin it out, keeping the edges straight and even.

To clean and starch Point Lace.— Fix the lace in a prepared tent, draw it straight, make a warm lather of Castille soap, and, with a fine brush dipped in, rub over the point gently; and when it is clean on one side, do the same to the other; then throw some clean water on it, in which a little alum has been dissolved, to take off the suds, and having some thin starch, go over with the same on the wrong side, and iron it on the same side when dry, then open it with a bodkin, and set it in order.

To clean point lace, if not very dirty, without washing; fix it in a tent as the former, and go over with fine bread, the crust being pared off, and when it is done, dust out the crumbs, &c.

To Wash and Starch Lawns.— Lawns may be done in the same manner as the former, only observe to iron them on the wrong side, and use gumarabic water instead of starch, and, according to what has been directed for sarcenets, any coloured silks may be starched, abating or augmenting the gum water, as may be thought fit according to the stiffness intended.

To make the celebrated Pomade Divine.— According to Dr. Beddoes, this composition is as follows, viz. beef marrow, twelve ounces, steeped in water ten days, and afterwards in rode water twenty-four hours; flowers of benjamin, pounded storax, and Florentine orris, and clove and nutmeg, a quarter of an ounce. The whole to be put in an earthen vessel, closely covered down, to keep in the fumes, and being suspended in water made to boil three hours; after which, the whole is to be strained and put into bottles.

To take out fruit spots.—Let the spotted part of the cloth imbibe a little water without dipping, and hold the part over a lighted common brimstone match at a proper distance. The sulphurous gas which is discharged, soon causes the spot to disappear.

To preserve Chesnuts and Filberts— The chesnut is to be treated like the walnut after the husk is removed, which, in the chesnut, opens of itslf. Chesnuts and walnuts may be preserved during the whole winter, by covering them with earth, as farmers do potatoes.

To clean Oil Paintings.— I. smoked, or very dirty, take stale urine, in which a little common salt is dissolved: rub them over with a woollen cloth dipped in that, till you think them quite clean, then with a sponge wash them over with fair water; then dry them, and rub them over with a clean cloth.

To prevent Danger from Wet Clothes. Keep if possible in motion, and take care not to go near a fire, or into any very warm place, so as to occasion a sudden heat, till some time after you have been able to procure dry clothes.

Method of preventing Hysterics.—Carraway seeds, finely pounded, with a small proportion of ginger and salt, spread upon bread and butter, and eaten every day, especially early in the morning, and at night, before going to bed, are successfully used in Germany as a domestic remedy against hysterics.

To fumigate foul rooms.—To one table-spoonful of common salt and a little powdered maganese in a glass cup, add three or four different times, a quarter of a wine glass of vitriolic acid. At every addition of the acid, the vapour will come in contact with the malignant miasmata, and destroy them.

To cure a bruise in the eye.—Take conserve of red roses, and also a rotten apple, put them in a fold of thin cambric, apply it to the eye, and it will draw the bruise out.

Easy and almost instantaneous cure for the ague.—When the fit is on, take a new laid egg, in a glass of brandy, and go to bed immediately. This very simple recipe has cured a great many, after more celebrated preparations have proved unsuccessful.

Remedy for burns.—A little spirit of turpentine, applied to recent burns, will mitigate the pain, if not wholly remove it.

For a pain in the ear.—Oil of sweet almonds two drachms, and oil of amber four drops; apply four drops of this mixture when in pain, to the part affected.

For Chilblains. Soak them in warm bran and water, then rub them well with mustard seed flour; but it will be better if they are done before they break.

To prevent corns from growing on the feet. — Easy shoes; frequently bathing the feet in luke-warm water, with a little salt or pot-ashes dissolved in it.

The corn itself will be completely destroyed by rubbing it daily with a little caustic solution of pot ash, till a soft skin is formed.

Cure for Warts.—The milky juice of the stalks of spurge, or of the common fig leaf, by persevering application, will, to a certainty, soon remove them.

To destroy snails and slugs.—A few turnips sliced and laid on the borders of the garden they infest, will attract them in the evening.

To change Hair to a deep Brown.—A solution of the silver caustic in water is the foundation of all the nostrums for this purpose, it must be well diluted before used.

To take off a Gold Ring sticking tight on a Finger.— Touch it with mercury, and it becomes so brittle that a slight blow with a hammer will break it.

To destroy Grubs.— Cut a turf, and lay it with the grass downwards near the plant destroyed by the grub, and it will attract him.

To discharge Grease from Leather.— The white of an egg applied to the spot, and dried in the sun; or, to two table spoonsful of spirit of turpentine, add half an ounce of mealy potatoes with some of the best Durham mustard. Apply this mixture to the spot and rub it off when dry. A little vinegar added, revives, and is perhaps more efficacious.

Economical Use of Nutmeg.—If a person begin to grate a nutmeg at the stalk end, it will prove hollow throughout; whereas the same nutmeg, grated from the other end, would have proved sound and solid to the last. This circumstance may be thus accounted for:—The centre of a nutmeg consists of a number of fibres issuing from the stalk, and its continuation through the centre of the fruit, the other ends of which fibres though closely surrounded and pressed by the fruit, do not adhere to it when the stalk is grated away.

To increase the Growth of Hair.—Hartshorn beat small, and mixed with oil being rubbed upon the head of persons who have lost their hair, will cause it to grow again as at first.

Composition for restoring scorched Linen.—Boil, to a good consistency, in half a pint of vinegar, tow ounces of Fuller's earth, an ounce of hen's dung, half an ounce of cake soap, and the juice of tow onions. Spread this composition over the whole of the damaged part; and if the scorching were not quite through, and the threads actually consumed, after suffering it to dry on, and letting it receive a subsequent good washing or tow the place will appear full as white and perfect as any other part of the linen.

To preserve Furs, Woollens, &c.—Many woollen-drapers put bits of camphor, the size of a nutmeg, in papers, on different parts of their shelves in their shop; and as they brush their cloths every two, three, or four months, this keeps them free from moths; and this should be done in boxes where furs, &c. are put. A tallow candle is frequently put between each muff when laid by.

To keep Moths, Beetles, &c. from clothes.—Put a piece of camphor in a linen bag, or some aromatic herbs, in the drawers, among linen or woolen clothes, and neither moth nor worm will come near them.

To prevent Brass Vessels from contracting Verdigris after being used.—Instead of wiping them dry, it has been found, that by constantly immersing them in water, they are kept perfectly innoxious, and will remain for years, fully as clean, and nearly as bright, as when they first came out of the hands of the workmen.

Useful Knife-Board.—A common knife board, covered with thick buff leather, on which are put emery, one part; crocus martis, three parts; in very fine powder, mixed into a thick paste with a little lard or sweet oil, and spread on the leather to the thickness of a shilling, gives a far superior edge and polish to knives; and will not wear the knife nearly so much as the common method of using brick dust on a board.

To clean candlesticks and snuffers.—If silver or plated, care must be taken that they are not scratched in getting off the wax or grease: therefore never use a knife for that purpose, nor hold them before the fire to melt the wax or grease, as in general the hollow part of the candlesticks, towards the bottom, is filled with a composition that will melt if made too hot. Pour boiling water over them; this will take all the grease off without injury if wiped directly with an old cloth, and save the brushes from being greased; let them in all other respects be cleaned like the rest of the plate.

If japanned bed-room candlesticks, never hold them near the fire, or scrape them with a knife; the best way is to pour water upon them just hot enough to melt the grease; then wipe them with a cloth, and if they look smeary, sprinkle a little whiting or flour upon them and rub it clean off.

Be very particular in cleaning the patent snuffers, as they go with a spring, and are easily broken. The part which shuts up the snuffing has in general a small hole in it, where a pin can be put, to keep it open while cleaning it; be sure to have them well cleaned, that the snuff may not drop about when using them. The extinguishers likewise must be well cleaned in the inside, and be put ready with the snuffers, that the candlesticks may not be taken up without them.

If the sockets of the candlesticks be too large for the candles, put a piece of paper round the end, but do not let it be seen above the nozzle of the candlestick. Be particular in putting them in straight, and having clean hands, that they may not be dirtied. Always light the candles to burn off the cotton, before setting them up; but leave the ends long enough to be lighted with ease when wanted.

E 2

To clean looking-glasses, mirrors, &c.—If they should be hung so high that they cannot be conveniently reached, have a pair of steps to stand upon; but mind that they stand steady. Then take a piece of soft sponge, well washed and cleaned from every thing gritty, just dip it into water and squeeze it out again, and then dip it into some spirits of wine. Rub it over the glass; dust it over with some powder blue, or whiting sifted through muslin; rub it lightly and quickly off again, with a cloth : then take a clean cloth, and rub it well again, and finish by rubbing it with a silk handkerchief.

If the glass be very large, clean one half at a time, as otherwise the spirit of wine will dry before it can be rubbed off. If the frames are not varnished, the greatest care is necessary to keep them quite dry, so as not to touch them with the sponge, as this will discolor or take off the gilding.

To clean the frames, take a little raw cotton in the state of wool, and rub the frames with it; this will take off all the dust and dirt without injuring the gilding. If the frames are well varnished, rub them with spirit of wine, which will take out all spots, and give them a fine polish. Varnished doors may be done in the same manner. Never use any cloth to frames, or drawings, or unvarnished oil paintings, when cleaning and dusting them.

To avoid Sunburn and Freckles.—females liable to freckle or sunburn should never wear white veils, as they increase the power of the sun's light.

To keep warm.—Wear flannel, it will keep the body warm in winter, and ice from melting in the Summer: as it prevents the passage of heat from the man and to the ice.

Linen good for colds, or catarrh in the head.—Persons with catarrh in the eyes or nose will experience more relief on applying a linen or cambric handkerchief to the face than from one made of cotton : because the linen, conducting readily absorbes the heat and diminishes the inflamation, while the cotton repulsing to the heat increases the temperature, and the pain.

Loose clothing warmer than close fits.—Loose clothing is much warmer than that which fits tight because the quantity of imperfectly conducting air thus confined around the body resists the escape of animal heat.

To Wash White Merino Shawls.—Wash the shawl in fair suds made beforehand, rub no soap on the shawl rinse in clear warm water, with two changes if you please; then take solution of gum arabic, and add to it warm water till you think it will produce a little stiffness like starch when dry. Press with a moderately hot iron, before quite dry, laying a clean cotton or linen cloth between the iron and the shawl.

To clean tea trays—Do not pour boiling water over them, particularly on japanned ones, as it will make the varnish crack and peel off; but have a sponge wetted with warm water and a little soap, if the tray be very dirty; then rub it with a cloth; if it looks smeary, dust on a little flour, then rub it with a dry cloth. If the proper tray gets marked take a piece of woolen cloth, with a little sweet oil, and rub it over the marks, if any thing will take them out this will. Let the urn be emptied and the top wiped dry, particularly the outside, for if any wet be suffered to dry on it will leave a mark.

Renovation of Manuscripts.—Take a hair pencil and wash the part which has been effaced with a solution of prussiate of potash in water, and the writing will again appear, if the paper has not been destroyed.

A cure for sore backs of horses.—The best method of curing sore backs, is to dissolve half an ounce of blue vitriol in a pint of water, and dab the injured parts with it four or five times a day.

To wash and clean Gentlemen's Gloves. — Wash them in soap and water till the dirt is got out, then stretch them on wooden hands, or pull them out in their proper shape. Never wring them, as that puts them out of form, and makes them shrink; put them one upon another and press the water out. Then rub the following mixture over the outside of the gloves. If wanted quite yellow, take yellow ochre; if quite white, pipe clay; if between the two, mix a little of each together. By proper mixtures of these any shade may be produced. Mix the color with beer or vinegar.

Let them dry gradually, not too near the fire, nor in too hot a sun; when they are about half dried, rub them well, and stretch them out to keep them from shrinking, and to soften them. When they are well rubbed and dried, take a small cane and beat them, then brush them; when this is done, iron them rather warm, with a piece of paper over them, but do not let the iron be too hot.

To preserve hats. — Hats require great care or they will soon look shabby. Brush them with a soft camel-hair brush, this will keep the fur smooth. Have a stick for each hat to keep it in proper shape, especially if the hat has got wet; put the stick in as soon as the hat is taken off, and when dry put it into a hat box, particularly if not in constant use, as the air and dust soon turn hats brown. If the hat is very wet, handle it as lightly as possible; wipe it dry with a cloth, or silk handkerchief; then brush it with the soft brush. If the fur sticks so close when almost dry, that it cannot be got loose with the soft brushes, then use the hard ones; but if the fur still sticks, damp it a little with a sponge dipped in beer or vinegar; then brush it with a hard brush till dry.

An infallible lotion for blows, bruises and sprains in horses. — Take of spirit of wine, eight ounces; dissolve one ounce of camphor first, in the spirits of wine, then add one ounce of oil of turpentine, one ounce of spirit of sal ammoniac, oil of origanum half an ounce, and one large table spoonful of liquid laudanum. It must be well rubbed in with the hand, for full a quarter of an hour, every time it is used; which must be four times each day. You will be astonished at its efficacy when you try it.

How to know the age of a Dog until he be six years old. — A dog has a very visible mark in his teeth, as well as a horse, which mark does not disappear until he be very near, or full six years old. Look to the four front teeth, both in the upper and lower jaw, but particularly to the teeth in the upper jaw; for, in those four front teeth, the mark remains longest: at twelve months old, you will observe every one of the four front teeth, both in the upper and under jaw, jagged and uneven, nearly in the form of a *flower de luce*, but not quite so pointed, at the edge of the jags, as a flower de luce is. As the dog advances in age, these marks will wear away, gradually decrease, and grow smoother and less jagged every year. Between three and four years old, these marks will be full half worn down; and when you observe all the four front, both in the upper and lower jaw, quite worn smooth and even, and not in the least jagged, then you may conclude that the dog is nearly, if not full six years old. When those marks are worn quite flat and even, and those teeth quite level and even, you can no longer judge the age of a dog. Many huntsmen and game-keepers ignorantly look at the side and eye teeth of a dog; there are many dogs not two years old, which have had the canker in the mouth, with hardly one sound tooth in their heads.

An effectual preventive against flies settling upon, or biting animals — Boil 1 oz. of coloquintida half an hour in 3 pints of water, dip a sponge in the liquid and rub the animal over the parts liable to be attacked.

To stain Leather Gloves.—Those pleasing hues of yellow, brown, or tan colour, are readily imparted to leather gloves by this simple process:—steep saffron in boiling-hot water for twelve hours then having sewd up the tops of the gloves to prevent the dye from staining the in sides wet them over with a sponge dipped in the liquid; the quantity of saffron as well as of water depends on how much dye may be wanted and their relative proportions on the depth of colour required A common tea cup will contain sufficient in quantity, for a single pair of gloves

To make old Gold appear like new.—Dissolve sal ammoniac in urine, coil the chain in it, and it will have the desired effect.

To varnish drawings or carn-work Boil some parchment in soft clear water, in a glazed pipkin, till it becomes a fine clear size strain, and keep it for use; give your work two coats, observing to do it quickly and lightly; when dry apply your varnish.

Medicated Cephalic snuff.—Take half an ounce each of rosemary, sage, lillies of the valley, and the tops of sweet marjoram, with a drachm each of asaracca root, lavender flowers and nutmeg. Reduce the whole to a fine powder, and take it like common snuff, as often as may be necessary for the relief of the head, &c. There are many more powerful snuffs for medicinal purposes, but few so useful, agreeable, and innocent, to be used at pleasure.

Easy method of restoring and rendering legible damaged parchment deeds, &c.—When a parchment deed becomes obliterated and discolored by moisture, on simply immersing it in spring water, for about a minute, then pressing it between sheets of bloting paper, to prevent its shrivelling up while getting dry: it will generally, when it has nearly approached that state, be found to have resumed its original colour, and appear as perfectly plain, but should the characters not prove legible on its becoming moderately dry

the operation must be repeated as often as it may be necessary. The following mixture, it is asserted will make writing which has been obliterated, faded, or sunk, either on paper or on parchment, immediately legible,—Bruise two or three nutgalls, infuse them in half a pint of wine, and let the bottle stand for two days in the sun or in any other equally warm situation: then wash the part of the parchment or paper which is wanted to have the writing recovered, by means of a sponge or soft brush, dipped in the vinous infusion; and the purpose will be immediately answered if it be sufficiently strong. Should that not happen, its power must be increased by an additional quantity of galls; and, perhaps, in some cases, stronger heat and even stronger wine, may also be necessary.

Method of cleaning Playing-cards.—Nothing soils sooner than playing cards, and fine ones are an expensive article to re-place. The following method will be found to remove every thing from them but a stain, and will give the dirtiest pack possible the appearance of being new. Rub the soiled card with a piece of flannel and good fresh butter, until the butter shall have cleaned off all the dirt. So soon as the dirt is removed, wipe off the butter with a clean rag; and to restore the card to its former gloss, rub the surface sharply with a piece of flannel and some flour: rub the edges neatly with fine sand paper and the operation is completed.

To stain beech of a mahogany color.—Take two ounces of dragon's blood, break it in pieces, and put it into a quart of rectified spirits of wine; let the bottle stand in a warm place, shake it frequently, and when dissolved it is fit for use.

Another.—Take one pound of logwood, boil it in four quarts of water, add a double handful of walnut peeling; boil it up again, take out the chips, and add a pint of the best vinegar, and it will be fit for use.

Curious method of separating Gold and Silver from Lace.—Cut in pieces the gold or silver lace, intended to be divested of any thing but the pure metal; tie it up tightly in linen and boil it in soap ley, till the size appears diminished; then take the cloth out of the liquid, and, after repeatedly rinsing it in cold water, beat it well with a mallet, to draw out all the alkaline particles. On opening the linen, to the astonishment of those who have never before witnessed the process, the metallic part will be found pure and undiminished, in all its natural brightness.

To detect copper in Pickles or Green Tea.—Put a few leaves of the tea, or some of the pickles cut small, into a phial, with two or three drachms of liquid ammonia diluted with one half the quantity of water. Shake the phial, when if the most minute portion of copper be present, the liquid will asssume a fine blue color.

An easy method of breaking Glass to any required Figure.—Make a small notch by means of a file, on the edge of a piece of glass, then make the end of a tobacco-pipe, or of a red iron of the same size, red hot in the fire, apply the hot iron to the notch, and draw it slowly along the surface of the glass, in any direction you please; a crack will be made in the glass, and will follow the direction of the iron. Round glass bottles or flasks, may be cut in the middle, by wrapping round them a worsted thread, dipped in spirits of turpentine, and setting it on fire, when fastened on the glass.

Ready mode of mending cracks in stoves, pipes, and iron ovens, as practised in Germany.—When a crack is discovered in a stove, through which the fire or smoke penetrates, the aperture may be completely closed in a moment with a composition consisting of wood ashes and common salt, made up into paste with a little water, and plastered over the crack. The good effect is equally certain, whether the stove, &c. be cold or hot.

To clear houses, barns, &c. of rats and mice.—Gather the plant dog's tongue, the cynoglossum officinale of Linnæus, which grows abundantly in every field; at the period when the sap is in its full vigour, bruise it with a hammer, or otherwise, and lay it in the house, barn or granary, infested by rats or mice, and those troublesome animals will immediately shift their quarters.

To bleach straw bonnets.—Take a common plate, fill it with water, set a small piece of sheet iron, with the ends bent down to raise the top above the water, place in the middle of the plate; on which tin plate you must place a piece of brimstone, set it on fire and cover it over tight with a large bell or large tumbler or bowl that will just shut down close within the brim of the plate; at first raise the cover a little to admit a current of air to cause the sulphur to burn, until you fill the whole with a white vapor; then shut down tight about ten minutes; and the water will absorb the sulphurus acid gas, with which straw hats are washed over to bleach in the most approved manner. It will also remove fruit and vegetable stains from dress.

A Water-proof Varnish for Prints, and Pictures.—Dilute one quarter of a pound of Venice Turpentine, with a gill, or thereabouts, of spirits wine. If too thick, add a little more of this last; if not enough, a little of the former, so that it has no more thickness than milk. Lay one coat on the right side of the print, and when dry it will shine like glass. If it be not to your liking lay on another.

A black varnish for Straw or Chip Hats.—Half an ounce of the best black sealing wax, two ounces of rectified spirits of wine. Powder the wax, put it with the spirits into a four ounce vial; digest them in a small heat, or near the fire till the wax is dissolved; lay it on warm with a fine soft hair brush, before a fire or the sun. It gives stiffness to old straw hats, and a beautiful gloss, and resists wet.

To clean and restore the elacticity of cane chair bottoms, coaches, &c.—Turn up the chair bottom, &c. and with hot water and a sponge wash the cane work well, so that it may be well soaked; Should it be dirty you must add soap; let it dry in the air, and you will find it as tight and firm as when new, provided the cane is not broken.

A green paint for garden stands, Venetian blinds, trelisses, &c.—Take mineral green and white lead ground in turpentine, mix up a quantity to your mind, with a small quantity of turpentine varnish for the first coat; for the second you must put as much varnish in the colour as will produce a good gloss. N. B. By adding a small quantity of Prussian blue, you will have the color much brighter.

To stain Horn to imitate Tortoisshell.—Take an equal quantity of quick lime and red lead, mix it up with strong soap lyes, lay it on the horn with a small brush, like the mottle in tortoiseshell; when it is dry, repeat it two or three times.

To take Ink spots out of Mahogany, &c.—Apply spirits of salts with a bit of rag till the ink disappears.

Another.—Put a few drops of spirits of nitre in a tea spoonful of water, touch the spots with a feather dipped in the mixture, and on the ink disappearing, rub it over immediately with a rag wetted in cold water, or there will be a white mark which will not be easily effaced.

To damask Leather for Table covers and other purposes.—Provide yourself with a block glued up, two feet six inches long, and two feet wide, faced with pear tree, five-eighths of an inch thick, upon which have some pretty patterns drawn, that has a good effect in the light and dark shades only, but it must be so divided that it must match end for end and side for side; which pattern must be sunk in the paper stainer or printer's block, and may be done by ony one that knows a little of chair carving; then strain your leather dry on the block with tack and with a glass-ball rubber of about four pounds weight pass to and fro over the leather, rubbing hard till you produce the pattern perfectly glazed on the leather. N. B.—If your cover is larger than the block, be very careful in shifting it, that you may not injure the pattern. I have made a pattern in wood, which was afterwards cast in brass, repaired, and fixed upon a block, (for a leather gilder) which is much better than one of wood; the pattern comes off much sharper and cleaner.

To clean black Feathers.—Pour a pennyworth of bullock's gall into a wash-hand basin; pour warm water on this, and run your feathers through it; rinse in cold water, and finish them as you would other feathers.

How to take the stain of the dye from the hands—Take a small quantity of oil of vitriol and pour it into some cold water, in a wash-hand basin, and wash your hands in it without soap; the dye will then come off. You may afterwards cleanse them completely in hot soap and water, taking care that all the acid is washed away before the soap is applied

To take off the stains of light colors, reds, greens, blues, &c. from the hands.—Wash your hands in soap and water, in which some pearl-ash is dissolved.—N. B. If the vitriol water is not made very strong, it will not injure the most delicate hand, nor leave any red or coarse appearance.

Freckles on the Face.—To disperse freckles, take two ounces of lemon juice, half a drachm of powdered borax, and one drachm of sugar, mix them, and let them stand a few days in a glass bottle, till the liquor is fit for use; then rub it on the hands and face occasionally.

Windsor Soap.—Cut some new white soap into thin slices, melt it over a slow fire, and scent it with oil of carraway; when perfectly dissolved, pour it into a mould and let it remain a week, then cut it into such sized squares as you may require

To stain Harps, Violins, or any other Musical Instrument.—A Crimson stain.—Take one pound of ground Brazil and boil it in three quarts of water for an hour; strain it and add half an ounce of cochineal, boil it again for half an hour gently, and it will be fit for use.—N. B. If you would have it of the scarlet tint, boil half an ounce of saffron in a quart of water. and pass over the work previous to the red strain. Observe the work must be very clean and of air-wood, or good sycamore without blemish; when varnished it will look very rich.

For a Purple stain.—Take a pound of chip-logwood, to which put three quarts of water, boil it well for an hour add four ounces of pearl-ash, and two ounces of indigo pounded, and you will have a good purple.

For a fine Black.—When black is required in musical instruments, it is produced by japanning, the work being well prepared with size and lamp-black; take some black japan, (form the varnish makers and give it two coats,) after which varnish and polish it.

A fine Blue stain.—Take a pound of oil of vitriol in a glass bottle, in which put four ounces of indigo, and proceed as before directed in dying.

A fine Green stain.—Take three pints of strong vinegar, to which put four ounces of the best verdigris ground fine, half an ounce of sap-green, and half an ounce of indigo.

For a bright Yellow.—There is no need whatever to stain the wood, as a very small bit of aloes put in the varnish will make it of a good color, and has the desired effect.

To make varnish for Violins, &c.—Take half a gallon of rectified spirits of wine, to which put six ounces of gum sundrach, three ounces of gum-mastich, and half a pint of turpentine varnish; put the above in a tin can, in a warm place, frequently shaking it until it is dissolved, strain it and keep it for use. If you find it harder than you wish, add a little more turpentine varnish.

To stain Box-wood Brown.—Hold your work to the fire, that it may receive a gentle warmth, then take aqua-fortis and with a feather pass over the work till you find it change to a fine brown (always keeping it near the fire,) you may then oil and polish it.

To varnish Harps, dulcinas, &c., in the Indian manner.—Prepare the work with size and red ochre, then take ochre, burnt umber, and red lead, well ground, and mix up a dark brown color in turpentine varnish, adding as much spirits of turpentine, that you may just be able to work it, pass over your work even, and while it is yet wet, take a muslin sieve, and sift as much Dutch metal (bronze) upon it as you may think requisite to produce the effect, after which varnish and polish it.

For dying Silk Stockings black.—These are dyed like other silks, excepting that they must be steeped a day or two in bark liquor, before they are put in the black silk dye. At first they will look like an iron grey; but to finish and black them, they must be put on wooden legs, laid on a table, and rubbed with your oily rubber or flannel, upon which is oil of olives, and then the more they are rubbed the better. Each pair of stockings will require half a table spoonful of oil at least, and half an hour's rubbing, to finish them well. Sweet oil is the best in this process, as it leaves no disagreeable smell.

For the bite of a snake.—Take the bark of yellow poplar and bruise it, and make a poultice of it and apply it to the wound, bathing the arm or leg that is bitten with a strong decoction of the same, and let the person afflicted drink half a pint every hour. This is a safe and easy remedy, and will effect a cure in a short time.

Another.—Charcoal made into a paste with hog's lard, is a grand antidote for snake-bites. In bad cases it should be changed often. It will probably prove effectual for the sting of bees and all other similar cases of poison.

Substitute for Cream.—Beat up the whole of a fresh egg in a basin, and then pour boiling tea or water over it gradually, to prevent it curdling. In flavor and richness this preparation resembles cream.

To destroy Snails and Slugs—A few turnips sliced and laid on the borders of the garden they infest, will attract them in the evening.

To prevent Paper from sinking.—If the paper used in superior editions of books, and which sinks so as to prevent its being written on, be dipped in alum-water, it may be written on. This practice was adopted by Peiresc.

Pearl White.—Bismuth dissolved in aquafortis is pearl white. This, though at first it whitens, afterwards blackens the skin, as all preparations from lead do; and therefore none of them are safely to be used.

To take off a Gold Ring sticking tight on a Finger.—Touch it with mercury, and it becomes so brittle that a slight blow with a hammer will break it.

To detect the mixture of Arsenic.—A solution of blue vitrol dropped into any liquid in which arsenic has been put will turn it green.

Chapped or sore Lips.—May be healed by the frequent application of honey-water and protecting them from the influence of cold air.

Approved Dentifrice.—A distinguished Chemist recommends the following compound as a safe and excellent dentifrice, viz: of white sugar and powdered charcoal, each one ounce; of Peruvian bark, half an ounce; of cream of tartar, one drachm and a half; and of canella, twenty-four grains; well rubbed together into an impalpable powder. He describes it as strengthening to the gums, and cleansing to the teeth, and as destroying the disagreeable odour in the breath, which so often arises from decaying teeth.—As a preventive of tooth-ache, we have heard washing the mouth and teeth twice a day with salt and water, strongly recommended by gentlemen who have experienced much benefit from it.

Rendering Lard.—A new mode of rendering lard, in operation in Cincinnati, is mentioned in the Atlas of that city, which has many advantages over the old. The lard, in leaf and strip, is thrown into a large wooden vat, some ten feet in diameter, where it is thoroughly melted by a volume of steam being poured upon it. It is then conveyed to another vat underneath the water, thoroughly evaporated, and the melted lard drawn off into kegs and barrels. One hundred and fifty barrels per day may be thus rendered, with the labor of two men; there is no possibility of the lard being burnt, and every particle of it in the hog is thus saved, which cannot be done by any press, however powerful.

Small Pox.—In Dr. Lott's copy of "Mead *de Variolis*," was written, what was termed "A curious and infallible preventive against ever catching the Small Pox," as follows:—Two spoonfuls of red ochre, such as is used for marking sheep, infused in half a pint of ale, and taken seven mornings successively, fasting.

The Stomach.—"I firmly believe that almost every malady of the human frame is, either by highways or by-ways, connected with the stomach. The woes of every other member are founded on your stomach, and I must own, I never see a fashionable physician mysteriously consulting the pulse of his patient, but I feel a desire to exclaim—Why not tell the poor gentleman at once, 'Sir, you have eaten too much, you've drunk too much, and you have not taken exercise enough?'" The human frame was not created imperfect; it is we ourselves who have made it so. There exists no donkey in creation so overladen as our stomach."

To preserve Clothes.—As clothes when laid up for a time, acquire an unpleasant odour, which required considerable exposure to the atmospheric air, it will be prevented by laying recently made charcoal between the folds of the garments; and even when the odour has taken place, the charcoal will absorb

Cure for a Run-round on the Finger.—The first symptom of the disease is a heat, from swelling and pain, and a redness at the top of the nail. *Cure*—first open with a needle; then, with the point of a penknife, scratch the whole surface of the nail, both lengthwise and across. This alone, it is said, will check and cure the complaint.

Remedy for Sore Throat.—Take 5 spoonfuls of syrup of elder-berries and mix with 1 spoonful of honey, and as much salt prunel (in powder) as well lie on a ten cent piece: take a tea-spoonful of this as often as you can.

Opodeldoc, or Camphorated Soap Liniment.—Take common white soap, three ounces; camphor, one ounce; oil of rosemary, oil of origanum, each half an ounce; alcohol, one pint; cut the soap fine, and with a gentle heat dissolve it in the alcohol in which the other articles had been previously dissolved Pour into wide-mouthed vials or jars, to cool.

If liquid opodeldoc is preferred, two ounces of castile soap, in place of three ounces of common soap. N. B.—Troy ounces are designated. If not practicable to have the articles weighed by that standard, bear in mind that the Troy ounce is nearly equal to 1 1-9 ounce Avordupois.

Opodeldoc, made according to the above recipes, is altogether superior to that usually sold in vials, at exorbitant prices.

To cure Grubs in Horses.—Take 1 pint strong vinegar, 1 ounce chalk in powder, stir it well and drench the animal.

To stop Bleeding at the Nose.—To cure it, apply to the neck behind and on each side, a cloth dipped in cold water : or, put the legs and arms in cold water : or wash the temples, nose and neck, with vinegar : or, snuff up vinegar and water.

To Improve the Complexion.—Take bitter almonds whitened, 1 part ; rose-water, 16 parts,—Mix and strain, then add five grains of bichloride of mercury to every eight-ounce vial of the mixture, and scent with rose or violet, to suit the fancy.

To Fatten Poultry.—Boil rice in sweet milk, and feed them with it.

Tomatoes a Cure for Scours in Pigs.—This plant, the Tomatoe, is generally at first disliked by many ; but it nevertheless is much cultivated and admired. Last fall (says the Maine Farmer) we had a pig that was taken with the scours badly. We tried various remedies for it, but with little effect. One day we threw over to it two or three tomatoes, which it ate readily, and which we found gave it relief. By following this course a few days it was finally cured.

To cure Rheumatism.— One of the most generally useful of all remedies, in a large proportion of rheumatic cases, is the mistura guaiaci of the London Pharmacopœia : and it is observed that it is usually most beneficial when it acts on the bowels and on the kidneys. The vinum colchici, or the Dover's powder, may often be added with much advantage to it. Moderate bloodletting, and the exhibition of calomel at bed time with or without opium, should seldom be neglected at the same time

Prussic Acid.—A short time ago a gentleman residing in Hertford-shire, wishing to destroy a useless dog, administered to it about twenty drops of prussic acid. The animal almost immediately became paralyzed but appearing likely to linger for a short time, the owner, intending to put it out of its misery, threw it into a pond ; the dog, however, having felt the effect of the water immediately swam out, shook itself, and appeared as if nothing whatever had occurred. It may not be generally known that throwing cold water over the head of animal completely neutralizes this deadly poison.

To revive a dull Fire.—Powdered nitre strewed on the fire, is the best bellows that can be used.

Growth of Hair increased, and Baldness prevented.—Take 4 ounces of castor oil, 8 do. good Jamaica rum, 30 drops oil of lavender, or 10 do. oil of rose, annoint occasionally the head, shaking well the bottle previously.

F

Making Soap.—Mr. Tomlinson, writing to Judge Buel, says.—"My wife has no trouble about soap.—The grease is put into a cask, and strong lye added. During the year, as the fat increases, more lye is stirred in, and occasionally stirred with a stick that is kept in it. By the time the cask is full, the soap is made ready for use. It is made hard by boiling and adding a quart of fine salt to three gallons of soap. It is put into a tub to cool, and the froth scraped off. It is afterwards melted to a boiling heat, and a little rosin or turpentine given, which improves the quality."

Horse-Raddish.—It is easy to have a supply of horse-raddish all winter. Have a quantity grated while the root is in perfection; put it in bottles, fill it with vinegar, and keep it corked tight. *Note*—It is very much improved by keeping it in this way if kept from the action of the air.

Cure for Deafness.—It is said that mixing sulphuric æther and ammonia, and allowing it to stand fourteen days, a solution is formed which, if properly applied to the internal ear will remove in almost every case this hitherto considered incurable affection.

Never Kill a Bee.—The smoke of the " fungus maxims," or common puff ball, when dried so as to hold fire, has a stupifying effect on the bees, and renders them as harmless as brimstone does, without any of its deadly effects. By means of this, weak swarms, which would not live through the winter, may be united to strong stocks. It is a fact, borne out by experiment, that a hive that has doubled will not consume more honey in the winter than a stock in its natural state. This was discovered by a Swiss pastor, De Gelior. The additional heat seems to serve, instead of additional food, to keep up the vitality of the half torpid bees. A cold, dry, dark room, is the best winter quarters for bees. They will consume less honey than if left on their stands, and will not be weakened by the loss of thousands, which tempted out by the premature warmth, are caught by the cold winds, fall to the ground and never rise again.

Dryness is essential; and ventilation or proper airing of the hives in summer, is the most valuable improvements in bee keeping.

To clear closets from cock-roaches. Remove every article from the closet, scrub the shelves with lye, and then white-wash the closet walls. Next take a sufficient quantity of black wadding, or of old soft newspaper, and soak it in spirits of camphor or turpentine—camphor will be best. Then with a fork or a knife stuff it closely and hard into all the crevices, cracks, and holes, however small. United with the copperas that is in the black wadding, and in the printing ink of the newspaper, the camphor or turpentine will destroy or expel the cock-roaches, so that for a long time you will see no more of them. If they return, repeat the remedy. Black wadding is rather better than newspaper, as you can stuff it in more effectivly, and the roaches will be unable to eat their way through it. You may clear them out in the same manner from the kitchen, &c., but as they are generally more numerous in kitchens than elsewhere, set also for them every night a large earthen cock roach trap baited with molassess and water. You can buy these traps in market, or at a pottery shop. If your house is much infested with these disgusting and intolerable insects, have several traps, and set them in different places where the roaches most abound. A mixture of painter's white lead, indian meal, and brown sugar, wet to a paste with water, and set about on old plates or saucers is very poisonous to them; but as it soon dries up you must make a fresh mixture every night.

To expel Rats from Houses.— Smear their holes and haunts with a mixture of two parts of tar to one of lamp oil, gently boiled together. They will not approach it.

To remove dark stains from silver. —There are many substances that communicate a dark inky stain to silver spoons, forks, &c., a stain that is sometimes so inveterate as to resist all common applications. A certain remedy, is to obtain from a druggist's a small phial of sulphuric acid, and pouring a little of it into a saucer, wet with it a soft linen rag, and rub it on the blackened silver till the stain disappears. Then brighten the article with whiting, finely powdered and sifted, and wetted with whiskey or spirits of wine. When the whiting has dried on, and rested a quarter of an hour or more, wipe it off with a silk handkerchief, and polish with a soft buckskin.

To take off wall-paper. —To clear a wall from paper, previous to painting or white-washing, wet the paper thoroughly, with a long-handled brush dipped in a bucket of warm water. While the paper is quite wet, so that it blisters and loosens, you can pull it off with your hands. If any small bits are found still adhering, wet them afresh, and scrape them off with a case-knife.

A Remedy for Scarlet Fever —A respectable citizen, who has seen the remedy alluded to tried with success, has requested us to publish the following recipe for the cure of Scarlet Fever. *Administer Yeast.* —To an adult give two table spoonfulls, and to a child of two or three years of age, one spoonfull, to be taken once in two hours; by gargling the throat with, yeast, when it is sore, immediate relief is afforded,

To prevent the Clothes of Children from taking fire. — 'The danger and difficulty can very easily be avoided by the use of alum.

" When clothes are washed they should be rinsed out in alum water — the solution should be made tolerably strong. If the clothing, which has been newly washed, should require starch, the alum may be put in the starch water.

" Alum should be used on all occasions; it renders the clothing fireproof. All clothing about a house or a steamboat made of cotton should be impregnated with alum. For instance, bed and window curtains, &c., such articles generally having much fringe about them.

" This hint, if attended to, will prove a perfect safety to clothing from fire."

Important Remedy for Cancers. — Colonel Ussey, of the Parish of De Soto, informs the editor of the Caddo Gazette, that he has fully tested a remedy for this very troublesome disease, recommended to him by a Spanish woman, a native of the country. The remedy is this —Take an egg and break it, then pour out the white, retaining the yolk in the shell, put in salt, and mix with the yolk as long as it will receive it; stir them together until a salve is formed, put a portion of this on a sticking plaster, and apply it to the cancer about twice a day. He has made the experiment in two instances in his own family with complete success.

Hoarsness. —One drachm of freshly scraped horse-radish root, to be infused with four ounces of water, in a close vessel, for two hours, and made into a syrup, with double its weight in vinegar, is an approved remedy for hoarseness ; a teaspoonful has often proved effectual ; a few teaspoons, it is said, have never been known to fail in removing hoarseness.

Cure for Consumption. —Tea made of St. John's worth, used as a constant drink, has cured the consumption, and what has been done, may be done again. The tea may be made as you would make peppermint or any other herb tea to drink —by merely steeping the herb in warm water The herb may be gathered at any time after it is large enough—but the best time for gathering it is during the month of July. It may be found in almost every meadow.

Mice vs Spearmint. —Mice have such an aversion to the common spearmint, that they will not approach a crib or granary in which a few sprigs of this herb are strewed.

Excellent Varnish for Umbrellas, &c.—Great coats, and other articles much exposed to the weather, are rendered both sun and rain proof, by the following excellent varnish: Boil well together two pounds of turpentine, one pound of litharge in powder, and two or three pounds of linseed oil. When the article is brushed over with this varnish, it must be dried in the sun; after which, the greatest heat will not effect it.

To try the purity of Spirits.—See if the liquor will burn away without leaving any moisture behind. As spirits is much lighter than water, place a hollow ivory ball in it; the deeper the ball sinks, the lighter the liquor, and consequently the more spirituous.

A Corn Plaster.—One ounce of naval pitch, half an ounce of galbanum, dissolved in vinegar, one scruple of ammonia, and one drachm and a half of diachylon, mixed together.

To prevent Wounds from mortifying—Sprinkle sugar on them. The Turks wash fresh wounds with wine, and sprinkle sugar on them. Obstinate ulcers may be cured with sugar dissolved in strong decoction of walnut leaves.

Useful Knife-Board.—A common knife-board, covered with thick buff-leather, on which are put emery, one part, crocus martis, three parts, in very fine powder, mixed into a thick paste with a little lard or sweet oil, and spread on the leather to the thickness of a shilling, gives a far superior edge and polish to knives; and will not wear the knife nearly so much as the common method of using brick-dust on a board.

Economical Use of Nutmeg.—If a person begin to grate a nutmeg at the stalk end, it will prove hollow throughout; whereas the same nutmeg, grated from the other end, would have proved sound and solid to the last. This circumstance may be thus accounted for:—The centre of a nutmeg consists of a number of fibres issuing from the stalk, and its continuation through the centre of the fruit, the other ends of which fibres, through closely surrounded and pressed by the fruit, do not adhere to it. When the stalk is grated away, those fibres having lost their hold, gradualy drop out, and the nutmeg appears hollow; as more of the stalk is grated away, others drop out in succession, and the hollow continues through the whole nut. By beginning at the contrary end, the fibres above mentioned are grated off a their core end, with the surrounded fruit, and do not drop out and cause a hole.

Preservation of Apples—The following practical observations, contained in a letter from Noah Webster, Esq. have been published in the Massachusetts Agricultural Repository.

It is the practice with some persons to pick apples in October, and first spread them on the floor of an upper room. This practice is said to render apples more durable, by drying them. But I can affirm this to be a mistake. Apples, after remaining on trees as long as safety from the frost will admit, should be taken directly from trees to close casks, and kept dry and close as possible. If suffered to lie on the floor for weeks, they wither and loose their flavor, without acquiring an additional durability. The best mode of preserving apples for spring use, I have found to be, the putting of them in dry sand as soon as picked. For this purpose, dry sand in the heat of summer, and late in October, put down the apples in layers, with a covering of sand upon each layer.—The singular advantages of this mode of treatment are these: 1st. The sand keeps the apples from the air, which is essential to their preservation. 2d. The sand checks the evaporation of the apples, thus preserving in them their full flavor—at the same time any moisture yielded by the apples, (and some there will be,) is absorbed by the sand, so that the apples are kept dry, and all mustiness is prevented. My pippins in May and June, are as fresh as when first picked, even the ends of the stems looked as if just separated from the twig.

Important Cure for Bronchitis.—Croton oil, it is said, will entirely remove this complaint. A minister who had been laid aside from his pastoral office by the bronchitis, for three years, has entirely recovered his voice by the application of croton oil to the surface of the throat, against the organ affected. One drop, daily rubbed over the surface, produced a singular but powerful eruption of the skin, which, as it progressed, restored his voice to its full tone and vigour.

To Prevent the Smoking of Lamps. —Soak the wick in strong vinegar and dry it well. They will of course smoke, even after this preparation, if the wicks are put up too high.

To make Liquorice Lozenges.—1. Take extract of liquorice, 1 pound; powdered white sugar, 2 pounds. Mix with mucilage made with rose-water.

2. Take lump sugar, 100 parts; liquorice, 150 parts; powdered starch, 40 parts; mucilage, to mix.

To Perfume Clothes.—Take dried red roses, and to increase their smell, pour on them fresh rose-water, and still drying between in the shade; then take cloves, cinnamon, spikenards seed, storax, calamita, benjaman, violet root nutmegs aa3iij. to a pound of roses; beat them all into small pieces, and mix them with the roses, and put them into perfuming bags.

Stains in Mahogany.—Take two ounces of oil of vitriol, and one of muriatic acid; mix by shaking in a phial, and when to be used, lay it over the spotted part by means of a feather or woollen rag. Afterwards wash the part over with water, and polish as usual.

To discharge Grease from Paper. Burn bones of sheep; with the powder rub both sides of the spot; and, putting white pieces of paper on each side, lay the whole in a press. Repeat this process till the spot disappears.

Scours in Animals.—A writer in the Farmer, recommends for this disease finely pulverized bones.

How to make Blacking.—Take one gallon of vinegar, put it into a stone jug; add one pound of ivory black, well pulverized, half a pound of loaf sugar; half on ounce of oil of vitriol, and one ounce of sweet-oil; incorporate the whole by stirring. This blacking, if well made, is an excellent article.

To Wagoners.—Take hogs's lard. melt it over a gentle fire, and then stir it in flour until it becomes a paste Grease your wagons or carriages with it—and you will never use tar again.

To cure Gapes in Chickens.—Gaps in chickens may be easily cured by giving them small crums of dough impregneted with a little soft soap; once or twice is sufficient, in most cases.

Whitewash.—There is nothing which so much improves the appearance of a house and the premises, as painting and white-washing the tenements and fences. The following recipes for white-washing, have been found by experience to answer the same purpose on wood, brick and stone, as oil-paint, and are much cheaper. The first is the recipe used for the President's house at Washington, improved by further experiments. The second is a simpler and cheaper one, which the writer has known to succeed in a variety of cases, lasting as long and looking as well as white oil-paint.

Recipe—Take half a bushel of unslacked lime, and slack it with boiling hot water, covering it during the process. Strain it, and add a peck of salt dissolved in warm water; three pounds of ground rice boiled to a thin paste, put in boiling hot; half a pound of powdred Spanish whiting, and a pound of clear glue, dissolved in warm water. Mix, and let it stand several days. Then keep it in a kettle on a portable furnace, and put on as hot as possible, with a painter's or a white-wash brush.

A fine Yellow Wash.—Lime-water, 1 pound; bichloride of mercury, 40 grains. Rub together, Shake the bottle before use. Used for syphiltic ulcers.

Face Ache.—This common affection, so often supposed to be excited by a diseased tooth, although the latter fails to be detected—a rheumatic, chronic kind of pain, wholly different from that of tic-douloureux, is often speedily curable by *muriate of ammonia.* This salt should be given in doses of half a drachm, dissolved in water, three or four times daily. About four doses will be sufficient to test the potency of the remedy. At other times the oxide of potassium, in five or six-grain doses, is quickly effective towards a cure. The efficiency of the latter remedy renders it probable that the affection is of the nature of periosteal inflamation.

To Housewives.—A correspondent of the South Western Farmer gives the following recipe for removing grease spots from clothes, &c. He says: " Will you allow a gentleman of an indefinite age, an admirer of domestic economy, to tell you how to remove grease spots from your merinos, silks, &c., without injuring their color? Or the cuffs and collars of your husbands' coats can also be cleaned in the same manner ; in short any article that may be desired, but it is more particularly applicable to such as are made up of wool, or of which it forms a part. Take the yolk of an egg, entirely free from the white, mix it with a little warm water, (be sure not to scald the egg,) and with a soft brush apply the mixture, and rub it on the spot until the grease appears removed or loose. Wash off the egg with moderately warm water,, and finally rinse off the whole with clean cold water.— Should not all the grease be removed, which may arise from being on a long time, or not sufficiently washed, dry and repeat the operation."

To change Hair to a deep Brown. —A solution of the silver caustic in water is the foundation of all the nostrums for this purpose. It must be well diluted before used.

Corns and Warts—Apply soft brown paper moistened with spittle. A few dressings will remove them.

Mr. Yearsley's Advice for the Deaf.—1. Never syringe your ear nor allow it to be done by others unless for the removal of an accumulation of wax.

2. Be sure that such accumulation forms an obstacle to the transmission of sound, otherwise it had better remain where it is, for it should always be borne in mind that wax is a natural secretion placed in the passage of the ear for a specific purpose. Its presence, in a moderate quantity, indicates a healthy condition of the outer passage of the ear. Its absence is the effect, and not, as is generally supposed, the cause of the disease which produces the deafness. Like deafness, want of wax is only a symtom of ear disease; hence the absurdity of attempting its restoration by stimulating drops and ointments.

3. Never pick the ears.

4 Never wet the hair, nor wash the head with cold water. A most pernicious practice!

5. Never bathe, nor use a shower bath, without carfully protecting the head and ears. Even then I question its propriety.

6. Never attempt to stop a discharge from the ears but under proper advice; for it may be that the drum of your ear may be open, and then, the employment of a stimulating or astringent injection will risk even fatal consequences.

7. Never apply, or suffer to be applied, anything to the outer passages of the ear, which causes heat or pain. Such applications may prove of temporary benefit ; but when the stimulus has subsided, you will be left worse than before.

8. Be strict in diet. Stomach derangements are a most prolific source of deafness.

9. Never expose yourself to wet or windy weather,

10. Never consult an aurist who is not an educated and diplomatised surgeon, who does not admit that deafness is an infirmity often difficult of removal, and very often incurable

RARE AND VALUABLE RECEIPTS.

Removing large ink stains.—Get some oxalic acid from the druggist's, put it into a pan, pour on some hot water, and stir it well. Wash the ink stain in this, and rinse it off with cold water twice repeated. Then put it in the sun. If the ink has not entirely disappeared, repeat the process. It is safest to try this with white articles only, as it will fade the colours in removing the ink. There are, however, many colours that when faded by the application of oxalic acid can be restored by rubbing the place with hartshorn, which, if very strong, should be a little diluted with cold water. If you have a piece of the same article try the experiment on a small scale, first upon that, by wetting it with oxalic acid, and then rubbing on some hartshorn. In removing ink stains from *white* things, the washing in oxalic acid and hot water is a certain remedy if persisted in. Ink spots on a carpet or table-cover may sometimes be removed by washing the place *immediately* with a cloth and cold water mixed with soap or oxgalic first taking up all you can with a teaspoon, if the ink has fallen in a large quantity. Finish with plain cold water.

To remove paint from the wall of a room.—If you intend papering a painted wall, you must first get off all the paint—otherwise the paper will not stick. To do this, mix in a bucket a sufficient quantity of pearlash with either warm or cold water so as to make a strong solution. Dip a flannel into this, and with it wash off the paint.

To Destroy Rats.—Equal parts of ox-gall and oil of amber made into a paste with oat meal ; make it up into little balls, lay them about, and set plenty of vessels of water close at hand.

Grafting.—Melt beeswax and tallow together, stirring in a little chalk if handy ; while hot dip in some strips of rags ; then tear them into strips suitable to prevent the escape of the sap or the introduction of water, and the work is finished

A Secret for a Farmer's Wife.— While the milking of your cows is going on, see that your pans are clean, and let them be placed in a kettle of boiling water.—Strain the milk into one of the pans taken hot from the kettle, and cover the same with another of the hot pans, and proceed in like manner with the whole mess of milk, and you will find that you will have double the quantity of good rich cream, and get double the quantity of sweet and delicious butter. This was given by a farmer friend.

An Effectual Cure for a Felon.— Bathe the part effected in ashes and water—take the yolk of an egg, six drops of the spirits of turpentine, a few beet leaves cut fine, a small quantity of hard soap, add one teaspoonful of burnt salt, and one of Indian meal ; it never fails to effect a cure, if applied in season.

To Preserve Cheese from Mites.— Paste over it coarse brown paper to cover every part.

To Clean Carpets.—Having well beaten and brushed, scour with ox gall, which will both extract grease and refresh the colours. A pint of gall in three gallons of soft water, warm, will do a large carpet.

To Revive Gilt Frames.—Beat up three oz. of the white of egg with one oz. of soda, blow off the dust from the frames, and then do them over with a soft brush dipped in this mixture, and they will immediately become bright and fresh.

To Cure Scratches in Horses.— Wash the feet or parts affected, with soap suds ; wipe them clean dry ; apply white lead ground in oil, as thick as can be evenly and smoothly laid on.—Exercise moderately ; keep the animal dry ; and in most cases the first application will cure effectually. Should a second be necessary, wash off the old lead, and apply with a brush as at first. Six or eight days should intervene between the applications.

To prevent the Hair falling off.— Wash the head once a day with good old Jamaica rum.

A Cure for Consumption.—Mr. Adam Mott gives the following statement in the Maine Farmer:

"A friend of mine who resides in Industry, in this State, told me that his wife was sick of what the Doctors call Consumption. She was visited by five physicians, who gave her over.—She was very sick—was unable to sit up—had a very severe cough—and grew no better, 'but rather worse'—she failed very fast. She recollected that she had before received benefit from the use of St. John's wort; her husband procured some of it; it was steeped, and she made it her constant drink. For four or five days there appeared to be but little alteration; But after this she grew better very fast; her health was so much improved, that in the course of six or eight weeks she was able to resume her customary occupation—she commenced weaving, and wove about 40 yards of cloth. During this time, she made constant use of St. John's wort tea. What has been done may again be done. It helped her—it may help others.

"The tea may be made as you would make pepper-mint or any herb tea to drink—by merely steeping the herb in water. The herb may be gathered any time after it is large enough; but the best time for gathering it is in the seventh month. A supply may then doubtless be found in almost every hay mow where there is any hay. I much approve of this simple remedy."

To extinguish a recent Fire.—A mop and a pail of water are generally the most efficacious remedies; but if it has gained head, then keep out the air, and remove all ascending or perpendicular combustibles, upon which the fire creeps and increases in force as it rises.

A secret worth knowing.—How to make three pair of boots last as long as six, and longer.—The following extract from Colonel Macerone's "Seasonable Hints," which appeared in the *Mechanics' Magazine,* dated February 3d, 1838. After stating the utility of sheep skin clothing, for persons whose employment renders it necessary that they should be much out of doors, &c., he says—

"I will not conclude without inviting the attention of our readers to a cheap and easy method of preserving their feet from wet, and their boots from wear. I have only had three pair of boots for the last six years (no shoes) and I think that I shall not require any others for the next six years to come. The reason is that I treat them in the following manner:—I put a pound of tallow and a half a pound rosin, into a pot on the fire; when melted and mixed, I warm the boots and apply the hot stuff with a painter's brush, until neither the sole nor upper leathers will suck in any more. If it is desired that the boots should immediately take a polish, dissolve an ounce of bees' wax in an ounce of spirits of turpentine, to which add a teaspoonful of lamp-black. A day or two after the boots have been treated with the tallow and rosin, rub over them the wax in turpentine, but not before the fire. Thus the exterior will have a coat of wax, alone, and shine like a mirror. Tallow, or any other grease, becomes rancid, and rots the stitching as well as the leather; but the rosin gives it an antiseptic quality which preserves the whole. Boots or shoes should be so large as to admit of wearing in them cork soles. Cork is so bad a conductor of heat, that with it in the boot, the feet are always warm on the coldest stone floor."

To prevent Brass Vessels from contracting Verdigris after being used.—Instead of wiping them dry, it has been found, that by by constantly immersing them in water, they are kept perfectly innoxious, and will remain for years, fully as clean, and nearly as bright, as when they first came out of the hands of the workmen.

Method of Cleaning China.—Mix a little pearl-ash, or a potter's clay, or soda with your water, and it will give them a bright appearance.

An excellent tooth Powder.—A distinguished chemist recommends the following compound as a safe and excellent dentirfrice, viz, white sugar and powdered charcoal, each one ounce, of Peruvian bark half an ounce, of cream of tarter one drachm and a half, and of canella twenty four grains, well rubbed together into an impalpable powder. He describes it as strengthening to the gums, and cleansing to the teeth, and as destroying the disagreeable odor in the breath, which so often arises from decaying teeth. As a preventive of toothache, we have heard washing the mouth and teeth twice a day with salt and water strongly recommended by gentlemen who have experienced much benefit from it.

To Stain Paper.—Paper may be stained a beautiful yellow, by the tincture of tumeric formed by the infusion of an ounce or more of the powdered tumeric in a pint of alcohol. This may be made to give any tint of yellow, from the lightest straw, to he bright orange yellow, and is equal in brightness, to the best died silks. A solution of gambouge, also makes a good yellow.

Crimson—A fine crimson stain may be given by a tincture of the Indian Lac, or lake, which is to be infused some days in alcohol, and then straining off the infusion through a flannel. The juice of the common blood beet, also stains a beautiful crimson, which may be reduced to a delicate rose color. The beets are to be bruised, and mashed to a pulp, with a little vinegar, after which, water may be added.

Blue.—For this purpose, the common, or rather the best blue ink, makes a delicate blue stain. For a very deep blue, indigo, finely ground on a stone with water, and a little gum arabic, or sugar may be used.

Green, or Purple.—May be made by mixing the blue with either the red or yellow, as the case may require, The expressed juice of green leaves, also makes a delicate, and tolerable durably green.

A Water Proof Glue.—Melt common glue in the smallest possible quantity of water, and add by drops, linseed oil that has been rendered drying by having a small quantity of litharge boiled in it; the glue being briskly stirred when the oil is added

Glue will resist water to a considerable extent by being dissolved in skimmed milk.

The addition of finely levigated chalk, to a solution of common glue in water, strengthens it and renders it suitable for signs or other work that is exposed to the weather.

A glue or cement that will hold against fire or water, may be made by mixing and boiling together linseed oil and quick lime. This mixture must be reduced to the consistence of soft putty, and then spread on tin plates and dried in the shade, where it will dry very hard. This may afterwards be melted like common glue, and must be used while hot.

Artificial Moonlight—We can tell how to get up a very pretty imitation of moonlight in a room. It is somewhere stated that a luminous bottle may be prepared which will give sufficient light in the night to admit of the hour being easily told on the dial of a watch. The process is as follows: a clear phial of white glass, of a long form, must be chosen, and some fine olive oil heated to ebulition in another vessel, a piece of phosphorus, of the size of a pea, must be put into the phial, and the boiling oil carefully poured over it, till the phial is one-third filled.—The phial must then be carefully corked, when it is to be used it must be unstopped, to admit the external air, and then closed again. The empty space of the phial will then appear luminous, and will give as much light as a dull moon. Each time the light disappears, on removing the stopper it will instantly reappear. In cold weather the bottle must be warmed in the hands before the stopper is removed. A phial prepared in this way may be used ever night for six months with success.

To stop a fit of Coughing.—A correspondent of the London Medical Gazette, states that to close the nostrils with the thumb and finger during expiration, leaving them free during inspiration, will relieve a fit of coughing in a short time.

In addition to the above, we can state from persons knowledge, that to press the finger on the upper lip just below the nose, will make the severest premonitory symptoms of a sneeze pass off harmless. We have found the remedy useful many a time n creeping on game in the woods.

Crush them in the egg.—If you look over your fruit trees carefully, you will occasionally find a patch of greenish substance closely adhering to some of the branches, and sometimes encircling them.

Within this substance you will find a great number of blueish green eggs, very nicely packed in the smallest possible space. These are the eggs of the moth which was produced from the caterpillar that devoured the leaves of the tree so voraciously in the spring, will produce another swarm of the same species, as active and as hungry as were those. By a little labor and attention they may very easily be destroyed now, and your trees protected from their ravages.

An Important Discovery.—The means of instantly stopping a horse when he runs away, has been discovered in France. It is simple. A sudden transition from light to total darkness, is the principle. It is contrived, by means of a spring connected with the reins, to cover the horse's eyes. This was done in an instance when the animals were at the top of their speed, and the result was their instantaneous stoppage; for the light being suddenly excluded, horses no more rush forward, says the discoverer, without seeing their way, than would a man afflicted with blindness.

Tomato Pickles.—Take tomatoes when two thirds ripe; prick them full of holes with a fork; then make a strong brine, boil and skim it.

When cool, put your tomatoes in; let them remain eight days, and then take out and put them in weak vinegar.—Let them lay twenty-four hours; then take them out and lay a layer of tomatoes, then a thin layer of onions, with a tea spoonful each of cinnamon, cloves and pepper, and a table spoonful of mustard; then pour on sharp vinegar. You may put them in jars, if you like.

Laryngeal Phthisis and Bronchitis.—Dr. Mott, of New York, has come out in favor of the use of Tobacco; he says it is a preventive or perhaps a cure for Laryngeal Phthisis and Bronchitis. If that is the case, there will be less difficulty in answering the question why the clergymen fifty years since were not troubled with broncheal complaints as much as they now are, as we believe in olden time few clergymen neglected the weed.

Grafting Grape Vines.—In Hovey's Magazine, a simple mode of grafting grape vines is described, which in substance is as follows:—Cut off the vine below the surface of the earth; split the stock, as in cleft grafting; let the scion be of one year's wood, with two or three buds; make it wedge shaped and insert it in the cleft; if the cleft does not hold it sufficiently firm, secure it by binding it tight; draw the earth over the whole, leaving the second bud from the top uncovered; take off all the sprouts from the stock and scion, except one, and train that as usual. We think those who have unproductive, or wild vines, would do well to try this method. The time is after the vines cease to bleed.

To destroy Grubs.—Cut a turf, and lay it with the grass downwards near the plant destroyed by the grubs, and it will attract them.

To remove Stains from Mourning Dresses.—Boil a good handful of fig-leaves in two quarts of water till reduced to a pint. Rombazine, crape, cloth, &c. need only be rubbed with a sponge dipped in the liquor, and the effect will be instantly produced.

To ascertain the Quality of Nutmegs.—Oil of nutmegs being of great value, it is often extracted from the nuts which are exposed to sale, and which are thereby rendered of very little value. To ascertain the quality of nutmegs, force a pin into them; and if good, however dry they may appear, the oil will be seen oozing out all round the pin, from the compression occasioned in the surrounding parts,

An effectual Method of retaining good Apples in the Country without grafting.—In every perfectly ripe apple, there will be found one, and sometimes two round seeds; the others will have one or more flatted sides. The round ones will produce the improved fruit from which they are taken, and those with flatted sides will produce the fruit of the crab, upon which the crab was inserted. It requires not a long time to ascertain the difference; for if a circle is drawn in rich ground, and the flat sided seeds planted therein, and the round seeds in the centre, the variations of quality will be discovered in two or three years; the first will throw out the leaves of a crab, and the latter the leaves of an improved tree, distinguished in shape, fibre, and languinous appearance, and, in due time, the fruit of each will prove every thing beyond doubt. It is to be observed, moreover, that the seeds of crabs, being originals, are mostly, if not altogether, round.

To make Ginger Beer.—To every gallon of spring water, add one ounce of sliced white ginger, one pound of common loaf sugar, and two ounces of lemon juice, or three large table spoonfulls; boil it near an hour and take off the scum; then run it through a hair sieve into a tub, and when cool (viz. 70°) add yeast in proportion of half a pint to nine gallons; keep it in a temperate situation two days, during which it may be stirred six or eight times; then put it into a cask, which must be kept full, and the yeast taken off at the bung hole with a spoon. In a fortnight add half a pint of fining (isinglass picked and steeped in beer) which will, if it has been properly fermented, clear it by ascent. The cask must be kept full, and the rising particles taken off at the bung-hole. When fine (which may be expected in twenty-four hours) bottle it, cork it well, and in summer it will be ripe, and fit to drink in a fortnight.

To preserve Milk.—Provide bottles which must be perfectly clean, sweet, and dry; draw the milk from the cow into the bottles, and as they are filled, immediately cork them well up, and fasten the corks with pack-thread or wire, Then spread a little straw on the bottom of a boiler, on which place bottles with straw between them, until the boiler contains a sufficient quantity. Fill it up with cold water; heat the water, and as soon as it begins to boil, draw the fire, and let the whole gradually cool. When quite cold, take out the bottles, and pack them with straw or saw-dust in hampers and stow them in the coolest part of the house or ship. Milk preserved in this manner, although eighteen months in the bottles, will be as sweet as when first milked from the cow.

To preserve Brass Ornaments.—Brass ornaments, when not gilt or luckered, may be cleaned in the same way, and a fine colour may be given to them by two simple processes. The first is to beat salammoniac into a fine powder, then to moisten it with soft water, rubbing it on the ornaments, which must be heated over charcoal, and rubbed dry with bran and whiting. The second is to wash the brass work with roche alum boiled in strong ley, in the proportion of an ounce to a pint; when dry it must be rubbed with fine tripoli. Either of these processes will give to brass the brilliancy of gold.

Method of destroying Insects on Fruit Trees.—Flour of brimstone, sprinkled by a puff, dredging box, or otherwise, on the leaves of vegetables, will effectually destroy worms and insects, and likewise promote the growth of the plants—Peach trees are particularly improved by the application.

GENERAL RULES FOR DIET.

Shun meat that's salt, it's never good,
The weak in health should take their food,
When livers make men billious.
Or stomachs grow rebellious,
Shun much vegetable diet,
Or your nerves will ne'er be quiet.
When you've had a good repast,
For just five hours you should fast.
And just before and after meals.
Avoid hard work with head or heels:
Nor eat too slow, nor yet too fast—
Especially beware the last.
Yet dawdling o'er a meal an hour,
Will sorely try the stomach's power.
Eat but three meals, shun varied plates,
Keep your heart merry with your mates ;
A gloomy brain brews languid blood,
Which never can digest your food.
Friendly be not with the kettle,
Take no soups, and drink but little;
Too much liquid mars digestion,
And, this is no point to jest on.
A strong censure I must utter
On new bread, hot toast and butter.
Cheese is unwholesome in excess,
The less the better. I confess.
Mind if you'd have slumbers light,
Let your evening meal be slight.
Observe these rules and you'll do right ;
Neglect, and you'll soon be a sprite.
If you are weak, soon strong you'll grow,
If you are strong, they'll keep you so.

GEORGE EDMONDS.

N. B. There is a sort of rhyme we learn at school to remember the number of days in the month, and the rhymes are great help to memory. Thousands grow diseased, and miserably live and miserably die, from not attending to these few plain rules for diet which I have set to rhyme and reason. Dr. Paris' book on diet, and Abernethy's Essays, merely inculcate the advice I have given in a short space.

Russian Mode of Curing Drunkenness. — The following singular means of curing habitual drunkenness is employed by a Russian physician, Dr. Schreiber, of Brzesc-Litewski:—It consists in confining the drunkard in a room and furnishing him, at discretion, with brandy diluted with two-thirds of water, as much wine, beer, and coffee as he desires, but containing one-third of brandy; all the food—the bread, meat, &c , are steeped in brandy and water. The poor wight is continually drunk and *dort.* On the fifth day of this regimen he has an extreme disgust for brandy; he earnestly requests other diet, but his desires must not be yielded to, until the poor wretch no longer desires to eat or drink ; he is then certainly cured of his *penchant* for drunkenness. He acquires such a disgust for brandy that he is ready to vomit at the sight of it.

To promote the Growth of Hair.— Mix equal parts of olive oil and spirits of rosemary and add a few drops of oil of nutmeg. If the hair be rubbed every night with a little of this liniment, and the proportion be very gradually augmented, it will answer every purpose of increasing the growth of hair, much more effectually than can be attained by any of the boasting emperical preparations which are imposed on the credulous purchaser.

Paste for the Piles.—Powder of elecampane 4 ounces ; black pepper 4 ounces ; fennel seed 6 ounces ; honey 8 ounces ; sugar 8 ounces ; mix and take a spoonful two or three times a day.

To make Pigs very Fat.—Feed them on boiled rice.

A Recipe to make Yeast.—To two middling sized boiled round potatoes, add one pint of boiling water, and two table spoonfuls of brown sugar When cool, add a small quantity of common yeast. One pint of hot water should be applied to every half pint of the compound. Hot water is better in warm weather, This yeast, being made without flour, will keep longer, and is said to be much better than any previously in use.

To discharge Grease from Leather —The white of an egg applied to the spot, and dried in the sun ; or, to two table spoonfuls of spirits of turpentine, add half an ounce of mealy potatoes, with some of the best Durham mustard. Apply this mixture to the spot, and rub it off when dry. A little vinegar added, revives, and is perhaps more efficacious.

Against Burns and Scalds— Plunge the part scalded into cold water as soon as possible. Wet it with linen steeped in rectified spirits or common brandy. Poultices and oily application are to be avoided.

To Clean Plate.—The best material for cleaning plate that is in constant use, is soap and water, with a soft cloth; if a dark, tarnished spot should appear, a little damp whitening on a small brush will soon remove it. For plate that has long lain by, liquor castors, cruet stands, &c., first wash it with soap and water, and if needful, (in consequence of tarnish,) smear it all over with whitening and spirits of wine, or common gin, set it to dry, and then brush it off. Decanter stands, and other articles which must not be washed, on account of the varnished satin wood and green baize, should be subject to the latter treatment only.

The best plate powder is the purest whitening; because it is soft, and not a metalic preparation, as rouge is, and other advertised plate powders; these act upon the silver, and wear it rapidly away.

After the plate has been washed with hot water, rub it over with a mixture of levigated hartshorn and spirits of turpentine, which is the best preparation I have known for cleansing plate and renewing its polish. Remember, that two good sized leathers are required for cleaning plate, one of which should be kept for rubbing off the hartshorn powder, and the other for polishing up the silver afterwards.

To keep Pickles and Sweetmeats.—Pickles should be kept in unglazed jars; unglazed stone pots answer very well for common fruit. A paper wet in brandy, or proof spirit, and laid on the preserved fruit, tends to keep it from fermenting. Both pickles and sweetmeats should be watched, to see that they do not ferment, particularly when the weather is warm. Whenever they ferment, turn off the vinegar syrup, scald and turn it back while hot. When pickles grow soft, it is owing to the vinegar being too weak. To strengthen it, heat it scalding hot, turn it back on the pickles, and, when luke-warm, put in a little alum, and a brown paper wet in molasses. If it does not grow sharp in the course of three weeks it is past recovery, and should be thrown away, and fresh vinegar turned on, scalding hot to the pickles

To Clean Woollen and Silk Shawls.—Pare and grate raw, mealy potatoes, and put to each pint of the potatoe pulp a couple of quarts of cold water. Let it stand five hours, then strain the water through a sieve, and rub as much of the potato pulp through as possible—let the strained water stand to settle again—when very clear, turn the water off from the dregs carefully. Put a clean white cotton sheet on a perfectly clean table, lay on the shawl which you wish to clean, and pin it down tight. Dip a sponge, that has never been used, into the potato water, and rub the shawl with it till clean; then rinse the shawl in clear water, with a tea-cup of salt to a pailful of water. Spread it on a clean, level place, where it will dry quick—if hung up to dry, the colors are apt to run, and make the shawl streaked. Fold it up while damp, and let it remain half an hour, then put it into a mangler—if you have not one, wrap it in a clean white cloth, and put it under a weight, and let it remain till dry. If there are any grease spots on the shawl, they should be extracted before the shawl is washed.

To prevent Moths.—In the month of April beat your fur garment well with a small cane or elastic stick, then lap them up in linen without pressing the fur too hard, and put between the folds some camphor in small lumps; then put your furs in this state in boxes well closed.

When the furs are wanted for use, beat them well as before, and expose them for twenty-four hours to the air, which will take away the smell of the camphor.

If the fur has long hair, as bear or fox, add to the camphor an equal quanity of black pepper in powder.

A Strong Paste for Paper.—To two large spoonfuls of fine flour put as much pounded rosin as will lie on a shilling; mix with as much strong beer as will make it of a due consistence, and boil half an hour. Let it be cold before it is used.

To Clean Papered Walls.—The very best method is to rub them with stale bread. Cut the crust off very thick, and wipe straight down from the top, then go to the top again, and so on. The staler the bread the better.

To Preserve ripe Peaches.—October is the best month, as they are then harder and larger. Put them into a preserving-pan full of cold water, with a slice or two of lemon; set them on a slow fire; have ready a sieve and a napkin; be careful not to do them too much; some will be ready sooner than others. When they begin to be soft they are done enough; drain them on the sieve, and let them stand until cold; then put them into glasses; pound sugar-candy very fine in a mortar, dissolve it in brandy, and fill up the glasses with it.

To Preserve whole or half Quinces.—Into two quarts of boiling water put a quantity of the fairest goldon pippins, in slices not very thin, and not pared, but wiped clean. Boil them very quick, close covered, till the water becomes a thick jelly: then scald the quinces, To every pint of pippin-jelly put a pound of the finest sugar; boil it, and skim it clear. Put those quinces that are to be done whole into the syrup at once, and let it boil very fast; and those that are to be done in halves by themselves: skim it, and when the fruit is clear put some of the syrup into a glass to try whether it jellies before taking off the fire. The quantity of quinces is to be a pound to a pound of sugar, and a pound of jelly already boiled with the sugar.

Biffins.—Take the red biffin apple, and put them into a cool oven six or seven times, flattening them gently by degrees, when they are soft enough to bear it. If the oven should be hot they will waste, and they ought to be put at first into a very cool one.

To Preserve Jarganel Pears most beautifully.—Pare them very thin, and simmer in a thin syrup; let them lie a day or two. Make the syrup richer, and simmer again, and repeat this till they are clear; then drain and dry them in the sun or a cool oven a very little time. They may be kept in syrup, and dried as wanted, which makes them more moist and rich.

To Preserve Siberian Crabs.—Rub the fruit with a dry flannel, taking care not to break the skin. Prick each with a needle all over to prevent their bursting. Boil a pound of sugar in a pint of water, then put in the fruit and boil it until the skin begins to crack slightly; then take up the crabs, drain them separately upon a dish; boil the syrup again, and, if not strong enough, add more sugar; when cold pour it over the fruit, which must be put into jars, tied down closely, and kept in a cool dry place.

Fruit Pie.—Cover the bottom of a pie-dish, well buttered, with a thickness of light paste, (*pate feuilletee*,) make a border of three or four thicknesses of the same paste, and place upon this crust your fruits, in the following manner. The apples having been pared, cored, and cut in slices; the apricots or peaches in halves or quarters, and freed from their stones; the prunes or cherries without stones, but otherwise entire, the pears remaining entire, arranged upon the pie, with their stems upward; the grains of verjuice, muscat raisins, and raspberries, remaining whole;—according as you would make your pie with either, you proceed to submit your fruits to the following operation. Boil in a sauce-pan a glass of wine with a quarter of a pound of sugar: put in your fruit for five minutes, and add a small glass of brandy. Let them drain; place on the paste, and put the pie in the oven. When it is baked, you pour over it the syrup in which you have boiled the fruit. This is the manner in which you must make pies with all sorts of fruits, marmelades and preserves.

Spinnage Pie.—Prepare the paste and the sauce as for a fruit pie, described as above; bake it, and fill it up, at the moment it is served, with a stuffing or filling of spinnage, with cream and sugar; glaze with a red-hot shovel, and serve.

Cream Pie.—Prepare your pie dish with a crust, and high border of light pastry, as for a fruit pie, fill it with a cream made beforehand. Observe that it is necessary that your cream should be cold, before it is turned upon the pastry. Wash the border crust with yolk of egg, and bake it in an oven. Before serving, powder with sugar and glaze with a hot shovel.

Cautions relative to the use of Brass and Copper Cooking Utensils.—Cleanliness has been aptly styled the cardinal cooked in a cleanly manner. Many lives has been lost in consequence of carelessness in using brass, copper and glazed earthern cooking utensils. The two first should be throughly cleansed with salt and hot vinegar before cooking in them, and no oily or acid substance after being cooked, should be allowed to cool or remain in any of them.

Cement for the Mouths of Corked Bottles.—Melt together a quarter of a pound of sealing wax, the same quantity of rosin, a couple of ounces of bees' wax. When it froths, stir it with a tallow candle. As soon as it melts, dip the mouth of the corked bottles into it. This is an excellent thing to exclude the air from such things as are injured by being opposed to it.

Cement for Alabaster.—Take of white bees' wax one pound, of rosin a pound, and three-quarters of alabaster. Melt the wax and rosin, then strew the alabaster over it lightly, (which should be previously reduced to a fine powder.) Stir the whole well together, then knead the mass in water, in order to incorporate the alabaster throughly with the rosin and wax. The alabaster, when mended, should be perfectly dry, and heated. The cement, when applied, should also be heated. Join the broken pieces, bind them, and let them remain a week. This composition, when properly managed, forms an extremely strong cement.

To pot Cheese.—Cheese that has begun to mould, can be kept from becoming any more so, by being treated in the following manner: Cut off the mouldy part, and if the cheese is dry, grate it—if not, pound it fine into a mortar, together with the crust. To each pound of it, when fine put a table-spoonful of brandy—mix it in well with the cheese, then press it down tight, in a clean stone pot, and lay a paper wet with brandy on the top of it. Cover the pot up tight, and keep it in a cool dry place. This is also a good way to treat dry pieces of cheese. Potted cheese is best when a year old. It will keep several years without any danger of its breeding insects.

To Make Blacking.—Three ounces of ivory black; two ounces of treacle; half an ounce of vitriol; half an ounce of sweet oil; quarter of a pint of vinegar, and three-quarters of a pint of water. Mix the oil, treacle, and ivory black, gradually to a paste; then add the vitriol, and by degrees, the vinegar and water. It will produce a beautiful polish.

To clean Stone Stairs and Halls.—Boil a pound of pipe-maker's clay with a quart of water, a quart of small beer, and put in a bit of stone-blue. Wash with this mixture, and, when dry, rub the stones with flannel and a brush.

To take Iron Stains out of Marble.—An equal quantity of fresh spirit of vitriol and lemon-juice being mixed in a bottle, shake it well; wet the spots, and in a few minutes rub with soft linen till they disappear.

To take Stains out of Marble.—Mix unslaked lime in finest powder with the stronger soap-ley, pretty thick, and instantly with a painter's brush lay it on the whole of the marble. In two month's time wash it off perfectly clean; then have ready a fine thick lather of soft soap, boiled in soft water; dip a brush in it, and scour the marble with powder, not as common cleaning. This will, by very good rubbing, give a beautiful polish. Clear off the soap, and finish with a smooth hard brush till the end be effected.

Hazelnut Butter.—Having scalded and blanched some hazelnuts, pound them to a paste in a mortar, adding gradually a small quantity of butter. This is good to eat with wild fowl, or to flavor the most delicate sauces.

To prevent the Ill Effects of Charcoal.—Set an uncovered vessel filled with boiling water over the pan containing the charcoal, the vapour of which will counteract the deleterious fumes, and, while it keeps boiling, will make the charcoal as safe as any other fuel.

Soft and fine Draught for those who are weak and have a Cough.—Beat a fresh-laid egg, and mix it with a quarter of a pint of new milk warmed, a large spoonful of capillaire, the same of rose-water, and a little nutmeg scraped. Do not warm it after the eggs is put in. Take it the first and last thing.

To loosen the Stoppers of Decanters and Smelling Bottles that are wedged in tight.—Dip the end of a feather in oil, and rub it round the stopple, close to the mouth of the bottle; then put the bottle about a couple of feet from the fire, having the mouth towards it. The heat will cause the oil to run down between the stopple and mouth of the bottle. When warm, strike the bottle gently on both sides, with any light wooden instrument that you may happen to have. If the stopple cannot be taken out with the hand at the end of this process, repeat it, and you will finally succeed by persevering in it, however firmly it may be wedged in.

To Clean Marble Fire-Places.—If you happen to live in a house which has marble fireplaces, never wash them with suds: this destroys the polish, in time. They should be dusted; the spots taken off with a nice oiled cloth, and then rubbed dry with a soft rag.

To pot Butter for Winter Use.—Mix a large spoonful of salt, a table-spoonful of powdered white sugar, and one of saltpetre. Work this quantity into six pounds of fresh-made butter. Put the butter into a stone pot, that is throughly cleansed. When you have finished putting down your butter, cover it with a layer of salt, and let it remain covered until cold weather.

To render Shoes Water-Proof.—Mix a pint of drying oil, two ounces of yellow wax, two ounces of turpentine, and half an ounce of Burgur pitch, over a slow fire. Lay the mixture, whilst hot, on the boots or shoes with a sponge or soft brush; and, when they are dry, lay it on again and again, until the leather becomes quite saturated, this is to say, will hold no more. Let them then be put away, and not be worn until they are perfectly dry and elastic: they will afterwards be found not only impenetrable to wet, but soft and pliable, and of much longer duration.

Eggs in Winter.—The reason hens do not usually lay eggs in the winter is that the gravel is covered up with snow, and therefore they are not furnished with lime to form the shells. If the bones left of meat, poultry, &c, are pounded and mixed with their food, or given to them alone, they will eat them very eagerly, and will lay eggs as the same as in summer. Hens fed on oats are much more likely to lay well than these fed on corn.

To Candy Almonds.—Blanch any quantity of almonds, then fry them in butter till they are of a light-brown colour; wipe them nicely with a napkin, and put them into a pan. Make a syrup of white sugar, and boil it to a thread; care must be taken to boil it to the exact candying point: pour it boiling hot upon the almonds, and stir them till they are quite cold. This is an excellent method of preparing almonds for dessert, and much approved of in London by the guests of his highness Prince Ekbaladoola, the Nawaub of Oude, from whose cook it has been obtained.

Bottled Fruit.—The best way of preserving all the common fruit for tarts is by bottling, and if the following directions be exactly observed it will be found to answer admirably. Gather any kind of fruit on a dry day, currants, gooseberries, plums &c.; put it into wide-mouthed bottles, and let it be fully ripe. Mix currants and raspberries in the same bottle, and put two ounces of sugar into each; then have bladders cut so large, that when they are tied over the bottles they will hang an inch all round below the string. Let the bladders be wet, and tied tightly then put the bottles up to their necks into a copper of cold water, with some straw between. Light a fire under the copper, and, when the juice of the fruit has boiled up, let the fire go gradually out, and leave the bottles in the water until it is cold. The bladders will have sprung up to their extent, making the bottles perfectly air-tight. Some persons put two bladders and turn the bottles upside down; but this is unnecessary, one being sufficient if properly managed. Fruit, thus preserved, will keep for any number of years retaining all its original freshness: the contents of every bottle must be used at once, for the air getting in will spoil, and they will require more sugar when put into tarts or puddings.

Larding.—Larding with slips of fat bacon greatly improves the tastes and appearance of meat, poultry, game, &c., and is much used in French cookery.

For this purpose, you must have a larding-pin; (which may be purchased at the hardware stores;) it is a steel instrument about a foot in length, sharp at one end, and cleft at the other into four divisions which are near two inches long, and resembling tweezers.

Bacon is the proper meat to lard with; the fat only is used. Cut it into slips not exceeding two inches in length, half an inch in breadth, and half an inch in thickness, and smaller if intended for poultry; they will diminish in cooking. Put these slips of bacon (one at a time) into the cleft or split end of the larding-pin. Give each slip a slight twist and press it down hard into the pin, with your fingers.—Then run the pin through meat or fowl (avoiding the bones,) and when you draw it out on the under side it will have left the slip of bacon sticking in the upper side. Take care to arrange the slips in regular rows and at equal distances; have them all of the same size, and let every one stick up about an inch from the surface of the meat. If any are wrong, take them out and do them over again.

Carpets.—Carpets should be taken up and shook thoroughly, if in constant use, as often as three or four times in a year, as the dirt that collects underneath them wears them out very fast. Straw kept under carpets, will make them wear much longer, as the dirt will sift through, and keep it from grinding out. Carpets should be taken up as often as once a year, even if not much used, as there is much danger of moths getting into them. If there is any appearance of moths in carpets when they are taken up, sprinkle tobacco or black pepper on the floor before the carpets are put down, and let it remain after they are laid down. When the dust is well shaken out of carpets, if there are grease spots on them, grate on potter's clay very thick, cover them with brown paper, and set on a warm iron. It will be necessary to repeat this process several times to get out all the grease

G 2

If the carpets are so much soiled as to require cleaning all over, after the dirt has been shaken out, spread them on a clean floor, and rub on them, with a new broom, pared and grated raw potatoes. Let the carpets remain till perfectly dry, before walking on them.

Burnt Rhubarb in Diarrhœa.—It may be useful to know the value of burnt rhubarb in diarrhœa. It has been used with the same pleasing effects for more than twenty years.—After one or two doses the pains quickly subside, and the bowels return to their natural state. The manner of preparing it, is to burn rhubarb powder in an iron pot, stirring it until it blackens; then smother it in a covered jar 't looses two-thirds of its weight by incineration. It is nearly tasteless. In no case has it failed where given. It may be given in port wine, milk and water.

To preserve Cheese from Insects.—Cover the cheese, while whole, with a paste made of wheat flour; then wrap a cloth round it, and cover it with the paste. Keep the cheese in a cool dry place. Cheese that has skippers in it, if kept till cold weather, will be freed of them.

To Preserve Green Currants.—Currants may be kept fresh for a year or more, if they are gathered when green, separated from the stems, put into dry, clean junk bottles, and corked very carefully, so as to exclude the air. They should be kept in a cool place in the cellar.

Garlic Butter.—Take two large cloves of garlic and pound them to a paste in a mortar, adding, by degrees, a piece of butter the size of an egg. You may with a little of this butter give the taste of garlic to sauces. Some persons like a piece of garlic butter on the table, to eat with roast meat.

Spinach for Coloring Green.—Take three handfuls of spinach, and pound it in a mortar to extract the juice. Then put it into a saucepan, and set it over a slow fire. When it is just ready to boil, take it off and strain it. By stirring in a small quantity of spinach-juice, you may give any sauce a green color.

To Prevent the Creaking of a Door—Rub a bit of soap on the hinges.

Domestic Yeast.—The following is copied from the London Gardener's Chronicle, and must be cheap and easy:—Boil one pound of good flour, quarter of a pound of brown sugar, and a little salt, in two gallons of water, for an hour. When milk warm, bottle it and cork it closely, and it will be fit for use in twenty-four hours. One pound of this yeast will make eighteen pounds of bread.

Hints for Health.—If the blood has stagnated, take exercise, and if you still feel chilly, a glass of good old country ale will be worth a thousand drams. Brown bread is the best occasional food at breakfast that can be taken; nature never intended that glorious husk, which envelopes the wheaten grain, to be thrown where Macbeth wisely recommends physic to be sent.—Laugh as loud as you can, and as frequently as possible. Depression of spirits, besides its immediate effect on the nervous system, deranges the respiration, and mars the proper oxygenation and circulation of the blood, causing diminished vitality, and leading to consumption. Avoid all articles of food when decomposed; a love for putrid game is the vilest instance of morbid tastes.

To Fatten Fowls or Chickens in four or five days.—Set rice over the fire with skimmed milk, only as much as will serve one day. Let it boil till the rice is quite swelled out; you may add a teaspoonful or two of sugar, but it will do well without. Feed them three times a-day in common pans; give them only as much as will quite fill them at once. When you put fresh, let the pans be set in water, that no sourness may be conveyed to the fowls, as that prevents them from fattening. Give them clean water, or the milk of the rice, to drink; but the less wet the latter is when perfectly soaked the better. By this method the flesh will have a clear whiteness which no other food gives; and when it is considered how far a pound of rice will go, and how much time is saved by this mode, it will be found to be as cheap as barley meal, or more so. The pen should be daily cleaned, and no food given for sixteen hours before the poultry be killed.

Feathers.—In towns, poultry being usually sold ready picked, the feathers, which may occasionally come in small quantities, are neglected; but orders should be given to put them into a tub free from damp, and as they dry to change them into paper bags, a few in each; they should hang in a dry kitchen to season; fresh ones must not be added to those in part dried, or they will occasion a musty smell, but they should go through the same process. In a few months they will be fit to add to beds or to make pillows, without the usual mode of drying them in a cool oven, which may be pursued if they are wanted before five or six months.

To Choose Eggs at Market, and Preserve them.—Put the large end of the egg to your tongue; if it feels warm, it is new. In new-laid eggs there is a small division of the skin from the shell, which is filled with air, and is perceptible to the eye at the end. On looking through them against the sun or candle, if fresh, eggs will be pretty clear. If they shake, they are not fresh.

Eggs may be bought cheapest when the hens first begin to lay in the spring, before they sit; in Lent and at Easter they become dear. They may be preserved fresh by dipping them in boiling water and instantly taking them out, or by oiling the shell; either of which ways is to prevent the air passing through it; or kept on shelves with small holes to receive one in each, and be turned every other day; or close, packed in a keg, and covered with strong lime-water.

A very supporting Broth against any kind of Weakness.—Boil two pounds of loin of mutton, with a very large handful of chervil in two quarts of water to one. Take off part of the fat. Any other herbs or roots may be added. Take half a pint three or four times a day.

To Extract Oil from Boards or Stone.—Make a strong ley of pearl-ashes and soft water, and add as much unslacked lime as it will take up; stir it together, and then let it settle a few minutes; bottle it, and stop close; have ready some water to lower it as used, and scour the part with it. If the liquor should lie long on the boards, it will draw out the colour of them: therefore do it with care and expedition.

RARE AND VALUABLE RECIPES.

Housekeepers would do well to remember the fact, that by putting a piece of loaf sugar, the size of a walnut, into the teapot, the tea will be made to infuse, or "draw," in one half the usual time.

To Clean the Backs of the Grate, the Inner Hearth, and the Fronts of Cast-Iron Stoves.—Boil about a quarter of a pound of the best black-lead with a pint of small beer and a bit of soap the size of a walnut. When that is melted, dip a painter's brush, and wet the grate, having first brushed off all the soot and dust; then take a hard brush and rub it till of a beautiful brightness.

Another way.—Mix black-lead and whites of eggs well beaten together; dip a painter's brush. wet all over; then rub it bright w... a hard brush.

To preserve Irons from Rust.—Melt fresh mutton-suet, smear over the iron with it while hot; then dust it well with unslacked lime pounded and tied up in a muslin. Irons so prepared will keep many months. Use no oil for them, at any time, except salad oil, there being water in all other.

Fire-irons should be kept wrapped in baize, in a dry place, when not used.

The best time to apply paint.—It has long been a subject of inquiry, says a valuable paper, as to the best time to apply paint to the clapboards of houses for durability. Repeated experiments have been made, within twenty-five years past, which have resulted in the conviction that paint applied between November and March, will stand more than twice as long as that which is spread in the warmest weather. The reason is obvious, for in cold weather the oil, and component parts of the paint form a hard substance on the surface of the clapboard, nearly as hard as glass, and not easily erased, or even cut with a sharp knife, and will not soon wear off; whereas paints applied in the months of July and August, and more especially if in a severe drought, the oil penetrates into the wood like water into a sponge, and leaves the lead nearly dry, which will soon crumble off.

"I hesitate not to say, that of females not one in fifty, I fear not in five hundred, dresses sufficiently loose to suffer no ill consequence from ligature or compression." So says Mrs. Gore, and we believe she is more than half right. Suposing our ladies had always been in the habit of dressing perfectly loose, what could they say if they were compelled to lace themselves up after the present fashion as a punishment? Why they would raise the very old nick about it.

A Cure for the Toothache—(When not arising from Rheumatism.) Take two parts of powdered alum, and seven parts of nitric æther. One or two grains are to be inserted in the cavity of the tooth, and repeated whenever the pain returns; in a short time the pain will cease to return, and the chemical action which produces the *caries* (decay of the bone) will cease.

For a Cut.—Wash off the blood in cold water, and bind it up with a clean cotton bandage; if it inclines to bleed, put on scraped lint, after bringing the edges of the wound together as closely as possible, and bind it rather tight. Or use sticking-plaster.

When a Nail or Pin has been run into the Foot, instantly bind on a rind of salt pork; if the foot swell bathe it in a strong decoction of wormwood, then bind on another rind of pork, and keep quiet till the wound is well. The lockjaw is often caused by such wounds, if neglected

For a Bruise or Sprain.—Bathe the part in cold water, till you can get ready a decoction of wormwood. This is one of the best remedies for sprains and bruises. When the wormwood is fresh gathered, pound the leaves and wet them either with water or vinegar, and bind them on the bruise; when the herb is dry, put it into cold water, and let it boil a short time, then bathe the bruise and bind on the herb.

Always keep cotton wool, scraped lint, and wormwood on hand.

To take Wax out of Cloth.—Hold a red hot iron (a poker will do) steadily within an inch or so of the cloth, and in a few minutes the wax will wholly evaporate; then rub the cloth with some whitish brown paper to remove any mark that may remain.

To Wash White Cotton Clothes.— Table cloths, or any white clothes that have coffee or fruit stains on them, before being put into soap-suds, should have boiling water turned on them, and remain in it till the water is cold—The spots should be then rubbed out in it. If they are put into soap-suds with the stains in, they will be set by it, so that no subsequent washing will remove them. Table cloths will be less likely to get stained up, if they are always rinsed in thin starch water, as it tends to keep coffee and fruit from sinking into the texture of the cloth. White clothes that are very dirty, will come clean easily if put into strong, cool suds, and hung on the fire the night previous to the day in which they are to be washed. If they get to boiling, it will not do them any harm, provided the suds are cool when they are put in; if it is hot at first, it will set the dirt in. The following method of washing clothes is a saving of great labor. Soak the clothes in lukewarm soap-suds; if they are quite dirty, soak them over night. To every three pails of water put a pint of soft soap, and table-spoonful of the salts of soda. Heat it till mildly warm, then put in the clothes without any rubbing, and boil them an hour. Drain the suds out of them as much as possible, as it is bad for the hands; then add water till cool enough for the hands. The dirt will be loose, so that they will require but a little rubbing. Rinse them thoroughly in clear water, then in indigo water. The soda can be produced cheap, by purchasing it in large quantities—soda is an excellent thing to soften hard water. The soda suds will not do to wash calicoes in. It is a good plan to save your suds, after washing, to water your garden, if you have one, or to harden cellars and yards, when sandy.

To Wash Woollens.—If you do not wish to have white flannels shrink when washed, make a good suds of hard soap, and wash the flannels in it, without rubbing any soap on them; rub them out in another suds, then wring them out of it, and put them in a clean tub, and turn on sufficient boiling water to cover them, and let them remain till the water is cold. A little indigo in the boiling water makes the flannels look nicer. If you wish to have your white flannels shrink, so as to have them thick, wash them in soft soap-suds, and rinse them in cold water. Colored woollens that incline to fade, should be washed with beef's gall and warm water before they are put into soap-suds. Colored pantaloons looks very well washed with beef's gall and fair warm water, and pressed on the wrong side while damp.

Cream.—The quantity of cream on milk may be greatly increased by the following process:—Have two pans ready in boiling hot water, and when the new milk is brought in, put it into one of these hot pans and cover it with the other. The quality as well as the thickness of the cream is improved.

Paste.—To make common paste, mix one table-spoonful of flour with one of cold, stir it well together, and add two more table-spoonfuls of water; set it over the fire and give it a boil, stirring it all the time, or it will burn at the bottom of the saucepan.

Chloride of Lime.—A room may be purified from offensive smells of any kind by a few spoonfuls of chloride of lime dissolved in water. A good sized saucer, or some similar vessel, is large enough for all common purposes. The article is cheap, and is invaluable in the apartment of an invalid.

A new and excellent Cement.— Three parts of ashes, three parts of clay, and one part of sand, is said to make a cement as hard as marble, and impervious to water.

To Blacken the Fronts of Stone Chimney-Pieces. — Mix oil-varnish with lamp-black, and a little spirit of turpentine to thin it to the consistence of paint. Wash the stone with soap and water very clean; then sponge it with clear water; and when perfectly dry, brush it over twice with this colour, letting it dry between the times. It looks extremly well. The lamp-black must be sifted first.

Feathers.—It is said that tumbled plumes may be restored to elasticity and beauty by dipping them in hot water, then shaking and drying them.

RARE AND VALUABLE RECIPES.

To Clean Silk Goods.—When silk cushions, or silk coverings to furniture, become dingy, rub dry bran on them gently, with a woollen cloth, till clean. Remove grease spots and stains as in direction. Silk garments should have the spots extracted before being washed—use hard soap for all colors but yellow, for which hard soap is the best. Put the soap into hot water, beat it till it is perfectly dissolved, then add sufficient cold water to make it just lukewarm water. Rinse it in another water, and for bright yellows, crimsons, and maroons, add sulphuric acid enough to the water to give it an acid taste, before rinsing the garment in it. To restore the colors of the different shades of pink, put in the second rinsing water a little vinegar or lemon-juice. For scarlet, use a solution of tin; for blues, purples, and their shades, use pearl-ash; and for olive-greens, dissolve verdigris in the rinsing water—fawn and browns should be rinsed in pure water. Dip the silks up and down in the rinsing water; take them out of it without wringing, and dry them in the shade. Fold them up while damp; let them remain to have the dampness strike through all parts of them alike, then put them in a mangle—if you have not one, iron them on the wrong side, with an iron just hot enough to smooth them. A little isinglass or gum arabic, dissolved in the rinsing water of gauze shawls and ribbons, is good to stiffen them. The water in which pared potatoes have been boiled, is an excellent thing to wash black silk in—it stiffens, and makes them glossy and black. Beef's gall and lukewarm water is also a nice thing to restore rusty silk, and soap-suds answer very well. They look better not to be rinsed in clear water, but they should be washed in two different waters.

To Cleanse Feather Beds and Mattresses.—When feather beds become solid or heavy, they may be made clean and light by being treated in the following manner:—Rub them over with a stiff brush, dipped in hot soap-suds. When clean, lay them on a shed, or any other clean place, where the rain will fall on them. When thoroughly soaked, let them dry in a hot sun for six or seven successive days, shaking them up well, and turning them over each day. They should be covered over with a thick cloth during the night: if exposed to the night air, they will become damp and mildew. This way of washing the bed-ticking and feathers, makes them very fresh and light, and is much easier than the old fashioned way, of emptying the beds, and washing the feathers separately, while it answers quite as well. Care must be taken to dry the bed perfectly, before sleeping on it. Hair mattresses that have become hard and dirty, can be made nearly as good as new by ripping them, washing the ticking, and picking the hair free from bunches, and keeping it in a dry airy place, several days. Whenever the tickings gets dry, fill it lightly with the hair, and tack it together.

To Cleanse Vials and Pie Plates.—Bottles and vials that have had medicines in them, may be cleansed by putting ashes in each one, and immersing them in a pot of cold water, then heating the water gradually until it boils. When they have boiled in it an hour, take it from the fire, and let them remain in it till cold; then wash them in soap suds, and rinse them in fair water till clean. Pie plates that have been used much for baking, are apt to impart an unpleasant taste to the pies, which is owing to the lard and butter of the crust soaking into them, and becoming rancid. It may be removed by putting them in a brass kettle, with ashes and cold water, and boiling them in it an hour.

To prevent the formation of a Crust on Tea-Kettles.—Keep an oyster-shell in your tea-kettle, and it will prevent the formation of a crust on the inside of it, by attracting the stony particles to itself.

To take Rust out of Steel.—Cover the steel with sweet oil well rubbed on it, and in forty-eight hours use unslacked lime finely powdered, to rub until all the rust disappears.

Candles.—Very hard and durable candles, are made in the following manner: Melt together ten ounces of mutton tallow, a quarter of an ounce of camphor, four ounces of beeswax, and two ounces of alum. Candles made of these materials burn with very clear light.

A cheap paint.—Take one bushel of unslacked lime and slack it with cold water ; when slacked, add to it 20 lbs, of spanish whiting, 17 lbs of salt, and 12 lbs. of sugar, strain this mixture through a wire sive, and it will be fit for use after reducing with cold water. This is intended for the outside of buildings, or where it is exposed to the weather. In order to give a good color, three coats are necessary on brick, and two on wood. It may be laid on with a brush similar to whitewash. Each coat must have sufficient time to dry before the next is applied. For painting inside walks, as before, 1 bushel of unslacked lime. 3 lbs. of sugar, 5 lbs. salt, and prepare as above, and apply with a brush.

I have used it on brick and find it well calculated to preserve them—it is far preferable to oil paint. I have used it on wood, and assure you that it will last longer on rough siding than oil paint will on planed siding or boards.

You can make any color you please. If you wish straw color, use Yellow Ochre instead of whitening; for lemon color, Ochre and Chrome Yellow ; for lead and slate color, Lampblack; for blue, Indigo ; for green, Chrome Green. The different kinds of paint will not cost more than one fourth as much as oil paints, including the labor of putting on.

New Tooth Powder.—One of the commonest tooth powders of the present day consists of pulverised orris root, burnt hartshorn, charcoal, Armenian bole, and dragon's blood ; the orris root being used merely to give it a pleasant flavor, and to conceal any disagreeable effluvium emitted from the mouth. But the finest of all dentifrices is the plain camphorated tooth powder ; for while the camphor does no injury to the teeth, it instantly destroys those minute creatures which produce the tartar and green incrustation on the enamel. To promote a general cleanliness of the teeth, the fact cannot be too often repeated, that a microscopic observer, M. Mandl has discovered that not only the foul mucous covering of the tongue, but the tartar of the teeth, consists of the dead remains of millions of infusorial animalculæ. Leuwenhoek discovered long ago that the mucous secretion of the human mouth abounded in living specimens of these minute beings ; but it remained for M. Mandl to make known that the tartar of the teeth consists of their dead bodies compactly united together in one mass by chemical decomposition. When a portion of this tartar of the teeth is softened in clear water, and placed under a powerful microscope, it is found to consist of their delicate skeletons. M. Mandl, who is unable to account for their origin in the mouth, says they are most observable in those persons who live on spare diet, and here commends, as the quickest mode of destroying them, the application of a tooth-brush dipped in brandy or any other ardent spirit.

For Burns and Scalds.—Mix in a bottle three ounces of olive oil and four ounces of lime water. Apply the mixture to the part burned five or six times a day with a feather. Linseed oil is equally as good as olive oil.

Another.—Spread clarified honey upon a linen rag, and apply it to the burn immediately, and it will relieve the pain instantly, and heal the sore in a very short time.

Cuts.—All that is necessary to be done for triffing cuts, is to wash the blood out clean with cold water, and bring the edges of the wound together as closely as possible, and apply some straps of adhesive plaster. Shoemaker's wax spread upon strips of rags will make very good ones. Bleeding may usually be stopped by pressure ; but if not, apply a cobweb or puff-ball.

TEMPERANCE PLUM-PUDDING.

Take a pound of the best raisins, and cut them in half, after removing the seeds. Pick and wash clean a pound of currants, and dry them thoroughly before the fire, spread out on a large flat dish. Cut into slips half a pound of citron. Then mix together on the dish with the currants, the cut raisins and the slips of citron, and dredge them thickly with flour; tumbling them about in it till they are well coated all over. The flour will keep them properly dispersed throughout the pudding, and prevent their sinking to the bottom. Chop very fine a pound of beef-suet. Mix a pint of West India molasses with a pint of rich milk. Sift a pound of flour. Beat eight eggs till very thick and light. Stir the beaten eggs gradually into the mixed molasses and milk, alternately with the flour, and a half pound of brown sugar, (which should previously be crushed smooth by rolling it with a rolling pin,) a little of each at a time. Then add, by degrees, the fruit and the suet, a little of each alternately. Beat and stir the whole very hard, till all the ingredients are thoroughly mixed. Take a large clean square cloth of thick muslin or coarse linen, dip it in boiling water, then shake it out and dredge it with flour. Spread it out in a deep pan, and pour the pudding mixture into it.—Leave room for it to swell, and tie it firmly; plastering up the tying place with a small lump of flour and water mixed into a dough, to prevent any water from getting in. Have ready a large pot of hot water, boiling hard. Put in the pudding and boil it well from six to eight hours. Less than six will not be sufficient, and eight will not be too long. Turn it several times while boiling. Keep at hand a kettle of hot water to replenish that in the pudding pot, as it boils away. To put in cold water will make the pudding so heavy, as to be unfit to eat. Also, it will be spoiled if any water is allowed to get into the bag. Do not take it up till immediately before it is wanted on the table. Then untie the bag, and turn out

the pudding. Serve it up with a sauce-boat of cream, made very sweet with sugar, and seasoned with nutmeg. What is left of the pudding may be sliced and fried next day. The West India molasses (which will add to the lightness of any boiled or batter pudding,) is instead of the wine and brandy, generally put into plum-puddings. Instead of wheat flour, this pudding may be made of sifted yellow Indian meal.

In boiling a pudding in a tin mould (which must be previously buttered) see that the water does not rise above the top. To turn it out, dip the mould into a vessel of cold water; otherwise you will find it difficult to open.

TOMATO FIGS.

As this is the season of tomatoes, we republish the following recipe, and commend it to every good housewife who desires to have a rich conserve of domestic manufacture wherewith to treat her friends. And while we do so, would recommend to her, in putting up peaches, pears, quinces, &c., not to omit to preserve a few jars of *tomatoes* as they make the most spicy preserve of all.

Take six pounds of sugar to one peck (or sixteen pounds) of the fruit. Scald and remove the skin of the fruit in the usual way. Cook them over a fire, their own juice being sufficient without the addition of water, until the sugar penetrates and they are clarified. They are then taken out, spread on dishes, flattened and dried in the sun. A small quantity of the syrup should be occasionally sprinkled over them whilst drying; after which, pack them down in boxes, treating each layer with powdered sugar. The syrup is afterwards concentrated and bottled for use. They keep well from year to year and retain surprisingly their flavor, which is nearly that of the best quality of fresh figs. The pear shaped or single tomatoes answers the purpose best. Ordinary brown sugar may be used, a large portion of which is retained in syrup.

MERINGUED APPLES.

Take large ripe pippin apples. Pare them, and extract the cores with an apple - corer, (which no house should be without) so as to leave the apples whole.—Put them into a deep white dish. Rub off the yellow rind of some lemons on bits of loaf sugar; then crush or powder the sugar, and fill with it the holes where the cores came out.— Squeeze through a strainer the juice of the lemons, and pour it round the apples, in the bottom of the dish. If you have not enough of lemon-juice to keep the apples from burning when they bake, you may add to it a very little water. Set the dish into a moderate oven, and bake the apples till they are so tender that a straw or twig from a corn-broom can penetrate them through, but be careful not to let them break. When sufficiently done, set the dish on ice, or in a very cold place in the open air. Prepare a meringue or icing in the proportion of a quarter of a pound of the best loaf sugar, (*very* finely powdered) to every white of an egg. Beat the white of egg first, by itself, till it becomes a firm stiff froth, that will stand alone on the rods or whisk. Then beat in, gradually, the sugar (a teaspoonful at a time) till you have a thick stiff icing or meringue. Add to it a little lemon-juice. When the apples are quite cold, put a portion of this meringue on the top of each. With a broad knife (dipped frequently in cold water) spread the meringue thickly and evenly all over them, smoothing it with the knife-blade. Remember before you ice them to drain from them the juice, which you may save for some other purpose. When iced, set the apples into a moderate oven, and leave them there a few minutes, till they are very slightly browned, and the surface of the meringue hardened. Then take them out; and when cold, serve them up on a glass dish.

Instead of lemon grating you may use rose water to mix with the sugar that fills the holes, and to pour into the bottom of the dish to moisten the apples while baking.

In this case add a little extract of roses to the meringue or icing.

Fine apples prepared in this manner will be found a beautiful and delicious article for a dinner or supper party. They must be done with great care and nicety.

———

CORN BREAD.

Good corn bread being always in season, we republish the following recipe:

"Take as much corn meal as you wish to cook, scald it well, by pouring boiling water over it, and stirring it thoroughly, then mix it into the consistency of batter, with milk; if it is pretty rich it won't hurt it, but mind the mixing part, that it is thoroughly done, the more the better. Put in one egg, a tea spoonful of salæratus, and a table spoonful or more of lard. Mix the whole thoroughly together till the ingredients are entirely incorporated through the whole; mind I say, the mixing, the more the better. It is now to be baked as usual, about three quarters of an hour, and you will have the finest corn bread you ever ate."

———

TURBOT, OR A SHEEP'S HEAD FISH WITH CREAM.

Having cleaned the fish and washed it well through several waters, dry it in a towel; score it across the back, and lay it in a deep white baking-dish. Season it with powdered mace, nutmeg, cayenne, and a little salt, or a sufficient quantity of rich cream; adding some sweet marjoram and sweet basil; minced as finely as possible, and some grated bread crumbs. Pour this marinade over the fish; cover it, and let it stand half an hour. Then bake it in the marinade. Garnish with sliced lemon.

If you cannot conveniently obtain cream (which will be much the best,) cover the fish with bits of fresh butter, and then mix together, and strew over it the spices, herbs, and bread-crumbs.

———

RICE FLOUR POUND CAKE.

Weigh a pound of broken up loaf sugar of the best quality. Upon some of the largest lumps rub off the yellow rind of three large ripe lemons, that have been previously rolled under your hand on a table. Then powder finely all the pound of sugar. Cut the lemons and squeeze the juice through a strainer. Cut up, into a deep pan, a pound of the best fresh butter, and mix it with the sugar. Stir it with a wooden spaddle till perfectly light and creamy; then mix with it the lemon juice, adding a grated nutmeg. Sift a pound of rice flour into a broad shallow pan, and in another shallow pan beat twelve eggs till they are thick, smooth, and very light. Stir the beaten egg and the rice flour alternately into the butter and sugar, a little at a time of each. Having stirred the whole long and hard, put the mixture into a buttered tin pan that has straight or upright sides; set it immediately into a moderately brisk oven, and bake it thoroughly. It will require four or five hours in proportion to its thickness. When done, it will shrink from the sides of the pan, and the twig from a corn broom, or the blade of a knife plunged into it to the bottom will come out dry and clean. When cool, ice it, adding a little rose-water or lemon juice to the icing. As you spread on the icing, frequently dip the broad blade of your icing knife into a bowl of cold water—It will assist in smoothing it.

You may bake the mixture in little tins, like queen-cakes. For greasing cake-pans or pie-dishes, always use the best fresh butter. If the butter is salt or otherwise bad, it will communicate a disagreeable taste to the outside of the cakes, &c.

You may bake this mixture as a pudding or puddings—using only *half* a pound of rice flour, put the above quantities of all the other ingredients. Bake it in china as it must go to table in whatever dish it is baked in. Serve it up cold, with powdered sugar strewed over the top.

H

LEMON PUFFS.

Take a pound of the best loaf sugar, powdered. Grate upon a piece of the same sugar the yellow rind of four large ripe lemons; having first rolled each lemon under your hand upon a clean table. Then powder this sugar, and add it to the rest; mixing with it the juice of the lemons. Beat to a stiff froth the whites of four eggs, and then gradually and thoroughly beat it into the lemon and sugar, till thick and smooth. If too thin, add more powdered sugar : if too thick more beaten white of egg. Take a sheet or more of smooth white paper and lay it in a square tin pan, having first cut it to fit. Put on it at equal distances, a round spot of thinly spread powdered loaf sugar, about the size of a dollar. Upon each spot, place, with a spoon, a pile of the mixture, smoothing it and making the surface even. Sift over each a little powdered sugar. Set the pan in a moderate oven, and bake the puffs of a light brown. A few minutes baking will suffice They should rise very high. When cold loosen them carefully from the paper, by inserting a broad knife beneath them. Then spread them on a large dish, and keep them in a dry cold place till wanted. Orange puffs may be made in a similar manner; omitting the rind, and using instead, the juice of *five* large oranges. Very nice puffs can be made with the juice of raspberries, strawberries, currants or cherries.

BOILED EGGS.

It is a common opinion that eggs boiled above two or three minutes, become hard and unfit for use. The Hartford Times says:—" The late Dr. Remington, of this city, always boiled eggs when he eat them, at least thirty minutes. He said they then became mealy and tender, and much better than when boiled five minutes. He was an invalid, and careful of his health; probably he understood the nature of a boiled egg as well as anybody. Try one, boiled well for thirty minutes."

TEMPERANCE MINCE PIE

Take two pounds of the lean of a round of fresh beef that has been boiled the day before. It must be thoroughly boiled, and very tender. Mince it as finely as possible, with a chopping knife; and add to it two pounds of beef-suet, cleared from the skin and the filaments, and chopped very small. Mix the suet and the lean beef well together, and add a pound of brown sugar.— Pick, wash, and dry before the fire, two pounds of currants. Stone and chop two pounds of the best raisins. Sultana raisins have no seeds, and are therefore the most convenient. Grate the yellow rind of two large lemons or oranges into a saucer, and squeeze over it their juice. Mix this with the currants and raisins. Prepare a table-spoonful (heaped up) of powdered cinnamon; the same quantity of powdered cloves; the same of powdered ginger; a heaped tea spoonful of powdered nutmeg; and the same of powdered mace.—Mix the spices into a pint or more of the best *West India* molasses. Then mix well together the meat and fruit; and wet the whole with the spiced molasses, of which there must be enough to make the mixture very moist, but not too thin. If you want the mince-meat for immediate use, add to it four pounds of chopped apples. The apples for this purpose should be pippins or bell-flowers. Add, also, half a pound of citron, not minced but cut into slips. Having mixed the whole completely, bake it in a rich paste.

If you intend the mince-meat for keeping, do not add the apple and citron, till you are about to make the pies. Mix all the other articles thoroughly, and pack down the mince-meat hard into stone-jars. Lay upon the top of it a round of thin white paper, dipped in molasses, and cut to fit the inside of the jar.— Secure the top closely, first with a flat tight-fitting cork, and then with a lid.

West India molasses will be found an excellent substitute for the wine and brandy usually added to moisten mince-meat.

DAMSON JAMS.

Fill a stone jar with fine ripe damsons. Cover it, and set it in an open kettle of boiling water. Keep it over the fire, till the stones are all loose, and seperated from the pulp. Then transfer it to a broad pan, and when cool, carefully pick out the stones. Mash the pulp with a broad flat wooden ladle, or a potato-masher; and, when smooth, and of an even consistence throughout measure it, and to every quart of pulp allow a pound and a half of the best brown sugar. Stir the sugar and pulp well together. Then put the jam into a porcelain preserving-kettle, and boil it slowly an hour or more: skimming it well. When done, put it into broad flat stone jars, pressing it down, and smoothing the surface. Keep it open two days in a cool dry closet. Then lay over the top a piece of white paper cut to fit the jar, and dipped in brandy; and then cover it closely. If properly made, it will after awhile, be so firm that it can be cut down in slices, like cheese.

Plumb jam may be made as above; but damsons are better for this purpose, and also for jelly, as the juice is thicker and richer.

It is an old-fashioned error to use unripe fruit for any sort of sweet meat. When the fruit is thoroughly ripe, the sweetmeat is very superior in flavour, and also keeps better.

LOBSTER PATTIES.

Make some puff-paste, and spread it thinly on very deep patty-pans. Bake it empty, as shells. Having boiled two or three fine lobsters, extract the meat, and mince it very small, mixing it with the coral, smoothly mashed, and some yolk of hard-boiled eggs, grated. Season it with a little salt; some cayenne; and some powdered mace or nutmeg; adding, if you choose, a little grated lemon-peel. Moisten it well with cream or fresh butter. Put it into a stew-pan, add a very little water, and let it stew till it just comes to a boil. Then take it off and fill the patties with it.

STRAWBERRY CAKES.

Sift a quart of flour into a pan, and cut up in it half a pound of the best fresh butter—or a pint if the butter is soft enough to measure in that manner. Rub the butter into the flour with your hands, 'till the whole is crumbled fine. Beat two eggs 'till very light; and then mix with them two table-spoonfuls of powdered white sugar. Wet the flour and butter with the egg and sugar, so as to form a dough. If you find it too stiff, add *a very little* water—knead the dough till it quits your hands and leaves them clean. Spread some flour on your pasteboard (a marble slab is best for this purpose) and roll out the dough into a moderately thick sheet. Cut it into round cakes with the edge of a tumbler, or something similar, dipping the cutter frequently into flour to prevent its sticking. Butter some large square tin pans, or baking sheets. Lay the cakes in, not too close to each other. Set them in a brisk oven, and bake them a light brown. Have ready a sufficient quantity of fine ripe strawberries sweetened with loaf-sugar. When the cakes are cool, split them, place them on flat dishes and cover the bottom-piece of each cake with strawberries, slightly mashed or bruised—then lay on the top-piece, pressing it down on the strawberries.

Cover the whole top and sides with an icing made in the usual way, of beaten white of egg and powdered loaf-sugar. Before the icing is quite dry, ornament the top with whole strawberries, a large one in the centre, and a circle of smaller ones surrounding it.

These are delicious and beautiful cakes, if properly made. The strawberries are not to be baked, as the flavour of this fruit, like that of pine-apples, is much impaired by the action of fire—and its always best when not cooked.

Instead of strawberries, you may use raspberries. There is no raspberry so fine as the large white or yellow.

STEWED SALMON.

Having cleaned and washed the fish, cut it into slices or fillets about two inches thick. Lay them in a large dish; sprinkle a little salt very evenly over the slices; and in half an hour turn them on the other side.—Let them rest another half hour; then wash, drain, and wipe them dry with a clean towel. Spread some of the best fresh butter thickly over the strainer of a large fish-kettle; and lay the pieces of salmon upon it. Cover them almost all over with very thin slices of fresh lemon, from which all the seeds have been removed. Intersperse, among the lemon, a few slices of shalots or very small mild onions; a few sprigs of parsley; and some whole pepper corns. Set the kettle on a bed of live coals; and spread very hot ashes thickly over the lid, which must be previously well heated on the inside, by standing it up before the fire. The heat must be regularly kept up while the fish is stewing. It will not be done in less than three-quarters of an hour. When dishing it, remove the sliced lemon, shalots, parsley, &c., leaving them in the bottom of he kettle.—Cover the fish, and set the dish over a vessel of hot water while you are preparing the sauce. For this sauce, mix thoroughly a quarter of a pound of fresh butter with a table spoonful of flour.—Put it into a quart tin vessel with a lid, and add a table spoonful of water, and the seasoning that was left in the bottom o. the fish-kettle. Cover it, and set in a larger sauce pan or pot of boiling water. Shake it about till it comes to a boil. If you set it on coals the butter will oil.—Then remove the lemon and onion-slices; pour the sauce into a sauce-tureen; and send it to table with the stewed fish.—Garnish the dish with sprigs of curled parsley. This is a French mode of cooking salmon.

A PAIL full of ley, with a piece of copperas half as big as a hen's egg boiled in it, will produce a fine nankeen color, which will not wash out.

A PRESIDENT'S PUDDING.

Tie up closely in a bit of very thin muslin a vanilla bean cut into pieces, and a broken-up stick of cinnamon; and put the bag with its contents, into a quart of rich cream (not milk.) Boil the cream till highly flavoured; then take it off the fire; remove the bag; and pour the hot cream over half a pound of almond sponge-cake, sliced thin and laid in a deep dish. Cover the dish, and leave the cake to dissolve in the cream; afterwards set it in a cold place. Have ready two ounces or more of bitter almonds that have been blanched and pounded to a smooth paste (one at a time,) in a marble mortar; adding frequently, (as you pound them) a few drops of rose-water to keep them from oiling. Beat eight eggs till very light and thick; and stir them gradually into the mixture, in turn with the almond, and half a pound of pounded loaf sugar, a little at a time of each. Butter a deep dish, and put in the mixture.—Have ready a star cut out of a large piece of citron, a number of smaller stars, all of equal size, and a sufficiency of rays or long slips, also cut out of citron— Lay the large star on the top of the pudding, just in the centre, place the strips or rays so as to diverge from it towards the edge; within which, arrange the small stars at equal distances, in a circle. Set the pudding into a quick oven, and bake it well. Send it to table cold, with sugar grated over the top.

This quantity of ingredients will make two small puddings, soup-plate size. You may ornament the broad edge of the plates or deep dishes, with a rim of puff-paste, handsomely notched; but put no paste in the bottom or sides.

PERFUME FOR GLOVES.

Take of damask or rose scent, hal' an ounce, the spirit of cloves and mace, each a drachm; frankincense a quarter of an ounce. Mix them together, and lay them in papers, and when hard, press the gloves; they will take the scent in twenty-four hours, and hardly ever loose it.

PEACH CAKES.

Pick and wash a quart or more of dried peaches—stew them with as little water as possible, (barely sufficient to keep them from burning,) and stir them up occasionally from the bottom.—When they are entirely dissolved, mix in a quarter of a pound or more of brown sugar; and set the peaches out to cool. Soften a quarter of a pound of the best fresh butter in half a pint of warm milk, heated on the stove, but not allowed to simmer. Sift one pound of flour into a pan; pour in the warm milk and butter, (first stirring them well together,) add a salt-spoon of salt, and a wine-glass of strong fresh yeast.—Mix the whole into a dough.—Cover it, and set it by the fire to rise. When quite light, and cracked all over the top,—flour your paste-board, divide the dough, and make it up into small round cakes. Roll out each cake into a thin sheet—spread the half of each sheet thickly over with the stewed peach, (which must first be mashed very smooth;) then fold over the other half; bring the edges closely together and crimp them.—Lay the cakes in buttered square pans, and bake them brown. When done, grate sugar over the top. These cakes are very nice for children, being very light (if properly made and baked) and by no means rich. They are good substitutes for tarts.—Instead of peach, they may be made with stewed apple, flavoured with lemon and sweetened, or with raspberries, or any other convenient fruit, bottled or stewed to a jam.

TONGUE TOAST.

Take a cold smoked tongue that has been well boiled, and grate it with a coarse grater, or mince it fine. Mix it with cream and beaten yolk of egg, and give it a simmer over the fire. Having cut off all the crust, toast very nicely some slices of bread, and then butter them. Lay them on a dish, and cover each thickly with the tongue-mixture spread on hot. Lay them in a flat dish, that has been heated before the fire, and send them to table covered.

CROSS BUNS.

Pick clean a pound or half of dried currants; wash, drain, and dry them.— Then spread them on a large flat dish, and place it near the fire, or in the sun. When they are perfectly dry, dredge them thickly all over with flour, to prevent their sinking or clodding when baked. Sift into a deep pan two pounds of fine flour, and mix thoroughly with it a tablespoonful of powdered cinnamon, or of mixed nutmeg and cinnamon, and half a pound of powdered white sugar. Cut up half a pound of the best fresh butter in half a pint of milk. Warm it till the butter is quite soft, but not till it oils. While warm, stir into the milk and butter four tablespoonfuls of strong fresh yeast. Make a hole in the centre of the pan of flour; pour in the mixed liquid; then with a broad knife or a large spoon, mix the flour gradually in; beginning round the edge of the hole, and proceed till you have the entire mass of ingredients well incorporated. Cover the pan with a clean flannel or a thick towel, and set it in a warm place near the fire to rise. When it has risen well, and the surface of the dough is cracked all over, flour your pasteboard, divide the dough into equal portions and, mixing in the currants, knead it into round cakes about the size of a small saucer. Set them again to rise, covering them and placing them near the fire. When perfectly risen, brush them over lightly, with a glazing of warm milk, or of beaten white of eggs, sweetened with a little sugar, —and with the back of a knife mark every bun with a deep cross. Lay them in buttered square pans; set them in a rather brisk oven, and bake them well.—They should be a deep brown color. These buns (like all others) are best the day they are baked—In England, and in other parts of Europe, it is customary to have hot cross buns at breakfast on the morning of Good Friday. They are very good cakes at any season.

H 2 —

STEWED WILD DUCKS.

Having par-boiled the ducks for a quarter of an hour, with a large carrot in each to take off the sedgy or fishy taste, remove the carrots, cut up the ducks, and put them into a stew pan with just sufficient water to cover them. Cover the pan closely, and let them stew for a quarter of an hour or more. Have ready a mixture in the proportion of a glass of port-wine, a glass of mushroom catchup, the juice of two large lemons or oranges, a salt-spoonful of Cayenne, and a table-spoonful of powdered loaf sugar, all well stirred together. Pour this over the ducks, and let them stew in it about five minutes longer.—Then serve them up in a deep dish, with this gravy about them. Eat the stewed duck on plates with heaters under them. This mode of cooking them is excellent.

Cold roast duck that has been under done, is very fine stewed as above. Venison, also, and wild geese.

STEWED LAMB.

Take a quarter of lamb and cut it into steaks, removing the skin and part of the fat. Put the steaks into a large stew-pot, having seasoned them with a little salt and cayenne, and a grated nutmeg, or a tea spoonful of powdered mace. Place under the steaks a lettuce split in long quarters, and then pour on just sufficient boiling water to cover the whole. After it has stewed awhile, add a quart or more of green peas, a few sprigs of mint, and a bit of fresh butter, and let it cook about half an hour longer. Keep the stew closely covered, except when you remove the lid to take off the scum. In sending it to table, place the meat upon the lettuce, and the peas round it.

Cold ham sliced, and stewed in this manner with lettuce and peas will be found excellent.

MIXING SOILS.

"Some nine or ten years ago, in the early part of my farming, I had occasion to deepen a well about six or eight feet. The earth thrown out was a tenacious blue clay, just damp enough to cut into lumps, and adhesive enough to remain so. After finishing the well, the man who had charge of the farm was at a loss to know where to deposit it. Having a bare sandy knoll in one of the fields, which was not inaptly termed "personal property," from its being wafted about by every breeze, here to-day, and there to-morrow, it occurred to me that the clay would hold the sand and form a soil. I accordingly ordered it deposited there in heaps, the same as if manure. This was in the summer. In the fall the lumps were scattered over the surface and left to the action of the rain and frost In the spring it was found to have broken down, crumbled and slacked like lime. These heaps were reduced and the clay evenly spread over the surface. The field received a coat of manure, was ploughed, and sown with oats and peas. That where the clay was applied, produced the largest and most vigorous growth, of any other part of the field. In the fall it was sown with rye, and seeded down with timothy and clover. The rye as well as the clover was much more vigorous and heavier, on that than any part of the field. In fact, the person who occupied the farm after I left it, informed me that he lost his crop of grass on that part in consequence of its lodging. Thus the personal was made real or fast property, and remains so to the present day.

"Having experienced such beneficial effects from mixing clay with sand, I was afterwards induced to try what effect sand would have on a rather retentive soil. The garden at Three Hills Farm, is a stiff clay loam resting on a strong tenacious clay subsoil, rather inclining to moisture. The second year after I purchased and took possession of it, I caused a coat of sand, from six to eight inches depth, to be put on one of the squares, which was spaded in with the manure, and I had the satisfaction to witness the most gratifying and happy results—the crop on that square was far superior to any other in the garden. Since then I have caused over five hundred one-horse cart loads of sand to be put in the garden, and the effect is still visible although the sand has disappeared."

HOT BEDS.

Those who intend raising early vegetables, either for domestic use or for market, had better make some preparations for the business in February. Cabbages, tomatoes, cucumbers, egg-plants, &c., may be had three or four weeks earlier, if started in a hot bed in early spring, and put out after the weather has become steadily warm. In making a hot-bed, mark out the ground the size of the frame to be used, and make an excavation to the depth of a foot, or if the ground is quite dry, eighteen inches; put in good horse manure to the thickness of two feet, and put on the frame and glasses. When the heat is sufficiently raised, put on six or eight inches of good mould; that made from clean grass sods which have been piled and become entirely rotted the year before, is best; and when this is warmed to the proper degree, which can easily be told by applying the hand to it, plant the seeds. Care should be taken that there is not too much heat, especially when the sun shines. If there is too much, raise the glasses; and always let in as much air as practicable with keeping up the requisite degree of heat. Hot-bed plants require a great deal of water, which should be supplied from a watering-pot. If the weather should be so cold as to render it necessary, the bed should be protected by matt and straw.

Permanent hot-bed frames may be made of bricks. A false bottom is laid two or three feet from the

...ground, made of cast-iron, or iron bars, laid so closely together as to answer the purpose, on which is placed the earth for the plants. A door is left at one end of the brick-work, under the floor, to throw in manure, and another door at the opposite end, for taking the manure out. Thus a constant and regular supply of heart may be conveniently kept up, by only putting in fresh manure as the decomposition proceeds.

KEEP YOUR BEST STOCK.

Many farmers are in the habit of selling their best animals, as they bring the highest price. A greater mistake cannot be made. A difference of ten or even twenty per cent. in the price of a single animal, is a small affair compared with this difference in a whole herd.—By keeping the very best to propagate from, the whole may be made of equal excellence, and in the course of a few years, numerous animals might be produced, having the excellent properties that now distinguish some few of the best.

What should we say of a farmer who has several highly valuable varieties of potatoes, and other kinds that are inferior, and for the sake of ten cents extra for a bushel, sells for consumption all his best varieties, and plant those that are inferior, when in consequence of the imprudent measure, his next crop will fall short twenty-five per cent.! Every one will condemn this course, and few, if any, are so wanting in discretion as to pursue it; yet many take a similar course in selling their best animals, and propagating from the poor.

For the purposes of work, beef, and the dairy, there are probably no cattle superior to our own native breed, where attention has been given to improve them, though some improvement for certain purposes may be made by a cross with foreign breeds that excel in the qualities desired. There is a vast difference in our cattle in sections where much attention has been given to improvement by selecting the best, when contrasted with those where little or no attention has been paid to the subject, and as a matter of course, the best have been sold, or eaten up. Every man that raises stock has it in his power to make improvement, and he should avail himself of all the advantages around him to turn his power to the benefit of himself and posterity.

CARE OF ANIMALS IN WINTER.

In the colder climate of the various sections of our country, buildings, of some kind, are required for sheltering all domestic animals, and in general we think all should be fed under cover, or in yards attached to barns and sheds. There is much less waste in this way, and the animals are much more quiet and comfortable than when the food is thrown out in the dirt, and they are forced to eat under the exposure of wind and storm. In dry, cold weather, when the air is still, sheep may be sometimes foddered on clean, hard snow to good advantage—they will eat fodder here which they would refuse any where else. But it is only in dry weather that they can be fed in this way—as soon as the snow softens, or the weather becomes moist, they will not eat their fodder clean, out of doors, and they must be fed from racks or mangers in the house. Sheep do not like *wet*—they always prefer to keep both their food and their bodies *dry*.

Large flocks of sheep should be divided, putting the bucks and wethers together, the ewes in another lot, and the lambs and weak sheep in another. Subdivisions of these may be necessary, for too many must not be kept together. Some very good sheep-farmers think not more than a hundred should be allowed to run together—others allow more—but much depends on the room given them, the facilities for feeding, sheltering, &c. A *hospital* should be provided —self-interest, as well as humanity, demand it—and attention to the sick and feeble will be well repaid. A little nursing at the proper time often has such a magical effect on the invalid, that he comes out in the spring as brisk and hale as the best of the flock—a much more gratifying sight, truly, than to see his carcass hanging on a tree for the crows to pick.

If it is designed to raise early lambs for market, the ewes should be at once provided with warm, dry shelter, and fed with a little grain, and some roots, such as potatoes, turnips or beets. This will ensure a strong, healthy lamb, with plenty of milk to feed it.

Cold weather gives cattle and other stock sharp appetites, and this is the best time in the winter to feed out poor fodder. Give it to the stock in small quantities at a time, replenishing the mangers as often as they are cleaned, till they have get their fill. It is not good policy to make *milch cows* eat too much poor fodder—it had better be fed mostly to the young cattle—such as steers and two-year-old heifers.

Considerable advantage is sometimes derived from cutting fodder with a machine—Clover hay and straw, cut fine and mixed together, may be fed in this way without waste. Corn-fodder, if the stalks are small and well cured, will all be eaten if it is cut pretty fine. But it is not so with *large* stalks, which are very coarse and fibrous, and the sap of which becomes *sour* before they can be cured—cattle will not eat such, much sooner than they would eat their hoofs. It is of but little use to cut stuff for cattle to eat which is absolutely *uneatable*. It is true that animals will sometimes reject long fodder which is really nutritious, and which would be eaten if passed through a cutter; but the idea should never be taken from this, that cutting substances which are little else than woody fibre, will convert them into proper food for animals.

In the Western section of the country, where large herds are kept, sheltering and feeding under cover are attended with more in-convenience; but we are satisfied that the extension of the practice even there, would be followed by advantages more than counterbalancing the trouble. There is a great difference in the management of farmers in that region—the contrast between good and bad farming being as strikingly shown there as anywhere else—but it is often the case that the stock is permitted to range at will over the whole farm. The loss which is sustained from the waste of food, the injury done to the land by the treading of the cattle when it is wet and soft, and, as a matter of course, the great waste of flesh in the animals, are incalculable. The practice of feeding cattle almost entirely on corn fodder, which in that country is very long and coarse, is quite an obstacle to barn or yard feeding; but where this cannot be adopted, the stock should be fed on dry lands, with, if possible, a strong blue-grass sod, and by all means sheltered from the bleak and cutting winds, by forest or belt of trees.

CARROTS SUPERIOR TO OATS FOR HORSES.

This is a capital vegetable, full of nutritious substance, good for man and horse. A livery stable keeper says that he considers a peck of carrots and a peck of oats worth more for a horse than half a bushel of oats alone, and for horses that are not constantly employed, the carrots alone are far preferable to oats. He would purchase carrots for his horses in preference to oats, even if they cost the same by the bushel; the price of carrots, however, is generally about half that of oats. His horses eat the carrots with a far better relish than oats—so much so that if a peck of each are poured into the manger, they will eat all the carrots before they taste the oats. When fed constantly on carrots, a horse will drink scarcely a pail full of water in a week.

SIX REASONS FOR PLANTING AN ORCHARD.

[BY EDSON HARKNESS.]

1st. Would you leave an inheritance to your children,—plant an orchard. No other investment of money and labour will, in the long run pay so well.

2nd. Would you make home pleasant, the abode of the social virtues—plant an orchard. Nothing better promotes among neighbours a feeling of kindness and good will, than a treat of good fruit often repeated.

3rd. Would you remove from your children the strongest temptation to steal,—plant an orchard. If children cannot obtain fruit at home they are very apt to steal it; and when they have learned to steal fruit they are in a fair way to steal horses.

4th. Would you cultivate a constant feeling of thankfulness towards the Giver of all good,—plant an orchard. By having constantly before you one of the greatest blessings given to men, you must be hardened indeed if you are not influenced by a spirit of humility and thankfulness.

5th. Would you have your children love their home, respect their parents while living and venerate their memory when dead, in all wanderings look back upon the home of their youth as a sacred spot, an oasis in the great wilderness of the world, then—plant an orchard.

6th. In short, if you wish to avail yourself of the blessings of a bountiful Providence, which are within your reach, you must plant an orchard. And when you do it, see that you plant good fruit. Don't plant crab apple trees, nor wild plums, nor Indian peaches; the best are the cheapest.

Seriously, we have often wondered why our farmers did not devote more attention to the cultivation of fruit. It certainly would prove profitable and pleasant An orchard of an acre or so of choice fruit, properly taken care of, could not be the least profitable portion of a farm.

Upwards of a hundred bushels of fruit can be gathered annually, and without much trouble, from merely a small garden patch.

One great point to commence with, is to procure good sorts, for it requires no more labor to attend a tree that will bear apples worth seventy-five cents and a dollar a bushel, than one producing those not worth more than two shillings. Let our farmers think of these things.

DIG DEEP AND YOU'LL FIND TREASURE.

We commend the following anecdote to the particular consideration of those who are yet addicted to the practice of shallow ploughing, and who think that no good comes from deep stirring of the soil.— By adopting the practice of deep ploughing, a new source of wealth would be opened on many farms, which the "*skinning*" culture of a century or two has never developed. But to the anecdote—which, though old, is just as good as if it were "bran new:"

"An old farmer, on his death bed, told his sons who were not very industrious lads, that he had deeply buried his money in a particular field, which was the most barren land on his farm. In consequence of this information, soon after the old man's death, the sons began to dig (and they dug deeply too) all over the field—and this they did again and again, for it was long before they quite despaired of finding the money. At length, however, they gave up the search, and the land was planted with corn ; when, from the deep digging, pulverization and clearing which it had received in the search for the money, it produced a crop which was indeed a treasure."

It might result to the profit of some of our farmers' sons, should they imagine their fathers had deeply buried a bag of dollars in some barren field, and be led to dig in search of the treasure—and though they might not find the expected wealth, their exertions would be amply rewarded, as is illustrated in the anecdote.

In further evidence of the great utility of deep ploughing, we copy the following paragraph from the Report of the Hon. H. L. Ellsworth.

"Few individuals are aware of the extension of roots in pulverized soil. Von Thayer mentions finding roots of sanfoin from 10 to 15 feet deep in the ground. There are now in the National Gallery, corn roots taken from one side of a hill of corn laid bare by the freshet, and presented by the Hon. J. S. Skinner to the National Gallery. The corn was planted on the 20th of May, and roots gathered the 14th of July, 1842. In sixty days some of the large roots extended more than four feet, covered with lateral branches. I have caused the roots to be measured: the aggregate length of roots in the hill, is, by Mr. Skinner's estimate, over 8000 feet. The specimen alluded to, is open for examination. The fact is here mentioned to show the importance of deep ploughing, to enable the plant to find nourishment, so much below the surface as may avoid the effect of drought, give support to the stalk, and not expose the roots to be cut off by needed cultivation. Soil is made by exposure of earth to the atmosphere; and whoever wishes to make permanent improvements will not fail to *plough deep*."

HEMP.

According to a statement in the Western (Missouri) Journal, about 10,000 bales of hemp, the crop of this season, will be shipped from that place next spring. The same paper states that the aggregate amount, if the season had been favorable, would have reached 30,000 bales. It is thought 40,000 bales will be raised in that neighborhood this year.

COVERING VEGETABLES WITH LEAVES.

We would recommend every person, especially farmers, to cover their vegetables in the cellar with a good thick coat of leaves; besides protecting them from frost, they will keep the vegetables from the air and make them much better; and as the leaves are dry they will not rot them, nor produce any odor in the house, as sea weed does, and it will save the trouble of banking up around the cellar. Last winter, as usual, we used them in our cellar, and not a potatoe, turnip, beet, carrot, nor parsnip was frozen, nor did they rot, although water froze three inches in the cellar, and every thing uncovered was frozen as hard as ice.

EGGS AND POULTRY.

Mr. Ellsworth, Commissioner of Patents, in his annual report, embracing a vast amount of agricultural information, says it is supposed that there may be annually consumed in the United States 1,400,000,000 of eggs, and averaging the value at 6 cents per dozen, this would amount to $8,000,000. If we allow an average of five chickens, or other kinds of fowls, a year to each person, at a cost of 12½ cts. average, including turkeys, geese, ducks, &c., that will amount to more than 97,500,000—equal in value to $12,000,000 annually; making the aggregate value of the consumption of poultry, to say nothing of the amount which might be added for feathers. It is said to have been ascertained that half a million of eggs are consumed every month in the city of New York. One woman in the Fulton market, sold 175,000 eggs in ten weeks, supplying the Astor House each day with 1000 for five days and on Saturday with 2,500.

MANAGEMENT OF HENS.

A number of subscribers complain that their hens produce no eggs in cold weather, when they would be most acceptable, owing to their scarcity and high price, and they request an article on their winter management.

Owing to cold weather, which is unfavourable to most birds, and the ground being generally covered with snow, which deprives hens of a choice of food, they will not lay so well in winter as they will in summer. Yet in many cases they do very well at this season, and much may be done by good management to make them profitable.

By good shelter and proper food much may be done to remedy the inclemency and the inconveniences of the season, and render the keeping of poultry less expensive, if not profitable in winter.

When hens run at large in summer, they, in a measure, choose their own food and condiments ; but when confined to narrow limits in summer, or deprived of access to the ground in winter, and of insects as a part of their food, great care is necessary in order to supply them with proper food for the support of themselves and the production of eggs.

Hens should have a warm and dry shelter, a good supply of pure water, and a variety of food, which may be mostly of that kind that is cheapest. They should have two or more kinds of grain by them. Corn is very good, so are barley, oats, wheat and buckwheat.—Some prefer barley to oats; others say that as oats contain the most lime they are better. Wheat is an excellent food, as it contains lime, but it is generally too dear for this purpose.—Wheat bran or shorts, as it is commonly called in the market, is a good food in a moderate quantity, as it contains phosphate of lime, but much of it would have an unfavourable effect.

Besides grain constantly by them, hens should have occasionally a warm, mixed dish, in the cold season. It may be well to give this every morning, if it is convenient, covering up the grain at night, else they will eat freely of that before their warm breakfast is prepared.— Potatoes, with refuse apples, pieces of pumpkins, squashes, crusts of bread, &c , boiled with meal or bran mixed in while hot, make very good and acceptable food. As hens need some animal food when they do not roam about in warm weather to collect it, refuse fish, meat, or scraps, may be added to their *chowder*, or *conjunction*, as an old lady once called a dish which she had prepared with numerous ingredients. When hens have their own way and can get it, they eat freely of animal food.

Besides common food and water, hens need condiments, such as gravel, lime, charcoal, &c. Lime may be given in old plaster, pounded chalk, oyster shells, and bones. Bones should not be burned; as this operation will drive off the oleaginous matter, which is good animal food. Charcoal is good; and some give pounded bricks and crockery. Hens eat grass and other plants in summer, and they need green food in winter. Cabbages are the best. They should also have occasionally raw apples, potatoes and turnips i large pieces, which they will pick and eat.

Sometimes, after all the attention that can be given, hens will grow fat and lazy, and make no discounts to repay the kindness they receive. Perhaps they suffer from inaction. Then bury grain up in sand and gravel, or in the pulverized shells, mortar, &c., and let them work for a living, and dig it out as they want. This often has an excellent effect in winter, as it affords them a good exercise. Keep the hen-house clean and well ventilated in moderate weather. Let them have clean straw in their nests. Give them a chance to enjoy the sun-shine, and supply them with ashes or dry sand to roll in.

HOW TO GET NEW VARIE-TIES OF POTATOES.

When the vines are done growing and are turned brown, the seed is ripe: then take the balls and string with a large needle and strong thread; hang them in a dry place, where they will gradually dry and mature, without danger or injury from frost. In the month of April, soak the balls for several hours from the pulp; when washed and dried, they are fit for sowing in rows, in a bed well prepared in the garden; they will sprout in a fortnight; they must be attended to like other vegetables. When about two inches high, they may be thinned and transplanted into rows. As they increase in size, they should be hilled. In the autumn many of them will be of the size of a walnut, and from that to a pea. In the following spring, they should be planted in hills, placing the large ones together,—they will in the second season attain their full size, and will exhibit several varieties of form, and may then be selected to suit the judgment of the cultivator. I would prefer gathering the balls from potatoes of a good kind. The first crops from seeds thus obtained, will be productive, and will continue so for many years, gradually deteriorating, until they will need a renewal by the process.

PEACH TREES.

As good peaches have now become a profitable commodity, we here offer some seasonable hints relative to their culture.

Early in the spring remove the earth from the tree at its roots, make a close examination for worms with the aid of a knife, carefully cutting in where any gum is found and as far as there seems to be a hollow under the bark. When the worms, if any, are extracted, wash the whole stem of the tree with strong soap suds; when dry, apply a coating of whitewash, (in which salt has been dissolved,) around the stem near the roots. Then make a pyramid around the tree of powdered charcoal or fine coal cinder, or, in default of these, sand or dirt. Two or three times during the year, remove the pyramid, examine for worms, rub the stem near the roots with a piece of coarse cloth to destroy any moth eggs that may have been deposited, and finally restore the pyramid. An occasional application of salt and saltpetre or wood ashes may be made, and some rely altogether on these applications, with the addition of searching for worms in spring and autumn, and on these occasions carefully rubbing or scraping the tree. If trees are attended to for two or three years, they are not likely to be attacked by the worm. The tree becomes sound and healthy and the worm does not seem to be able to penetrate the bark."

TOBACCO AROUND PEACH TREES.

In the early part of spring, or early part of summer, scrape the earth from round the body of the tree to the depth of one or three inches, being particularly careful not to injure the crown of the roots; fill the cup thus formed with trash tobacco from the shops, and envelope the ball of the tree to the height of three or four inches with the stems or leaves. I do not offer this as a means to renovate a diseased tree, but as a preventive, the efficacy of which has been tested for nineteen years, by Samuel Wood, one of the most approved nurserymen and extensive fruit growers in this section of country; and also by other practical farmers, with unfailing success.

COLIC IN HORSES.

Horses attacked with this fearful disease are speedily and effectually relieved by the following simple remedy. Dissolve, in a quart of pure water, as much salt as will thoroughly saturate the liquid, and drench the animal thoroughly until you discover symptoms of relief. The same is good for the botts.

TO PREVENT HORSES JUMP-ING FENCES.

Some years ago I bought a good horse, which, among other fine qualities, was recommended as a great jumper, vaulting with ease "over a fence six feet high." I intended to take care of that part of the business myself, but for a time I found I was overmatched. I tied his head to his fore-feet, but that made no difference—over he went. I put a wooden clog on his fore-feet, as large as a man's leg, but he carried that over the high fence with him. I "hoppled" him, fastening his fore and hind feet within two feet of each other; but was very much surprised to find him, all chained as before, on the other side of the fence; and it was not till several repetitions of the experiment, that I saw how he did it—which was by drawing his two chained feet closely to his body, and throwing himself over with the other two. And when he chanced to be free from all restraint, it was very often hard to tell where he might be found, as he would soon pass half a dozen high fences to reach some favourite field. To try to catch him was very much like a boy's trying to catch the hawk,—he said he "did not expect to get him, but thought he might at least worry him."

But I have found a simple and efficient remedy. Pass a small and strong cord round his body just behind the shoulders, and tie the halter to this cord between the fore-legs, so as to leave a distance of about two feet from the cord to his head. If then he undertakes to jump, he is compelled to throw his head forward, which draws hard on the small cord, causing it to cut into his back, and he instantly desists. The cord should not be more than a quarter of an inch in diameter.

COAL TAR AS A PAINT.

This article, which is abundant and cheap, has long been used successfully as an economical paint.

A correspondent of the American Agriculturist says:—

"I think it would be well to call the attention of farmers to the use of coal tar as a paint. The tar produced in coal-gas works is used extensively in England for painting fences, out buildings, &c., and is being introduced in this country also. It never alters by exposure to the weather, and one or two good coats will last many years. It is the cheapest and best black paint that can be used. Our buildings are painted with it; all our apparatus also; and even the wrought-iron pipe we place in the ground is coated with it. I think if its advantages were fully known, it would be generally used throughout the United States. The government soak the bricks used in building the fort at Throg's Neck in this tar, which renders them impervious to water; and posts painted with it are protected from rot, when in the ground, as effectually as if they had been charred."

VALUE OF HENS IN A GARDEN.

At a late meeting of the New York Farmer's Club, Mr. Smyth, the projector of the Atlantic Steam Navigation Company, said that he had in England, trained two hens to destroy the insects in his garden, with great success. He would let the hens into the garden early in the morning, and as they had finished their work, call them off to feed them, and then keep them away until the next morning, when they would be hungry. He was now engaged in training a regiment of hens to destroy the insects in a corn field belonging to his nephew.

FEEDING HOGS.

In an experiment in Maryland in feeding hogs with shelled corn, and half the quantity in meal made into mush, those pigs fed on the mush, weighed five pounds heavier in a given time than those fed on raw corn, and their coats much better.

CORN SUGAR.

A correspondent of the Tocsin of Liberty, gives the following account of the mode of cultivating the common Indian corn for the purpose of making sugar from it, and the simple apparatus and process by which the sugar may be made, all as he saw it, in the pleasant little settlement called Quaker street, in the south-west part of Duanesburg, Schenectady county. The whole operation of tillage and manufacture is so simple and practical, and the results so desirable, that we trust our farmers will give a portion of their care and labor in this direction:—

I sat down to write of Corn Sugar, according to my promise, to several friends, who propose to try an experiment with it next spring, to the extent of an acre or two, at least. I have recently noticed several successful experiments to make sugar and molasses, in various parts of the country. They can be attended by no loss, for the stalks will make good fodder, if nothing else. The corn should be planted as early as the season will allow. Planted in rows, 7 or 12 inches apart, it will do well. Keep it well hoed, and when the ears begin to silk, carefully clip off every ear. Let the stalks grow till they are fully matured. Just as they begin to turn yellow a little, cut them up close to the ground.—All the strength and sweetness of the grain passes into the stalk, and it will grow larger and higher than usual. It should be planted on good, rich land, to secure the best results. It must be cut before it is touched by frost, or the sugar will not granulate.

A common cider mill, with three smooth rollers, placed a little nearer together than is usual in grinding apples, will answer very well in grinding the stalks. The juice is boiled down in copper or brass kettles, skimming it, as it may be necessary, till it is about as thick as common molasses. The yield of molasses is about one pint to five pints of juice.—To have the sugar chrystalize, the juice when boiled down, should be placed in shallow pans over a gentle heat, or in the sun, by day, and in a well warmed room by night. If, through want of experience, the experimenter does not get his sugar, the value of the molasses is not changed. It is much like honey, and contains much more saccharine than the best of New Orleans or Trinidad molasses. The flavor is very fine.

A machine for grinding, made with iron rollers, though more costly, would work rather better than one of wood; but it is not essential. A wooden one might be shod with iron.

The scum, taken off while boiling, will make capital vinegar. The value of the stalks, after grinding, as feed for cattle, is considerable. It may be fed out at once, or dried for future use.

NEW THEORY OF MILDEW.

We find it stated in the Canadian Agricultural Journal, that Mr. Haywood, lecturer on Chemistry at the Sheffield (England) Medical School, recently gave a lecture before the Norton Farmers' Club, wherein, among other things, he advanced what to us is a new theory for the formation of honey-dew and mildew.

Our readers are aware that many theories have been advanced; some attribute it to one thing, and some to another. Mr. Haywood explains the phenomenon in this way. Mildew is caused by the rapid evaporation of water from the leaves of plants after a wet spring, when the salts the water contained were left on the surface of such plants as were already matured, while others, which were in a growing state, appropriated them to their uses.

Honey-dew was caused by an excess of carbon in the plant, which could only occur in dry weather, when the other ingredients could not be furnished for it to combine with

---

CULTURE OF MILLET.

June is a good time to sow millet. It will do well sown any time in the month. It makes, when well cured, excellent fodder. One of the general advantages of this crop, is, that if the hay-crop is likely to come in light, this may be grown as a substitute. Half a bushel of seed, broadcast to the acre, is a proper quantity, though only a peck is sometimes sown on rich ground. It may if desired, de sown in drills, and if designed for seed, this is the best way. A common turnip-drill, will sow the seed well. It will yield bountifully, and the seed, when ground into meal, is excellent for fattening animals. Rather light ground is best for it—it will indeed do well on land that is too light for grass. In 1841, Mr. G. Jones received a premium from the Tompkins County Agricultural Society, for having raised on two acres, five and a half tons of millet fodder, and sixty-three bushels of seed. It was new land—the wood and timber from which was taken off in the month of April, and twenty quarts of seed sown to the acre the 8th of June succeeding.

Millet flour makes a very agreeable and digestive cake, and is in our opinion, in every respect, superior to that of buckwheat, as it is free from that gallous, spongy character which renders the latter injurious to a great number of people, particularly those living in large cities

WHITE DAISY.

In the summer of 1837, we observed for the first time, in a field of ten acres, about five completely covered with the white daisy—so much so that no domestic animal which we raise would graze among them, or even look for grass where the dasies grew. They were mowed off that summer, but apparently to no purpose. The next spring as soon as the grass had started, we turned about one hundred and twenty wethers and yearling lambs into the field, and kept them as long as there was anything green to be seen, when they were driven out, until the daisies and grass had again started up, when they were put back and the daisies again eaten off. We continued to change them in and out of that field throughout the summer—our object being to keep the ground where the daisies grew, as bare as sheep could be made to gnaw it. The end of this is, that there has not been a daisy there since. We would recommend to those who are troubled with the daisy, to use their sheep, (if they have any) not only for the comfort of themselves and families, but for the labor saving animal also. They should be confined to the daisy on its first appearance in the spring, and so many of them as to eat all clean in two weeks or less, when they may be changed into another field, till such time as the daisy again springs up. We have never known or heard of daisies destroyed in this way before.

REARING PEACH TREES.

Mr. Allen W. Dodge, says, in the Massachusetts Ploughman, that he prefers the following mode of planting peach stones:

"I deposit the stones, after being taken from the peach, in sand or dirt; put them in the ground, slightly covered, in the fall. As for the cotton bag, to keep them under the ground, I have never tried it, or any covering but the ground itself. Take up the stones early in the spring, crack them, and plant immediately the meats or pits. In a week, or ten days, they will be up without fail, just as certain as so many peas, or kernels of corn."

PEACH TREES.

Plant tansy around the roots of peach trees. The peach worm will not trouble them afterwards.

KEEPING CATTLE WARM.

If we look abroad at the habits or necessities of people, we find that as we advance from south to north, the consumption of animal food increases. It has been long known both to chemists and observing men, that a cold atmosphere requires an extra quantity of food to sustain life and health. And this observation is just as applicable to the cattle and horses whose home is at our barns, as it is to our own species. If they are kept warm, housed from the storm and shielded from unnecessary exposure, they will need less food than if left unprotected. The winter profit to be realized from milch cows, is unquestionably much affected by their treatment in this respect. I copy the following remarks from the fourth part of Johnston's Agricultural Lectures, as particularly in point.

"The degree of warmth in which the animal is kept, or the temperature of the atmosphere in which it lives, affects the quantity of food which the animal requires to eat. The heat of the animal is inseparably connected with its respiration. The more frequently it breathes, the warmer it becomes, and the more carbon it throws off from its lungs. Place a man in a cold situation, and he will either starve, or he will adopt some means of warming himself. He will probably take exercise, and by this means cause himself to breathe quicker. But to do this for a length of time, he must be supplied with more food. For not only does he give off more carbon from his lungs, but the exercise he takes, causes a greater natural waste also of the substance of his body.

'So it is with all animals. The greater the difference between the temperature of the body and that of the atmosphere in which they live, the more food they require to keep them warm, and to supply the natural waste. A proper attention to the warmth of his cattle or sheep, therefore, is of great practical consequence to the feeder of stock. By keeping them warm, he diminishes the quantity of food which is necessary to sustain them, and leaves a larger proportion for the production of beef or mutton.

"Various experiments have been lately published which confirm the opinions above deduced from theoretical considerations. On these I shall only mention one, by Mr. Childers, in which twenty sheep were folded in the open field, and twenty of nearly equal weight, were placed under a shed in a yard. Both lots were fed for three months —January, February and March— upon turnips, as many as they chose to eat, half a pound of linseed cake and half a pint of barley each sheep, per day, with a little hay and salt. The sheep in the field consumed the same quantity of food, all the barley and oil cake, and about 19 pounds of turnips per day, from the first to the last, and increased on the whole, 36 stone 8 lbs. Those under the shed consumed at first as much food as the others, but after the third week, they eat 2 lbs. less, or only 15 lbs. a day. Of the oil-cake, they also eat about one-third less than the other lot, and yet they increased in weight, 56 stone 6 pounds, or 20 stones more than the others.

"Thus the cold and exercise in the field, caused the one lot to convert more of their food into dung, the other, more of it into mutton.

"The absence of light, has also a material influence upon the effects of food in increasing the weight of animals."

AN INSECT TRAP.

Scoop out the inside of a turnip; scollop the edge of the shell, and place it downward on the earth. The insects will pass into it as a place of retreat, through the holes; and the beds of squashes, melons, cucumbers, &c., may thus soon be cleared of them.

POTATOES.

It is stated that if potatoes are sprinkled with slaked lime as soon as they are cut for seed, and shovelled over it, then immediately planted, it will prevent them from rot either in the round or in the cellar.

POTATOES.

The malady which has prevailed for a year or two, among potatoes, may operate as a discouragement to planting them as extensively as formerly. We venture not to give an opinion, from the little that is yet known, in regard to the origin of this disease, or to recommend any specific remedy; but from what we have seen should not hesitate to adopt the following rules in planting, cultivation, &c.

1. To plant on loamy soils of medium dryness. 2. If stable manure is used, let it be well mixed with the soil, and not left (especially if unfermented) in too great a quantity in the hill. 3. Plant good sized sound potatoes, cutting only the largest ones. Very small potatoes, or small pieces, are not likely to sprout so vigorously as large ones. The first food of the young plant is the substance of the old potatoe, and the greater the supply of this food, the more rapid, of course, is the early growth of this shoot. It is true, that under entirely favoruble circumstances of soil, season, &c., the shoot from a small potatoe, or from small pieces, may succeed, and the product from them in such cases, may not be much less; but it is reasonable that the shoot from a good sized round potatoe would be stronger and less predisposed to suffer from any unfavourable influences belonging either to the soil or atmosphere. 4. Plant as early as the ground is in a proper state. Many cases might be cited where early planted potatoes escaped the blight or disease, and produced a crop, when the variety, planted later on a piece immediately adjoining, were much injured. 5. Plant only varities of known hardiness. Much depends on this. Some kinds have always been remarkable for their healthy, hard constitutions; at the same time producing more than others under the same circumstances. Of the feeble sorts, there is the Mercer, called also Chenango, Meshanic, (corrupted from Nesnannock) which

I 2

from its supposed or acknowledged good qualities for the table, has been widely cultivated for several years past; but which has always been subject to blight—more so than most other kinds. We are not aware of any good qualities possessed by this potatoe that are not to be had in several other kinds, which have the advantage of greater hardiness and productiveness as well as soundness. 6. In cultivation, keep the crop clean from the "first start," but void ploughing or working it when the ground is so wet as to be in the least muddy, and do not use the plough or cultivator after the blossoms appear; as a mutilation of the roots after this may damage the setting of the tubers.

WARMING LANDS.

Mr. Josiah Levett, of Beverly, who has been remarkably successful in raising various kinds of vegetables, as has appeared from his superior exhibition at the Horticultural Rooms, in a late number of the New England Farmer, gives his mode of warming land, by which he gets vegetables almost as early as they are produced in the vicinity of Boston, though the season in Beverly is at least a week later, and Mr. Levett's land is moist and low.

His method is, to plough or spade, or in working the land in any way, to do it *while the sun shines clear*, and, if possible, from eleven to four o'clock. By this means the warmed surface earth is turned under, the cold earth brought up and warmed, and buried in turn. This is repeated two or three times on warm sunny days. Seeds planted on land thus warmed, a week or ten days later than ploughed or spaded but once, will mature their fruit earlier, and of a superior size, with the same manuring and attention.

This system is founded on the true principles of philosophy, as will appear evident to every person of reflection, and we doubt not may be turned to a good practical account.

To have early Potatoes.—The destruction of the Potato crop in England had been so extensive as to make it proper to look ahead for the best means of hastening the crop forward in the Spring, it being important to shorten as much as possible the period of privation. With a view to bring forward the next spring's crop at the earliest possible moment, the following suggestions have been made in the London Gardener's Chronicle.

Though not pressed by the same urgent necessity in this country, these suggestions may yet furnish hints to those who feel an ambition, both innocent and commendable, to have the earliest Potatoes on their own table—an ambition that deserves to be fostered, so long as it does not proceed from avaricious motives, or degenerate into envy of those who are winners in the race.

The writer recommends that recourse be had to the earliest known *varieties*, and then to keep in mind the following important facts, and the same general rules may be observed to get early sweet Potatoes:

1st. The eyes at the top of the Potato are the youngest and vegetate first; from them the crop will be about a fortnight earlier than that obtained from the lower part of the tuber.

2d. When the Potato is not cut, and the top eyes are allowed to proceed in their growth, the others push slowly, if at all.

3d. If the top sprout be removed, the others eyes will begin growing with greater vigor.

4th. It is, therefore, obvious that the top sprouts may be removed when they begin to show roots, and planted out for the earliest crop; whilst the rest of the tuber may be allowed to push the other eyes for a succession.

5th. In case of a scarcity of sets, the stems may be layered; they will root, and form a second crop of tubers; but this must be done early in the season, or before the first set tubers is fully ripe, although large enough to be fit for use.

Men who are skillful propagators of plants (as many gardeners are, and all ought to be) will readily imagine what important advantages may be taken of these properties of the Potatoe. We have long since been told that a Mr. Denson, in 1835,

propagated from three tubers, plants enough to crop half a rod of ground, and obtained from them an amount of produce equal to 16 tons per acre, in the same season. What may not be expected now, with the invaluable aid of cheap glass!

In the mild climates of Cornwall, Devonshire, and many parts of Ireland, Potatoes may be immediately sprouted in a warm place, as in a cottage near the fire, or on hurdles in cow-houses, &c.; and when the sprouts are two inches long, they may be cut off, together with a portion of the tuber, and planted out in a sheltered spot, covering the sprouts with two inches of light soil. A slight covering will be sufficient to protect them from such frosts as occur in those parts in ordinary winters. They will produce a crop fit for use in the beginning of May.

In cold situations, and where proper protection cannot be afforded, it may be advisable to defer sprouting the sets till the end of January. They may then be pushed four inches by the middle of March, and planted out as soon as the weather will permit.

In planting for the earliest crop, advantage should be taken of the most sheltered situations, such as the south side of walls, hedges, or fences. Where no such shelter can be obtained, ridges three feet apart should be formed, running east and west, and a furrow should then be made along the base on the south side for the dung, over which the sets should be placed, so that their tops on pushing, may appear half way up the side of the ridge. In such a position the roots derive warmth from the rays of the sun striking perpendicularly against the slope; and the top of the ridge affords shelter from northerly winds. If in addition furze, broom, straw, bunches of beech, spruce, &c., are struck in the top of the ridge so as to project over the young plants, slight frost will not injure them. If the soil about the plants can be covered with litter in cold nights, radiation of heat will be prevented; the litter should be removed during the day, and the surface frequently stirred. By these means an early crop may be taken off the ground in May, after which there is still time for a second crop.

THE FARMER.

Bees.—Statistics of Swarming—In this account of swarming, the Bees, being in the common straw-hive, were left to follow their natural inclination. The statement extends over a period of 10 years. 40 old hives produced 64 swarms; three swarms flew away, two of which were lost through inattention; 16 swarms were in May, 38 in June, 9 in July, and 1 in August. Five old hives did not swarm, one swarm swarmed once, and two swarms sent forth each two colonies; three of the old hives swarmed thrice each. The worst honey seasons were 1839, 1841, and 1845, in which years the average of swarms per old hive was the greatest, being respectively 2½, 2 1-5, and 2. In the best honey seasons there was less swarming, the average being 2, 1, 1⅔, and 1½. The earliest swarm in the 10 years was on May 9th, the latest on August 11th; the earliest hour of swarming, 9 o'clock, A. M.; the latest, half-past 3 o'clock. P. M. The greatest weight of first swarm 6 lbs.; of second swarm, 4¾ lbs. The second swarms, were generally, accompanied with more than one queen. This was also the case with two first swarms, which, doubtless, arose from the old queens, having died about the commencement of the swarming season. In one of the cases the queen was observed, dead in front of the hive. Many thousands of the Bees continued to cluster around the hive till the 10th or 11th day, when a swarm of 6 lbs. left, in company with several queens.

Disease in Potatoes.—The attention of every body is so absorbed by the Potato-Murrain, that we should be wanting in our duty towards the public if we did not continue to advert to the melancholy subject. Not that we have much to add either by way of advice or consolation; for the topics connected with the disease have all been already touched upon more or less amply, by ourselves or our correspondents; and every week's experience satisfies us that there is little, if anything, to modify in the opinions we have ourselves already expressed.

The mischief is, undoubtedly, extensive to a most alarming degree. If we estimate the amount of loss at five-sixth, we shall hardly exceed the fact. In many places the crop is hardly worth the digging; in others it is totally putrid; in many more, it seems to be spreading fast; and, as we mentioned last week, it has certainly broken out in Ireland. "All *my* Potatoes," says a correspondent near Dublin, "as well as those of the poor people here, are destroyed by the murrain. Two days ago, 12 acres were still safe; they are now gone." Germany, Holland and Belgium, are in the same state as England. A dysentery which has already appeared at Erfurt, is said, by the *Gazette de Cologne*, to be traceable to the use of bad Potatoes. The Belgian papers speak of cholera at Ghent, produced in the same way. Poland according to the same journals, is so threatened by famine, that the Prussian authorities on the frontier have been obliged to take precautionary measures for keeping the starving population out of the Prussian territory; and, finally, the authorities of some districts in France and Germany, have either prohibited or threatened to prohibit the exportation of Potatoes, lest there should be no seed for another year.

Such is the state of the case. It is useless now to speculate on the first cause of this murrain. Our original opinion was, we believe, correct; at least, we have not at present seen anything to shake our confidence in it; and we find that, with the single exception of Professor MORREN, the universal opinion among the Belgian cultivators is the same as ours, except when meteors, electricity, and other unknown forces, are appealed to. It is true that a minute fungus has made matters infinitely worse; but that is, we quite believe, a secondary cause. The consideration of this part of the question may, however be very well deferred. What we have now to look to is an immediate remedy for the evil.

To Purify Offensive Odors.—Pour a solution of copperas (sulphate of iron) upon any fecal matters, and it is rendered immediately inodorous. This cheap and efficient remedy should be in every family at this season of the year, and used wherever there is any decayed vegetable matter, privy-vaults, slops, or the like.

———

THE FARMER.

Planting Chesnuts.—The rapid growth of the Chesnut, the excellence of its timber, and its fine ornamental appearance, render it a desirable object of cultivation. The fruit which it produces too is not the least consideration.

Many, however, who attempt raising the trees, partially or wholly fail in causing the seeds to germinate. This is usually owing to the seeds becoming *dry* before they are planted. A few days exposure to dry air is sufficient to prevent their growing. Hence, as soon as they are taken from the tree they should be once planted before drying a day, or mixed with moist sand, and kept in that condition till planted. They should not be covered more than inch and a half deep, if the soil is heavy, nor more than two inches if it is light; but a still better way is to plant them half that depth, and then spread on a thin covering—say one inch of peat, or rotton leaves, which will keep the surface soft and moist.

It must be remembered that mice are exceedingly fond of the nuts, and if planted near grass lands, or other places frequented by mice, the young plants will be missing the next year.

Air Churn.—The Bishop of Derry has invented an atmospheric churn. Instead of the present unscientific mode of making butter by churning, his Lordship accomplishes this measure by the simpler manner of forcing a full current of atmospheric air through the cream, by means of an exceedingly well-devised forcing pump. The air passes through a glass tube connected with the air-pump, descending nearly to the bottom of the churn. The churn is of tin, and it fits into another tin cylinder provided with a funnel and stopcock, so as to heat the cream to the necessary temperature. The pump is worked by means of a wince, which is not so laborious as the usual churn. Independently of the happy application of science to this important department of domestic economy, in a practical point of view it is extremely valuable. The milk is not moved by a dasher, as in the common churn; but the oxygen of the atmosphere is brought into close contact with the cream, so as to effect a full combination of the butyra-

ceous part, and to convert it all into butter. On one occasion the churning was carried on for the space of one hour and forty-five minutes, and eleven gallons of cream produced 26 pounds of butter.

A Superior mode of Preparing Potatoes for Feeding Stock.—Mr. Boggild, of Copenhagen, washes his potatoes well, steams them thoroughly, and then, without allowing them to cool, he cuts them in a cylinder furnished internally with revolving knives, or crushes them in a mill, and mixes them with a small quantity of water and three pounds of ground malt to every one hundred pounds of raw potatoes.—This mixture is kept in motion, and at a temperature of one hundred and forty degrees to one hundred and eighty degrees F., for from one to five hours, when the thick gruel has acquired a sweet taste, and is ready for use Given in this state, the results of experimental trials are said to be—1st, That it is richer and better food for milch-cows, than twice the quantity of potatoes in the raw state.—2d, That it is excellent for fattening cattle and sheep, and for winter food; that it goes much farther than potatoes when merely steamed; and that it may be economically mixed up with chopped hay and straw.

More about Drying Potatoes.—A Glenburn Farmer says in a letter to the editor of the Bangor Courier, ' *Keep potatoes dry, and they will not rot.*' We copy the following :—

"I assume it to be a fact that the potatoe is not diseased. The tops of the potatoe have been killed extensively, the two past seasons, and, as a very natural consequence, the unripe, half-grown tubers, have rotted. The cause of the rot is fermentation. Prevent fermentation, and the frightful 'potatoe plague' is cured. This must be done by drying.—Any farmer who has a rotting field of potatoes, may save them by digging and *spreading them so thin as to dry the surface, and keep them dry until cold weather,* and he can then safely stow them away in the cellar. Drying any substance, as every one should know, will prevent fermentation. Fermentation in vegetable matter, produces decomposition, and decomposition is rot "

The Plough in the Garden.—Ten years experience in this country has convinced me, that an entirely different system of gardening should be pursued to that of Europe. In England, those who employ good gardeners, have generally a noble estate, descended from their ancestors, and together with it, an abundant income, to keep the estate in first-rate order. Here, where fortunes have to be acquired, generally, by personal industry and perseverance, it is not to be supposed that proprietors under these circumstances will be so lavish of expenditure. It appears to me then a mistake to lay out grounds after the plan of the English proprietors. The first expense may not be grudged, but the after expenses of keeping the place in repair *is always so.* I believe brother gardeners will bear me out in the assertion, that in nine cases out of ten, there is an unwillingness to allow sufficient help, or means to keep places in anything like order, either in England or here. The consequence is a disgust, rather than pleasure, on the part of both gardener and employer.

To obviate these difficulties, then, I would propose, that the vegetable garden, at any rate, should be without box-edgings and gravel walks, and so situated as to be easily worked with a plough, cultivator, &c.; a square or oblong is always best in form; and instead of the old fashioned four-quarters and subdivisions into beds, and alleys, for each kind of vegetable, let there be a continuous row of each the whole length or breadth of the garden, sown or planted, say two and a half feet apart, and worked with one horse and cultivator, or plough without mouldboard—a garden so worked will be found profitable, the bulk of the work being done by a farm laborer, it gives the gardener a little more time and opportunity to attend to the multiplicity of other matters that must not be neglected, and which occupy an immense amount of time, care, and attention, seldom noticed by his employer.

The objection of the plough in the garden on account of want of depth, is happily done away with, now that we have the subsoil plough—a plough that ought to be much more general in use. I noticed some fine ones at the Fair.

I know that gardeners generally have a prejudice against the plough in the garden, and till within a few years, I was among the number—but I can tell them, from five years experience with the plough, that it is far the easiest, most expeditious, and quite effectual; I raised good crops, and spent by far the most pleasant five years service in my life—pleasant, because by means of the plough, I could get crops in season, and my work always *before* me.

Peach Worm.—A sharp penknife, or a sharp wire is the best preventive for the worm. The insect insinuates itself under the *bark* of the tree, where ordinary poisonous applications will not reach it.

Sheep.—If you desire that your sheep shall pay you in *fleece* and *carcass* for your keep, let us, if you have not done so already, advise you to provide them with comfortable *sheds*, wherein they will be kept both warm and dry, as without this precaution, a large portion of their provender which should go to the increase of fat and wool, will be exhausted in furnishing heat to their bodies, and will consequently be lost to the owner. The salting of sheep, the giving them pine bows, and water regularly, are matters which should not be neglected through this and the succeeding winter and early spring months; nor is it less essential, that their bedding should be, at short intervals, renewed. In feeding them, *three* pounds of hay, daily, per head, will be enough. They should, however, occasionally, through the winter, receive as a part of their food, either beans, oats, barley, buckwheat, rye or corn meal, as also messes of roots of some kind In early spring, and indeed until the pastures are ready for their reception, these latter additions of food should be particularly attended to. In turning them to grass in the spring, care must be observed that, for some days, they be permitted to graze but a few hours at a time, and that they be furnished with hay during the residue of the day and night at their usual meals; as early grass is apt to bring on disorders of the intestines.

Keeping Pumpkins.—Pumpkins for stock are best kept in a dry loft with the flooring quite open, so as to allow the air to articulate as freely as possible between them. Were it not that they take up so much room we should prefer storing them at a single tier; but usually, for want of this when a large crop is to be secured, they must be piled upon each other. In this case, we would recommend their not being placed more than three or four deep. If piled together in too large heaps they gather moisture and rot rapidly. When frozen they may be preserved a long time; but they should be cooked before giving them to the stock, otherwise they may do them great injury. On the whole we prefer feeding our pumpkins as fast as possible after ripening, and before the cold weather sets in. They are of a cool watery nature, and unless cooked, we doubt whether they are near as beneficial to animals in frosty weather, as they are in milder, or, indeed, any kind of fruit, or root, though stock of a good breed usually do well upon them.

Cherry Leaves and Cattle.—A farmer lately turned his sheep into a lot occupied by some cherry trees, which had sent up shoots from the roots; the consequence was that the sheep partook of the leaves of these shoots, and were soon seen staggering about the lot and tumbling upon their heads. Many of them died, when their stomachs were found to contain large quantities of these leaves, which, all know, abound with *prussic acid*, fatal alike to man and animals. It should be known, too, that the stones and twigs, as well as the leaves of the peach, all contain prussic acid, and are poisonous.

Salt and Lime.—A mixture of salt and lime has been found to prove very valuable in raising wheat crops this season. The trials have realized the most sanguine expectations in many places. Turnips also prove well with this composition strewed upon the soil. Sulphate of soda (Epsom salts) has been of equally great value to potatoes. This, with an equal quantity of nitrate of soda, is thought by some even better.

About Peaches.— The following method is said not only to insure a plentiful crop of peaches, but greatly improves their size and flavor. A highly intelligent gentleman of Tennessee, who gave us the information, has practised it for the last twenty years, and has never known it to fail—it insures him a most plentiful crop every year.

The process is this:—In the fall of the year, about the time of the first freezing weather, draw the earth away from the roots, to a depth of some six inches, so as to expose the large roots at their junction with the tree. When the snows come, roll up large balls of it, and place them around the bottom of the tree, or, what is the same thing, shovel the snow into a heap around the tree, and in either case pack it or beat it down till it acquires almost the solidity of ice. Throw on this charcoal dust or saw dust, if you have it, and then cover it over with straw. This would preserve the snow till midsummer, or the straw alone will perhaps keep it from melting sufficiently long for all practical purposes. When snows do not fall a sufficient depth, ice packed up around the trees, and preserved as above stated, answers the same purpose. The object it will be at once perceived, is to prevent vegetation and bloom until all danger from frost is entirely past. After the spring has advanced, and the weather becomes decidedly settled and warm, whatever snow remains may be raked away from the trees, when, although they look to be dead in the midst of the surrounding vegetation, they will spring up into life and luxuriance, with a rapidity and vigor truly astonishing. The only inconvenience is, that the bloom is so redundant, that it is necessary, when the young fruit appears, to thin it out with a notched stick prepared for the purpose, so that the tree may have no more than it can bring to the utmost maturity and perfection. The same process is said to be equally applicable to apricots, plums, cherries, pears, apples, and indeed all fruit trees, apt to put forth blossoms before there is a certainty of having no more hard frost.

Destruction of Sparrows and other Birds.—Mr. Bradley, in his general treatise on Husbandry and Gardening, shows that a pair of sparrows during the time they have their young to feed, destroy on an avarage every week 3,360 caterpillars. The calcuation he founded on actual observation having remarked that the two parents carried to the nest forty caterpillars, &c., &c., in an hour. These birds likewise feed their young with butterflies and other winged insects, each of which, if not destroyed in this manner, would be the parent of hundreds of caterpillars.—[A correspondent of ours, who has paid much attention to the rearing of butterflies, &c., in order to obtain perfect specimens for an entomological cabinet, had 840 caterpillars hatched from the eggs laid by one female, of this tribe of insects, in the course of a few days.]—A gentleman writing on the use of birds, in the "Horticultural Register," states that the goldcrested wren, willow-wren, or hay-birds, and chiff-chaff, eat insects only. Where they are plentiful they may be of great use in thinning, on their first appearance, wheat-flies, blue dolphins, hop-flies, and the pea-plant aphides.—This is important, for one of these insects killed on their first appearance will prevent the breeding of thousands. Gardeners are prejudiced against the hay-bird, or cherry-chopper, but it does not taste either cherries or strawberries, but the cherry plant louse, which ravages cherry leaves in April. Nightingales eat insects only; so do the win-chat, the stone-chat, wheat-ear, pippips, and wag-tails. Every means should, therefore, be taken to encourage them to breed, by protecting their nests. The principal insecteating birds, which partially eat fruits or seeds, are the common wren, house and hedge-sparrows, redbreast, chaffinch, black-cap, garden-warbler, and the greater and lesser white-throats, also the tom-tits. The march-tits eat insects chiefly, but also eat farinaceous seeds, as those of the sun-flower, or peck a bit of ripe pear or apple; but such damage is trifling, and is a reward which should not be grudged, considering the great good which they do both to the farmer and gardener.

Lime.—If you wish to rot your sods as soon as possible, mix manure from the horse stable, or the strongest wood ashes that you can find.

If you desire to *preserve* your sods, unrotted, mix lime with them. Lime is a preserver, not a decomposer of vegetable matter. Lime is more suitable to be placed around fence posts to prevent their rotting,—than heaps of muck or sods, as many do—they know not why. Slacked lime creates no heap of muck, consequently it does not hasten or promote decomposition. Our opinion of lime is that it is no better than sand in a manure heap, though it cost more. It helps to kill worms, and it serves to correct certain acids in certain soils. In all red soils there is iron ore. In such soils lime has proved very valuable. The lands of Pennsylvania abound in iron ore, and it is there that lime is found useful.

Orchards.—Let the trees in the Orchard be carefully examined for dead limbs. These should be carefully cut off into the sound wood; the wound smoothly faced with a drawing knife—this done let a plaster of the following mixture be applied over the wound—Take equal parts of fresh cow dung, clay and slacked lime, to be mixed together into the consistence of mortar: face the plaster with a covering of thick paper to turn rain. The dead limbs being cut off and the wounds dressed, take a hard brush,—the clamp of a scrubbing brush will do,—and rub down the entire body of the tree, then with a paint or white-wash brush, apply the following mixture to the body of each tree as far as you can reach, extending down to the roots Mix together five gallons of soft soap, one pound of sulphur, and a gallon of salt. When perfectly incorporated together, it will be fit to be applied.

If the Orchard has not been recently manured and in culture, a gentle dressing of compost made of five parts forest-mould, two parts rotten dung, and one part lime, would greatly improve the quality of the fruit, by being ploughed in shallow—or if it should not be convenient to plough it in, harrowing will answer; but whether the plough or harrow be used, care must be taken not to injure the roots of the trees.

Preservation of Apples.—The following practical observations, contained in a letter from Noah Webster, have been published in the Massachusetts Agricultural Repository:—

"It is the practice with some persons to pick apples in October, and first spread them on the floor of an upper room. This practice is said to render apples more durable, by drying them. But I can affirm this to be a mistake. Apples after remaining on the trees as long as safety from the frost will admit, should be taken directly from trees to close casks, and kept dry and cool as possible. If suffered to lie on the floor for weeks, they wither and lose their flavour, without acquiring an additional durability. The best mode of preserving apples for spring use, I have found to be, the putting of them in dry sand as soon as picked. For this purpose, dry sand in the heat of summer; and late in October, put down the apples in layers, with a covering of sand upon each layer.— The singular advantage of this mode of treatment are these:—1st, the sand keeps the apples from the air, which is essential to their preservation.— 2d, the sand checks the evaporation of the apples, thus preserving them in their full flavour; at the same time, any moisture yielded by the apples, and some there will be, is absorbed by the sand, so that the apples are kept dry, and all mustiness is prevented.

Getting Poor on Rich Land, and Getting Rich on Poor Land.—A close observer of men and things, says the Ohio Cultivator, told us the following little history, which we hope will plough very deeply into the attention of all who plough very shallow in their soils:

Two brothers settled together in —— county. One of them on a cold, ugly, clay soil, covered with black-jack oak, not one of which was large enough to make a half dozen rails. This man would never drive any but large, powerful Conastoga horses, some seventeen hands high. He always put *three* horses to a large plough, and plunged it in some ten inches deep. This deep ploughing he invariably practiced and cultivated thoroughly afterwards. He raised his seventy bushels of corn to the acre.

This man had a brother about six miles off, settled on a rich white river bottom-land farm, and, while a black-jack clay soil yielded seventy bushels to the acre, this fine bottom land would not average fifty. One brother was steadily growing rich on poor land, and the other steadily growing poor on rich land.

One day the bottom land brother came down to see the black-jack-oak farmer, and they began to talk about their crops and farms, as farmers are very apt to do.

"How is it," said the first, "that you manage on this poor soil to beat me in crops?"

The reply was: "*I* WORK *my land!*"

That was it, exactly. Some men have such rich land that they won't *work* it; and they never get a step beyond where they began. They rely on the *soil*, not on labour, or skill, or care. *Some men expect their lands to work; and some men expect to work their land;* and that is just the difference between a good and bad farmer.

Potatoes.—Drying potatoes may be a good method to save them from the rot, and it may be well to save them in this way; yet by exposure to the air they will lose much of their good quality. If potatoes lay in a box or barrel, open to the air, and in a room, shed, or other place out of the cellar, they will lose much of their good qualities in five or six weeks. To preserve potatoes in good condition, they should be dug with as little exposure to the air as possible, and put in a cellar in a close bin, cask or box, and the cellar should be closed so as to exclude light and air. Yet it may be better to save them with a loss of a part of their good properties, than to let them decay; but we would caution the lovers of good potatoes against too much exposure, as it will cause too great a depreciation in their value.

Arrachia.—A vegetable indigenous in New Grenada, the arrachia, is said to be a valuable substitute for the potato. Each plant furnishes three or four pounds of root, of the nature of the carrot and potato united, and is said to be a wholesome food.

Biting Horses.—I never knew an instance of a biting horse being cured of the vice, and for this reason we have never hit upon an expedient (at least I never heard of one) that would make him, like the boy striking the wall, hurt himself. If we could find any mode of making him do so, he would be cured at once. A somewhat curious mode of doing this appeared in the public prints, the giving such a horse a hot roast leg of mutton to seize. Absurd as this appears, it is really not so much so as many things that are done towards horses. In fact, if a horse was addicted to biting legs of mutton, it would be a rational and certain way of curing him of the propensity, but, as legs of mutton do not often come in his way and arms of men frequently do, unless he was stupid enough not to be able to distinguish the one from the other, I fear the mutton plan could not avail much. Now, if we could cover a man with a coat of mail, with invisible spikes standing from it, two or three times seizing the man would, I doubt not, radically cure the horse, not of his disposition to bite, but of attempting to do so; but, as we cannot well do this, I think a short stick, and keeping an eye on him in approaching him or quitting him, is the only thing to be trusted to. Flogging him after he has been bitten will tend to increase his propensities to do it, for this reason, it is either dislike to man or fear of man that makes him bite: he seizes us for having hurt him, or in revenge for having been hurt. Consequently, punishing only confirms his fear and hate; so, probably, if we do this, and he finds he dares not bite, he tries the efficacy of a kick.

Weight of Corn per Acre.—Capt. Randall, of New-Bedford, has recently published in the N. E. Farmer an account of the weight of his corn sown broad-cast on a couple of acres and some rods. He says 35 tons of manure were spread upon each acre. Ten bushels of white, flat, Maryland corn were sown on two acres and 32 rods. The whole was well plowed and repeatedly harrowed, and a heavy roller was applied. Three separate rods of this corn were cut and weighed, and the average weight per rod was 388 lbs. This gives between 31 and 32 tons per acre, sown broadcast, very highly manured and land well prepared.

We think 40 tons per acre may be grown by sowing in drills, but the labor would be more, though the seed would not cost one quarter as much. Capt. Randall says he fed out his corn from 2 acres and 30 rods to 20 cows, three other cattle, and five calves, and it kept them 7 weeks and 5 days, with what they could pick in a dry pasture. And he is satisfied that his corn was equal to 15 tons of the very best of English hay.

But we think Capt. R. puts a wrong estate on this fodder from his corn field. Fifteen tons of hay would keep his stock through half the winter without any aid from the pasture ground, yet while all his stock could bite, bushes and all, his corn kept his stock but one third of the time that cattle are fed in winter.

Cattle will find something in the driest pasture and will partially fill themselves there, even though you feed out the richest products of the farm.

Again, the 2 acres and 32 rods of ground, with this high manuring, would have produced this season 160 bushels of shelled corn, beside all the stalks and husks. This corn dealt out in meal would make an allowance of 6⅔ bushels to each of the 24 cattle for 7 weeks and 5 days—or 213 quarts of meal each. That is, about three quarts of meal per day for each animal besides the husks and stalks. Should we not think it costly feeding to give out so much in addition to what could be obtained in the pasture ?

We wish to see more experiments made on feeding out green corn, and we therefore make these remarks on the experiment of Capt. Randall.

Removing Bees.—Where the queen-bee is put the rest of the bees will follow: set the hive where there is only a faint light; turn it up, and as the queen will make her appearance first, take and place her in an empty hive, and she will be followed by the rest of the bees.

———

Feeding Horses on the road.—Many persons in travelling, feed their horses too much and too often—continually stuffing them, not allowing them time to rest and digest their food; of course they suffer from over fullness and carrying unnecessary weight. Some make it a rule to bait every 10 miles, which is very inconsistent, as in some cases with a fleet animal, good road, favorable weather and load, this distance may be travelled in one third the time it can under unfavorable circumstaces, as to speed. It would be better to regulate the feeding by time, rather than distance.

Mr. S. B. Buckley, who made a botanical tour among the Cumberland mountains, says, in the Albany Cultivator, "four young men came in, travellers on horseback, who according to the Southern custom, rode all day without stopping to dine or feed their horses. Horses will do well and keep in good condition under such treatment, as I can testify from experience."

Horses should be well fed in the evening, and not stuffed too full in the morning, and the traveller should be moderate on starting with a horse having a full stomach. If a horse starts in good condition, and travels rather quick, he can go 25 miles without baiting; this is evident when we consider the time necessary to accomplish this space with tolerable speed.

If a horse starts, well fed, in the morning at seven o'clock, he can travel till noon, having a little water and a little rest occasionally, without food; or if he have any, a little meal in water, or two quarts of oats; if ground, the better; or a little lock of hay may be given instead of meal or oats. At noon, the horse should be pretty well fed, and rest two hours; then he can travel four or five hours with very little or no food.

Horses cannot well endure hard travelling on grass; therefore those that are generally kept on grass should be fed on hay the night previous to starting on a journey, or to a hard day's work. In taking horses from grass and feeding on dry fodder and grain, care must be had of their health as this change is liable to produce constipation of the bowels and cholic; which may be prevented by giving small quantities of wheat bran, or potatoes or other roots. Hay cut tolerable early, or that in which there is a good portion of clover, is more laxative, and may be preventive, but it is not so substantial food as well grown hay, or herds grass.

Vermin on Fowls.—Scattering slacked lime on the perches and floors of the hen-houses as often as once in ten days, will effectually eradicate the lice and promote the health of the fowls.

Disease among the Turnips.—The Liverpool Mercury of the 14 ult. publishes an extract of a letter from a magistrate of the county Louth, stating that "the destruction of the turnip crop is much more complete than that of the potato. All the Swedes are rotten at the core; yet the external appearance is as good as usual." Accounts from the south of England also states that the turnips there have been attacked in a similar way.

Ploughing Wet Land.—It is the opinion of some farmers, that ploughing grass land, which is inclined to wet, is of no benefit to it, but rather an injury. Such land probably requires draining, and if you are unable to do this, at present, perhaps it would be better to apply the dressing on the surface in the fall, and not attempt to break it up. Ploughing such land in the ordinary way renders it more flat and heavy, and not so well adapted to the English grasses as before. Perhaps ploughing, of itself, has sometimes been relied on too much, in attempting to renovate exhausted lands.

Apples.—Edmond Sears, of East Dennis, raised last year from a single limb of a tree, twenty-six greening apples, weighing twenty-six pounds. Who can beat this?

Fences, Bars, and Gates.—Personally inspect every pannel of fence upon your farm, and have every necessary repair promptly made. If the entrance to your fields are through *bars*, have those bars substituted by *gates*, for you may rest assured that the *time* occupied in taking down and putting up a set of bars, would in two years pay for a gate.

THE
FAMILY PHYSICIAN.

THE
FAMILY PHYSICIAN.

THE
FAMILY PHYSICIAN.

The great Preventives. — Keep the person clean, the clothing loose, the bowels open, the head cool, and the feet warm. This rule should be observed under all diseases, as well as in health.

Asthma, or Spasms of the lungs. — Tobacco, or skunk's cabbage smoked in a pipe, are the most safe and simple remedies. The leaves and pods of Lobelia or Indian Tobacco put in a quart bottle and covered with spirits, make a very beneficial tincture, which may be taken by the teaspoonful every three quarters of an hour till relieved.

Ascarides or seat Worms. — Dissolve a teaspoonful of table salt, in half a teacupful of warm water, and inject it into the bowels — or dissolve a teaspoonful of aloes in two tablespoonsful of brandy or vinegar, and take it in the morning and evening.

Appoplexy — Or falling down without sense, in a total prostration. — This is caused by a sudden rush of blood to the head, excessive heat, passion, heavy meals; about a pint of blood should be taken immediately, all tightness of the dress removed, the patient should be placed on a bed, with the head and shoulders raised: after which a dose of salts should be given, all severer treatment should be left to a physician.

Bleeding — How to do it. — If this operation is necessary and a practical bleeder is not at hand, let the person who is to perform it, tie a bandage around the arm about half way between the shoulder and elbow, this should never be so tightly drawn as to stop the pulsation at the wrist; the operator should select the most prominent vein in the bend of the arm, and observe that there is no pulsation near it, or he may strike an artery instead of a vein, and thereby endanger the life of the patient; after this, should he not have a lancet, he may open the vein with the point of any small sharp instrument; when a sufficient quantity of blood is drawn, the bandage should be gradually loosened, the wound pinched together with the thumb and finger, a small piece of lint or linen placed over it, and secured by a bandage passed over and under the arm drawn above and below the elbow, in the figure of an eight, and pinned tightly over the wound.

Bleeding from the Nose. — The patients head and body should be kept up, inclining slightly backwards, the dress kept open, apply iced water or vinegar to the back of the neck, and to the lower parts, and keep the head perfectly still — if the bleeding is very profuse let him draw a small portion of alum dissolved in water into the nostrils. if this should fail, the patient should be bled at the arm, and have a plug or roll of linen covered with powdered alum, or wet with a solution of alum and water, and gently introduced into the nostril.

Bleeding at the lungs, or spitting of blood. — Take a tablespoonful of table salt at intervals till relieved; if violent and obstinate take about five grains of sugar of lead, with about two of opium; let the diet be

THE FAMILY PHYSICIAN.

as cold and light as possible, such as the broth of rice or barley, when it is perfectly cool, and if the bleeding continues consult a physician as speedily as possible.

Billious fever.—The approach of this disease is indicated by a full hard and quick pulse, hot skin, white tongue, sickness of the stomach, and pain in the head. The patient should be bled till the pulse is reduced, and take from ten to fifteen grains of calomel, followed by a Seidlitz Powder; the bowels should still be kept open, by salts and senna, and the patient take no other nourishment than rice or barley, and cold lemonade.

Bronchitis.—Or soreness in the lower part of the throat, and in the breast. Take a dose of senna and salts, apply a plaster of Burgundy pitch to the breast, and use light diet; rub the throat with a coarse cloth, and avoid exposure and heavy exercise of the lungs. If the Burgundy pitch is not at hand, the ordinary pitch melted and spread on a piece of musklin or sheepskin may answer.

Biles.—Take frequent purges of salts—a poultice of soap and sugar is frequently used, and is active in drawing the bile to a head; but this preparation is generally too severe; a mush poultice, or one of bread and milk is generally the best: to this if the pain is severe a little sweet oil, and a teaspoonful of laudanum may be be added; if the bile does not break, it should be opened with a lancet, it should then be healed by a plaster of *simple cerate* a compound of bees wax and lard.

Bruises.—Bruises are too often neglected, from the fact that the extent of the injury is seldom visible. Soak a piece of bread in vinegar, then mash it into a poultice, add a few drops of laudanum, and apply it to the part, bruised wormwood and vinegar is also an effective application. Keep applying fresh poultices, and bathe the part with laudanum, sweet oil and vinegar.

Blotches on the skin—Pimples &c.—Take repeated doses of salts, or sulphur and cream of tartar; keep the person pure by frequent warm baths, avoid all stimulating drinks, and poisonous drugs and powders for the face, and use a light diet; if all this should fail use the syrup of Sarsaparilla.

Baldness.—If not from old age, may be cured by frequent shaving of the part, rubbing it repeatedly with a stiff brush, applying sweet oil, or beef's marrow, and wearing a cap over it made of beef's bladder.

Catarrh, or Cold.—This is attended with a cough, copious discharges of mucus from the nose, hoarseness and pain in the head—take a purge of senna manna and salts, drink freely of flaxseed tea, slightly accidulated with lemon and take about twenty drops of antimonial wine three times a day; if there is pain in the breast, the pitch plaster is very beneficial; a tea made of a teaspoonful of cayanne pepper is also very good. If it is attended with much cough make a mixture of an ounce of syrup squills, two drachms of antimonial wine, half an ounce of paragoric, with a half pint of water, and take two teaspoonsful every quarter of an hour till relieved.

Cholic.—A teaspoonful of lavender or essence of peppermint, with about twenty drops of laudanum, in ordinary cases, if severe, apply a mustard plaster over the lower part of the bowels or abdomen, keep it on till the skin is perfectly red, and take a dose of castor oil, with about fifteen drops of laudanum in it.

Cramp in the stomach.—A sharp violent darting and drawing pain in the stomach—apply hot bricks to the stomach and soles of the feet, and give a teaspoonful of ether with from forty to seventy drops of laudanum or paragoric.

Croup.—Give an emetic instantly, antimonial wine, from ten to fifteen drops, according to the age of the child; or five grains of ipecacuanha, and put the infant in a warm bath, about eight or ten drops of syrup of squills, or five of Coxe's hive syrup may be given, till vomiting takes place, if the throat is much swollen, a few leeches may be applied but at this stage a physician should be consulted if possible.

Cholera Morbus, or vomiting and purging.—Apply hot bricks or bottles filled with hot water to the feet, lay flannel cloths soaked in brandy or spirits of hartshorn over the stomach; take large draughts of rice, barley water, or chammomile tea; from forty to eighty drops of laudanum or paragoric in peppermint; after the attack is completely subdued, a small dose of castor oil with about ten drops of laudanum should be taken.

Costiveness, or tightness of the bowels. — Take light animal food such as mutton &c., eat mush and molasses once a day, take regular and moderate exercise, chew a small piece of rhubarb daily, and make an effort once a day to evacuate.

Chilblains, or Frost-bitten.—Soak the parts frequently in a solution of chloride of lime, and apply chicken fat, or pig's foot oil to them.

Cancer.—This is a small hard veiny tumour, attended with sharp burning pains; to avoid the necessity of the surgeon's knife, it demands the careful attention at its earliest stage. Bathe the part with a solution of the best brandy and common salt, apply mush poultice twice or thrice a day, or on the first appearance of the tumour touch it slightly with lunar caustic two or three times a day; a wash of strong lye made from hichory ashes, has been found efficacious; keep the surface covered from the cold air, use very light diet, and relieve the pain by laudanum or paragoric in large doses.

Dysentary, or Flux. — This is distinguished from Diarrhea, or common looseless of the bowels, by its being attended with a gripeing and bloody stools, and fever and thirst. The writer of this has known a moderate quantity of fresh ripe blackberries to effect a cure of this complaint in several instances; blackberry syrup is often successful, castor oil with about twenty drops of laudanum, is generally used, either in doses or glysters, followed by about twenty drops of laudanum; if very obstinate, apply a mustard plaster over the bowels, and take a table-spoonful of the following mixture every hour and a half:—one drachm of the tincture of Kino, three and a half ounces of chalk mixture, two ounces and a half of cinnamon water, and about fifty drops of laudanum. The drink should be weakened with port wine of the best quality, and the diet consist of chicken water, rice water, or arrow root gruel.

Diarrhœa, Lax, or looseness of the bowels. — This is most frequently brought on by the eating of too much vegetable food, and green fruit &c; or a cold; it is not unfrequently, an effort of nature to carry off some offensive matter, and should not be checked too suddenly. If occasioned by bad fruit, &c., take a dose of magnesia, and drink freely of boneset tea; if from cold, take a dose of castor oil, with about twenty or twenty-five drops of laudanum— bathe the feet in warm water; drink the tea as above, and promote perspiration; if obstinate pursue the same treatment as in similar stages of dysentary, using the same drinks and diet. Wear woolen stockings and flannel.

Dropsy of the belly.—This may be known by a swelling, or enlargement of the belly, a watery rattling when touched; hardly and scanty urine. It is a most obstinate disease to cure, except in the early stage and the early part of life; steaming and warm baths, such as promote free perspiration, are beneficial; it has been frequently cured by taking five grains of calomel with two of gamboge, every two days: an ounce and half of cream of tartar, taken in a little water, daily, has been found a valuable remedy; wear thick flannel, drink no more fluids than are absolutely necessary, and use light and digestable animal food, avoiding salted meats, &c., all such as create a thirst.

Dropsy of the chest.—This disease manifests itself by oppression on the breast, short and difficult breathing, cough, palpitation of the heart, and inability to lie down in the ordinary posture: accompanied with a sense of suffication.—This, like the above, is very difficult to cure: frequent emetics of about twenty grains of ipecacuanha, with one of antimony, or about twenty drops of spirits of turpentine, twice a day, to promote the flow of urine; in general the same treatment and diet as in dropsy in the belly is pursued o

Dropsy at the knee.—A swollen and baggy appearance of the flesh about the knee.—Apply the steam of vinegar, or chamomile,: or fly blister.

Dyspepsia or Indigestion.—Want of appetite, flatulence, or belching of wind, pain and sickness of the stomach, vomiting; disconsolate state of mind, disturbed s eep, debility, frightful dreams, &c.—There have been as many remedies recommended for this disease, as there are symtoms of its existence; but the following are known as the most effective:—Early rising, and moderate exercise in the pure open air, singing, reading, or speaking aloud; boiled mutton, or chicken and bran bread should be the principal diet, and a very small portion of this at a time; port wine may be moderately taken; take a Seidlitz Powder about twice a week; chew a small portion of rhubarb daily, spiced rhubarb is also good; avoid tobacco and ardent spirits, dress warm, and make an effort every day to evacuate the bowels, and a natural desire will generally follow.

Erysipelas, or St Anthony's F re. —An itching and burning of the face, ears, &c., followed by a redness of the skin, which finally breaks out in watery pimples, which extends sometimes entirely over the body.—The system must be reduced by salts and other cooling purgatives; take from six to ten grains of calomel in the same amount of jalap. The elixir of vitriol is frequently beneficial; this should be accompanied with the use of the Dovers Powder, chamomile and bonesct tea; external applications, as powdering the body over with scortched rye meal, sugar of lead water, &c. The following preparation, as a cooling mixture is of great value in affections of this nature:— One ounce and a half of Glauber salts, twenty grains of nitre, three grains of tartar emetic, in one pint of water. Take from one to three table spoonfuls every two hours; the food should be light, such as barley, tapioca, panada, &c., and the person kept as clean as possible.

Ear Ache.—This is generally caused by a severe cold in the head, by keeping the head too long under water in bathing, or by exposure to a current of cold and damp air.— Syringe the ear with warm water, and fill it with a mixture of laudanum and sweet oil, and cover the part with flannel; when this does not afford relief or a cure, apply a blister immediately back of the ear, and steam the ear with hot water, or vinegar, by means of a jug or bottle, and cool the system by a dose of salts; if matter forms in the ear apply poultices, keeping the parts washed clean by castile soap and warm water.

Epelepsy, or Fits.—The patient is suddenly thrown down in violent convulsions, clenching the hands, grinding the teeth, distorting the limbs, and the whole body.—The first effort should be to protect the patient from bruises, or other injury during the paroxysms; after these have subsided, place the body on a bed, with the head and shoulders elevated: if there is a quick and strong throbbing at the temple, take about twelve ounces of blood. In cases where the fit is felt creeping on, with a chilly sensation, about one of the limbs, wind a string

around it, and let the patient draw
it tight when the cold feeling comes
on, by twisting a stick which should
be worn about the person, attached
to the string. Persons subject to
this affection should carefully guard
against passion, great excitement,
and intemperance, and get bled
whenever they feel much fullness
in the blood vessels. A one grain
pill of the oxide of zinc taken twice
a day, and continued in for a long
period, increasing the doses until
four or five pills are taken daily,
has frequently effected a cure.

Eyes—Inflamation.—There are
two descriptions of this, a disease of
the eye ball, and of the eye-lid.
The inflamation of the eye ball
begins with an itching and burning,
and a feeling as if sand or dust had
been thrown in them; the white
turns red, or *blood shot.* In all
severe cases, if leeches can be obtained, apply three or four near the
eye every morning, till the inflamation subsides; this treatment should
be accompanied by the following
purgative every fourth day.—Ten
grains of calomel, with twenty
grains of jalap, or an ounce of salts.
For the heat of the eye, apply frequently a soft linen rag, dipped at
first in warm water, afterwards in
cold water; if the inflamation continues, dissolve four grains of white
vitriol, with the same quantity of
sugar of lead, in four ounces of
pure water, or six ounces of rose
water; if the pain and itching be
great, add about two drachms of
laudanum to the mixture, and bathe
the eyes. Abstain from all gross
and stimulating food and drinks;
keep the eye slightly covered, or
remain in a dark room—if this
fails, blisters behind the ears should
follow. In milder cases of opthal-
my, a moderate purgative is sufficient, using the rose water, or the
above mentioned washes. If particles of dirt, or gravel, or other
matter, fly into the eyes, they may
be removed by wrapping a piece of
wire with lint, and brushing under
the lids, or injections of warm milk.

Ulcers at the root of the eye-lashes,
should be touched with citron ointment, or with alum water, by means
of a hair pencil.

Fever and Ague.—The character
and symtoms of this disease are too
well known to require description.
The first step at a cure, is to empty
the stomach and bowels. An emetic, consisting of twenty grains of
Ipicac, with one of tartar emetic,
should be given immediately, with
large draughts of warm water, or
chamomile tea; and to insure the
operation on the bowels, take about
three grains of calomel; after this
soak the feet in warm water, take
about from forty to sixty drops of
laudanum, a large draught of chamomile tea, get into bed and cover
yourself up with blankets—this
treatment usually breaks the disease.
If the inflamatory symtoms continue,
blood may be taken, saline purgatives given, and the sulphate of
Quinia administered, or the great
remedy, *Peruvian Bark,* in about
two drachms every three hours—
if the stomach will not bear this
quantity, give half of it at a time,
and in half the time. In the
cold stages, or chills, use warm
drinks, apply bottles filled with hot
water to the soles of the feet, and
make use of every means to bring
on perspiration. During the fever
stage, spirits of nitre may be given
in doses of a teaspoonful, twice or
three times a day; after the disease
is broken, use a nourishing diet,
such as mutton and chicken soup—
eat moderately of the meat, and
drink moderately of wines and tonic
bitters.

Fistula.—An ulcer, or abcess in
the fundament; it is marked by
tumours, which give much pain,
particularly on going to stool, at
which time a yellowish matter is
discharged; this fact will distinguish it from piles; use a light diet,
such as mush, rice, and small doses
of castor oil, apply about fifty
leeches to the part, and a bread and
milk poultice, if this does not break
the tumour, and remove all obstruc-

tion, an operation must be performed.

Fever, Yellow.—Commences with brief chills, and flushes of heat, succeeded by a violent head-ache, pains in the back, weakness, prostration, sickness, and distressing feeling at the stomach; the eyes soon acquire a yellowish hue, which gradually spreads over the entire face—its first appearance on the skin is under the ears; the great distinguishing and alarming symtom is a constant vomiting, which at the third or fourth day, terminates in what is called the *Black vomit.* During the spontaneous vomiting which occurs in the early stage, the patient should drink freely of chamomile tea, then administer a cathartic—the most effectual of which is about 20 grains of calomel, which can be taken in any syrup, or mixed with crumbs of bread. If the patient is young and of free habit, and has a hard tremulous pulse, Dr. Rush recommends taking a small quantity of blood in the first twenty-four hours. Cold water applied externally is a powerful remedy, and very frequently arrests the disease at its commencement; it may be dashed over the patient from a bucket if his skin be hot, or cold application may be applied by a sponge or towel, to parts where the skin is particularly heated. Peruvian bark has been found very efficacious, if it can be kept on the stomach, which may be quieted by the Seidlitz Powder, or the following effevescing mixture, which is highly recommended, and may be given every two hours, adding ten drops of laudanum to each dose:—Dissolve a half teaspoonful of salts of tartar in two tablespoonsful of lemon juice, and drink it in its foaming or effervescing state; if this should fail to allay the vomiting, apply a blister to the stomach immediately. The bark should be given to the patient in the following form:—Take one ounce of powdered Peruvian bark, put it into a tin pot, pour a pint and a half of water on it, and let it boil for ten minutes; give, if the stomach will bear it, a tablespoonful, with three drops of peppermint, every half hour; should the stomach retain this, the quantity may be increased with ten drops of Elixir of vitriol added to it; if the stomach rejects bark in every form, it should be given in glysters of a half pint every two hours—if this succeeds throw the patient into a perspiration if possible; a powder consisting of one grain of calomel, camphor, and opium, will very often produce this effect, and give relief to the patient. To take inflamation from the vital parts, apply plasters to the legs, and poultices to the soul of the feet—drink lemonade, toast water, or orange juice, and eat only of gruel, sago, or panada.

Gravel.—This is known by a heavy bearing down pains in the small of the back, urine scanty and highly colored, sometimes tinged with blood; nausia, or sickness at the stomach; it is generally caused by any immoderate exercise of the parts, such as riding, jumping, &c., by gravel in the kidneys, cold, dissipation, &c.—Bleed from the arm according to the violence of the symtoms; oily cathartics, such as castor oil, sweet oil, &c.; put the patient in a warm bath—give about twenty-two grains of the uva-ursi, with fifty or sixty drops of laudanum three times a day, give large draughts of flaxseed tea; if the pain is very great, give a teaspoonful of laudanum in a glyster; the patient's back should be bathed with flannels dipped in hot water. Persons liable to this disease should avoid malt liquors, soused, pickled, or ascidulated food.

Gout—A stiffness of the small joints, accompanied by a painful swelling of the parts, which have a red or purple hue; it is generally caused by excessive indulgence in rich or highly seasoned food, and insufficient exercise.—Bleed occasionally in the first stages. take as much exercise as possible in pure air: drink pure water, and eat no gross food; let boiled lamb be the chief diet; keep the body open with light purgatives—if the complaint flies into the head or stomach, put mustard poultices to the feet and legs, bleed freely, and give active purges, such as salts and calomel.

Hiccups.—Spasms of the stomach: the symtoms are universally known —they may often be removed by large draughts of cold water; loud singing or speaking, or a sudden fright or surprise will also cure them; if they are very obstinate, and the patient is not otherwise affected, a blister should be applied to the stomach; when they attack a patient who has been long confined by a serious illness they generally denote the approach of death.

Head Ache.—The symtoms are too well known—the most common causes are foul stomach, indigestion, a billious state of the system, intemperance, and a determination of blood to the head.—Where a head ache is symptomatic of some other disease, it will readily cease on the removal thereof, as in the case of fever. When foul stomach or the presence of indigestible substances is apprehended, take a gentle emetic, and if costiveness exist, remove it by some mild laxative. If too great a determination of blood to the head be suspected, bleed, and subsist on a low diet; or soak the feet in hot water, containing a quart of wood ashes. If the head ache be rheumatic, apply blisters to the extremities, or to the back of the neck, and move the bowels by the common Aloectic pills. In case of slight head ache, it my be sufficient to bathe the feet in warm water, and wet the head with ether or spirit.

Heart Burn.—The symtoms are well known—it is generally caused by indigestion, or acid upon the stomach. Take a dose of magnesia, or Seidlitz Powder: the "Bitter Tonics," sold by different apothecaries, are efficacious; in obstinate cases, a blister or mustard poultice should be applied to the stomach; the bowels should be kept open daily, and the patient should subsist on light animal food.

Haemorrhoids, or Piles.— Are painful swellings at the lower extremity of the intestine or fundament, either internal or external.— the internal are most painful, especially while at stool. When external, they vary much in size, being sometimes as large as a nutmeg. Frequently they break and discharge blood, which relieves the pain: the swelling however, does not then entirely disappear, and soon increases again to its former size.— This complaint may preceed from habitual costiveness, plethora, hard riding on horseback, strong aloetic purges, or sitting on damp ground. As costiveness is the most frequent cause of piles, this must be obviated by mild laxatives, and none appears to be more efficacious than the use of the Flowers of Sulphur combined with an equal quanty of cream of tartar, mixed in molasses, in a dose of a tablespoonful every evening. Another excellent internal remedy is Balsam of Copaiva twelve drops, given twice in twenty-four hours, dropt on sugar or in a glass of water. Aloetic purgatives should be avoided.

As an application to the tumors, various ointments and washes are recommended, among which are the following:—Sulphur and hog's lard, equal parts, well mixed; nutgalls and hog's lard, equal parts, mercurial Ointment, or fresh butter; also, tar water, alum water, decoction of oak or Peruvian bark, lead water. A favorite application with many sailors is wet oakum. If the piles continue after the above treatment, and are very painful, apply leeches to the part, or if they are not to be had, make a small puncture in the tumors with a lancet, and after discharging their contents, apply warm poultices to the part.

When the bleeding piles return periodically, once in three or four weeks, the discharge may be con sidered salutary, and should not therefore be stopped, unless it becomes so excessive as to weaken the patient, in which case the decoction of bark may be taken in doses of three tablespoonsful every two hours, adding to each twenty drops of elixir of vitriol. Alum or lead water, added to a decoction of oak or Peruvian bark, is to be applied to the part, and injected in small quantity into the intestine, by means of a small syringe. In some instances, a falling down of the intestine will be a troublesome attendant on the piles, in which case the intestine must be immediately replaced after every evacuation, by pressing gently upon the part with the fingers, until it is reduced; and its return must be prevented by astringent applications, as alum dissolved in vinegar, decoction of bark, &c. All the known causes, particularly costiveness, both during the disease and afterwards, must be studiously avoided.

Inflamation of the throat, or Quinsy.—The throat internally, is red and swollen. There is generally some fever, a constant flow of viscid spittle, and pain in swallowing. When the inflamation is not subdued within five or six days from the first attack, a tumor containing matter will appear in the throat, and break. The usual causes of this inflamation; particularly sudden cold; occasioned by omitting some part of the covering usually worn about the neck; by sleeping in a damp bed; or wearing wet clothes. If the symtoms be severe, bleed freely and administer a dose of salts. Bathe the feet in warm water, with salt or ashes in it. Wear flannel around the neck; or, mash roasted potatoes and apply them in a stocking, as warm as the patient can bear. Gargle the throat every ten minutes, with a mixture of warm vinegar and water sweetened; or, with warm vinegar containing table-salt dissolved; or, with sage tea, honey, and with a piece of borax about the size of a

hickory nut to a pint. If this treatment fail to reduce the inflamation within the first forty-eight hours, the bleeding and purging are to be repeated, and a blister applied to the throat. Abstain from solid food and stimulants: If matter form, the difficulty of swallowing will be increased, and the patient in some danger of suffication. In this case, the suppuration must be hastened by inhaling the steam of warm water, from the nose of a tea-pot, And the application around the throat. Those who have had this disease once, are more liable to subsequent attacks.

In slight cases of sore throat, it may be sufficient to wear flannel around the throat, soaked frequently in a liniment made of hartshorn, sweet oil and laudanum.

Putrid Sore Throat.—It commences with cold shiverings—sickness and vomiting—heat and restlessness, great debility, flushed face, hoarseness and sore throat. Upon inspection, the internal surface appears of a fiery red color, which soon becomes darker and is interspersed with specks, of some shade between a light ash and a dark brown. There is considerable fever, which increases every evening—a small and irregular pulse, and oftentimes diarrhœa.—About the *second* or *third* day, large scarlet colored patches or stains appear upon the neck and face, and afterwards over the whole body. After continuing about four days, they depart with a scaling of the skin. In bad cases, the ulcers in the throat corrode deeper and deeper, debility increases to complete exhaustion, and the parts mortify. The patient expires usually before the seventh, often as early as the third or fourth day.

This disease is epidemic, often spreading through a whole village. Long exposure to a humid atmosphere and a debilitated habit predispose to an attack. This kind of sore throat may be distinguished from Quinsy, or common sore throat, by the eruption or specks above mentioned, by the weak fluttering pulse, general debility, and by the scarlet spots that appear on the skin. Each of these diseases however often partakes so much of the character of the other, that it is not always easy to distinguish them. It may be known from croup, by the absence of a croaking hoarseness, and by the presence of visible inflammation and specks above mentioned. The putrid sore- throat prevails mostly among children.

In the treatment of putrid sore throat, bleeding and active purging would be likely to increase the debility which is already very great. The stomach and bowels must however be cleansed; for which purpose take Ipecac: twenty-five grains of calomel, or some other purgative in small quantity. The principal indication of cure then are—

1. To counteract the putrid tendency that prevails.

2. To wash off frequently the acrid matter from the throat, and lastly, to obviate debility.

To correct the putrid tendency, Peruvian bark, mineral acids, and Cayanne pepper, are amongst the most valuable remedies. They may be taken in the following manner:—Take powder of bark, two table-spoonsful; Cayanne pepper, one table-spoonful; to which add three gills of boiling water, and after boiling it in a covered vessel ten minutes, add one gill of vinegar. Administer three tablespoonsful every two hours. Or, take decoction of bark, two table-spoonsful; tincture of bark, two tea-spoonsful; elixir vitriol, fifteen drops; mixed every two hours.

To cleanse the throat, use gargles of salt dissolved in vinegar;—or elixir vitriol, a teaspoonful to half a pint of warm water, sweetened every ten minutes. Inhale the steam of warm vinegar and water, from the nose of a teapot. Breathe the air, made by burning Nitre, thus: Close the patient's room, and upon a chafing dish of coals, throw powder of Nitre half an ounce; which will fill the room with a thick white cloud, that will last for some time. This process may be frequently repeated, in the course of the day.

If any particular symptom of an alarming nature arise during the progress of the disease, as diarrhœa, bleeding, &c. It must be checked immediately. For diarrhœa administer opium and brandy, or powder of Kino, thirty grains. Bleeding is also to be treated with astringents both locally and generally, as directed under the heads of differen. kinds of bleeding.

Inflammation of the Liver.—Pain in the right side, under the short ribs, which is increased by pressure; sometimes it extends to the chest, then resembling pleurisy, and often there is pain in the right shoulder. Irregular state of the bowels;—inability of lying on the left side ;—dry cough. The inflammation, if not reduced by the seventh or tenth day, usually ends in the formation of matter. In the former case, a billious looseness ensues; if an abscess form, it may break inwardly into the chest or abdomen, or outwardly through the skin.

Every exertion should be made to reduce the inflammation, as early as possible. Bleed and purge freely; —apply a large blister over the liver or part affected with soreness; and abstain from solid food and stimulants. If an abscess form and break, the patient's strength must be supported by bark and wine. If the abscess point outwardly, and threaten to break through the skin, the part should be poulticed.

Chronic Inflammation of the Liver. —The attack of this is generally so gradual, and the symptoms at its commencement so obscure, as to pass long unnoticed. There is dejection of mind; a loss of appetite; rumbling in the bowels; sense of weight and distention in the stomach; obstinate costiveness; clay colored stools: jaundice; and oftentimes an enlargement of the liver that can be felt.—Induce a slight

K

spitting with mercury, applied by friction, and given internally;—thus, a calomel pill or a grain of calomel, every night and morning, and rub Mercurial Ointment, of the bulk of a nutmeg, on the inside of the thighs, every evening. Apply to the part a plaster of mercury or of pitch, of the size of the hand and thickness of a dollar.

Jaw Ache.—Take a dose of salts, and apply a warm poultice of hops and vinegar to the part.—Steaming the part with the vapour of vinegar, keeping the body covered at the same time with blankets, till a perspiration comes on, is also very effectual.

Tetanus, or Locked-Jaw.—It commences with a sense of stiffness in the back part of the neck, rendering the motions of the head difficult and painful. This is soon succeeded by difficulty of swallowing; pain, often violent, about the breast bone and thence shooting to the back; rigidity of the lower jaw, which increasing, the teeth become so closely set together, as not to admit of the smallest opening. If the disease proceed further, a greater number of muscles become affected, and the body is forcibly bent either backwards, or forwards. At length the trunk, limbs, and countenance are distorted to a most painful and shocking degree. A remission of these symptoms occasionally takee place every ten or fifteen minutes, but they are renewed with aggravated force by the slightest causes, even the least motion of the patient, or the touch of an attendant. Finally a general convulsion puts a period to a most miserable state of existence. The duration of Lock-jaw is various. The disease is very common in hot climates, and is most frequent when a scorching sun is succeeded by a heavy rain or dew. But besides exposure to sudden changes of temperature, it is often caused by a wound of a nerve or tendon, or by a fractured bone. Give opium in large quantities, as four or five grains every hour, or three drachms of laudanum, every half hour. When the patient can no longer swallow, inject laudanum a table-spoonful in warm water every hour, and direct it to be retained as long as possible. With the first dose of opium, give ten grains of calomel, and follow it every six hours by a dose of five grains, till the mouth is affected. Use warm and cold bathing in succession. If the disease proceed from a wound, enlarge it pretty extensively, and pour into it hot spirits of turpentine, or burn the wound with an iron, brought to a white heat.

In one instance of locked-jaw, which proceeded from a wounded tendon, I succeeded in the cure by the sudden alternation of the hot and cold baths applied frequently, giving opium, and burning the wound with hot spirits of turpentine.

Jaundice.—Loss of appetite—aversion to exercise—yellowness of the eyes, and subsequently of the whole skin. The urine is highly colored and tinges the linen yellow; the stools are white, or of a clay color. The patient complains of a bitter taste, nausea and sickness at the stomach. Generally there is costiveness, which, however, is occasionally interrupted by diarrhœa. Frequently a sense of uneasiness and darting pain is felt under the short ribs of the right side, and at the pit of the stomach.

The *immediate* cause is an obstruction to the passage of bile, from the liver into the intestines, on account of which, it is thrown back into the circulation and diffused over the body, imparting to it the yellow color above mentioned. This obstruction may proceed:—1. From the lodgment of a stone in the gall-duct. This variety of jaundice may be known from the others, by occasional acute pains under the short ribs of the right side:—2. It may proceed from indurated mucus, lodged in the passage of the gall-duct. This variety follows a sedentary habit, debility, a long continued mercurial course for the venereal disease, and is generally unattended by pain. 3. The obstruction may proceed from enlargement of the liver, as in what is called the *ague cake*, which often succeeds the intermittent or remittent fever, or from that chronic inflammation of the liver, which is occasioned by hard drinking. In this variety of jaundice, the enlargement of the liver can be felt, which distinguishes it from other varieties.

Of the first variety. If pain and inflammation exist in considerable degree, bleed, and bathe the part with warm water; in addition to which, employ the remedies recommended in the second variety.

Second variety. Administer an emetic every other morning, and if it fail to move the bowels, give on the intervening days a mild cathartic, as, calomel, six grains; jalap, ten grains, mixed in syrup or other convenient vehicle, and repeat the dose every three hours, till it operates. Or, calomel pills, three or four, with castor oil, a table-spoonful; or calomel alone, twenty grains. The warm bath, by its relaxing powers, proves very useful in jaundice, and should be employed frequently. Exercise of the jolting kind, as running, dancing, jumping a rope, is very serviceable. To those who reside on shore, riding on horseback is an invaluable remedy.

In the third variety. Where the liver is enlarged, mercury should be employed, as recommended under the head of *Chronic affection of the Liver.* The diet should be light and nourishing.

Leeching.—The manner of applying leeches is too well known to require a description. Success is rendered more certain, by previously drying them, or allowing them to creep over a dry cloth; the part also to attract them, may be moistened with cream, sugar, or blood.

Inflammation of the Intestines.— Severe pain in the abdomen, increased upon pressure, and shooting in a twisting manner round the navel; hardness of the abdomen; obstinate costiveness. There is sometimes vomiting or straining at stool, according as the inflammation happens in the superior or inferior portion of the intestine. The pulse is quick, hard and contracted, and the urine high-colored, and there are other symptoms of fever, with great prostration of strength.

All those inducing inflammation of the stomach, also strangulated hernia—colic—long continued costiveness. It is distinguishable from colic by being accompanied with fever, and by increase of pain from pressure. The indications of cure are—

1 To reduce the inflammation by bleeding once or twice from the arm, by a large blister laid over the belly, by the warm bath, and by total abstinence from stimulating articles of diet or medicine.

2. To move the bowels by gentle purges, as castor oil, salts, or cream of tartar; and by glysters of salt water.

Inflammation of the Lungs—or Pleurisy.—Pleurisy, *pneumonia, peripneumonia,* and *lung fever,* are names given to inflammations of the lungs themselves, or of the membrane that covers them and lines the cavity of the chest. It is however improbable that either the lungs or this membrane are ever inflamed to a great degree separately, the disease of one being generally more or less extended to the other. On this account, and because the symptoms and treatment of the two diseases are nearly the same, they are both included here under the head of Pleurisy. It commonly commences with the usual symptoms of fever, accompanied or succeeded by a sense of weight, and afterwards pain in the chest. This begins in one side, ordinarily about the sixth or seventh rib, from which it shoots towards the breast-bone and shoulder-blade. The breathing is short and difficult and the pain is increased on drawing in the breath. There is constant inclination to cough, but every effort is interrupted by the pain it occasions, in consequence of which, viscid mucus collects in the air-passages, and causes a sort of a wheezing called rattles.

The disease begins to subside from the fourth to the seventh day; if not so soon as the latter period, the case may be considered dangerous. The abatement of the inflammation is marked by an amelioration of all the distressing symptoms, and a copious expectoration.

The great remedies in Pleurisy are bleeding, blistering and purging. In severe cases its rapid course and fatal tendency require that these should be employed with promptness and energy. Blood is to be drawn from a large orifice in the arm, till the patient is relieved of his pain, and difficult breathing, provided the quantity for this be short of two pints. If the the first bleeding fail to relieve, or if after relieving, the pain and difficult breathing return, the operation should, after twelve hours be repeated.

Move the bowels as early as convenient, by a mild laxative, as salts, one ounce.

Immediately after the first bleeding, apply a large blister upon the side, near the seat of the pain.

Bathe the feet in warm salt-water, and apply warm poultices to them.

Take very freely of warm barley-water, or flaxseed tea, made agreeable with sugar.

If the above fail to relieve the pain and other symptoms, within the first thirty-six hours, move the bowels again by the cooling mixture, taking two table-spoonsful every hour, till it operates. Another blister may be applied to the chest, and the bleeding repeated even a third time. As soon as the pain is relieved and expectoration has commenced, give Dover's powders ten grains, or Pectoral Mixture, a table-spoonful, every three hours, and continue the warm drinks.

Preserve a constant warmth of the skin by keeping in bed, and a uniform temperature of the apartment. During convalescence the patient may subsist on a generous diet and use wine.

Consumption. — The tubercular consumption which is by far the most common kind, may be divided into three stages or periods. In the *first* stage, the disease is slowly developed, ordinarily without being noticed. In this period it is very important to recognize it, but the physician is not often consulted so early. The first symptoms are a short dry cough, the breathing's being more easily hurried by bodily motion, the patient's becoming languid, indolent, and dyspeptic, and his gradually losing strength;—at length, from some fresh exciting cause, the cough becomes more considerable, and is particularly troublesome during the night;—breathing is more anxious;—sense of straitness and oppression across the chest is experienced;—an expectoration takes place, at first of frothy mucus, which afterwards becomes copious, viscid and opaque. These symptoms may be gradually progressing for months. The emaciation and weakness go on increasing; —a pain arises in some part of the breast, at first unsettled, but afterwards fixed in one or both sides, is increased by coughing, and sometimes becomes so acute as to prevent the patient's lying upon the affected side.

The disease now passes to a *second* period, in which it is easily recognized. Purulent matter resembling that made by a common ulcer, is coughed up. To distinguish whether it be such, or only mucus, mix some that is raised in the morning, in salt-water: if mucus or common phlegm, it swims and holds together; if pus, it sinks, and on stirring separates into particles; purulent matter is also opaque, has a greenish color, and is sweet to the patient's taste. Hectic fever takes place, known by a flushing of the face, by a hard, quick and frequen pulse, beating more than one hundred in a minute, and by high colored urine. The hectic has an exacerbation or increase twice in the day; the first time about noon, which is inconsiderable and soon suffers a remission; the other in the evening, which gradually increases until after midnight. Each of these fever fits is preceded by chills, and terminates in profuse perspiration. In the morning the patient is better, and thinks himself well. The cough and difficult breathing now go on increasing, and oftentimes there is a hoarseness or shrillness of the voice. After this stage is well established; by the appearance of the above symptoms, the patient may die in six or eight weeks. He is however able to go about, and when the expectoration of pus is first established, the appetite, that was lost in the first stage of the complaint, returns. During the fever fits, a circumscribed redness appears on each cheek, but at other times the face is pale, and countenance dejected.

The *third* period is that of general exhaustion, the countenance is peculiar and easily recognized by all. The cough becomes more hard and difficult, especially in the morning, when it often produces vomiting;— emaciation is extreme; diarrhœa comes on, and generally alternates with melting sweats; the legs swell; little ulcers appear in the throat; still the appetite often remains entire, and the patient flatters himself with hopes of speedy recovery, and is forming plans of interest or amusement, when death puts a period to his existence.

Spitting of blood sometimes induces the disease, or is the first symptom noticed. In other cases it occurs in the course of the disease, and sometimes terminates it.

Particular constitutions are more liable to consumption as where an hereditary predisposition exists, or particular formation of body, marked by long neck, prominent shoulders and narrow chest. The remote causes are, constitutional irritability of the lungs; sedentary life; a scrofulous habit, indicated by a clear skin, fair hair, delicate rosy complexion, large veins, thick upper lip, weak voice, and great sensibility. The more immediate or exciting causes are preceding disease—as spitting of blood, pneumonia, catarrh, scrofula, venereal disease, fistula—violent and depressing passions of the mind—intemperance—profuse evacuations as diarrhœa; or a large ulcer.

The cure should be accomplished early in the disease and before the hectic fever commences, or pus is expectorated. The treatment during this period should be regulated by the cause; if it be catarrh, pneumonia, spitting of blood, &c , attend to the directions given for the cure of those diseases.

The following are among the most approved remedies in the early stage of consumption.

1. Small bleedings, repeated when symptoms of inflammation run high.

2. A nourishing, easily digested, unstimulating diet; as milk, animal jellies, &c. The patient can best determine by his own experience what kind will be most agreeable and beneficial.

3. Mild laxatives, whenever there is the least tendency to costiveness.

4. Blisters on the chest, to counteract the inflammation of the lungs They should be large, and kept constantly running.

5. Emetics, every second or third day. The least debilitating is sulphate of copper or blue vitriol, in a dose of eight grains, dissolved in a gill of water; a vomiting is excited, as soon as it is swallowed, on which the patient should drink a pint of warm tea.

6. Expectorants; the best are such as nauseate and produce gentle perspiration, as Squills, Ipecac : Antimony, &c., to the use of which should be subjoined mucilaginous drinks, as flaxseed-tea, barley-water decoction of mallows, &c.

7. Anodynes, particularly Opium This may be given in combination with the expectorants, as in Pectoral Mixture and Dover's Powders; the former in a dose of a table-spoonful, and of the latter fifteen grains, on going to bed.

8. Exercise, especially on horseback. Long journeys are most serviceable.

9. Flannel worn next to the skin.

10. A sea voyage. Were I to speak of the effects of a sea voyage from my own observation, I should say it is very beneficial while the vessel is at sea; partly from the uniform temperature of the air, but more from the motion of the vessel.

Change of residence to a warm climate is often recommended. In two or three years' Mediterranean service however, nothing occurred within my observation to favor the opinion, that the climate of the sea would be beneficial ; on the contrary, among our sailors, consumptions were more frequent there, than I have ever known them to be in other climates.

In the frigate United States were ﬁ hteen deaths in one year, twelve . the Gueirriere, and eleven in the Constellation.   And what is still more in point, every case I met with in ships or on shore, was far more rapid in its progress, than I have ever known consumption to be in New England.

Several other remedies have acquired great celebrity, in every stage of consumption, as digitalis, the fumes of pitch inhaled, and a new medicine called Hydrocyanic Acid. The first and last of these are in certain cases worthy of a trial, but as it would be difficult, in a book like this, to make intelligible those particular cases, and all those circumstances to be regarded in the use of said remedies, I must recommend to the patient to consult a physician before he makes a trial of them.

If spitting of blood from the lungs occur at an early period, there is with it a tendency to inflammation.—

This must be prevented by measures of the most active kind. If the constitution do not positively forbid it, general bleeding should be employed, especially if the pulse be quick, although the patient may be feeble since the weakness induced by spitting blood is not occasioned by the quantity that is lost.   Blistering should then be employed; the patient should be confined to a mild diet and quietude, and should avoid speaking, coughing, &c.   The bowels are to be moved with cooling laxatives, as Glauber's or Epsom Salts, and the patient kept in a uniform temperature, of from sixty to sixty-five degrees, and take half a grain of Opium in the evening. After the above evacuations have been made, astringents and refrigerants will be proper; and when spitting of blood occurs in the latter stages of consumption, there are principally to be relied on.   The astringents are Elixir Vitriol and Alum ; the former in doses of twenty-five drops, in a gill of water, every three hours; the latter in doses of six grains. As a refrigerant, common salt is a very effectual remedy, and should be given when spitting of blood has commenced, in doses of two or three tea-spoonsful.

In the latter stages of consumption, nothing more can be done than to palliate distressing symptoms. For the cough, take Pectoral mixture and Opium Pills.

Diseases of Limbs and Large Joints ; or, Rheumatism.—There are two kinds :—*acute*, which is inflammatory, and of short duration ; and *chronic*, which is of long duration, and accompanied by debility.

Symptoms of Acute Rheumatism.— They commence with slight fever; very soon followed by an inflammation, sharp pain, and swelling in the neighborhood of one or more of the large joints, and this pain increases when the patient becomes warm in bed. It is variable, shifts from joint to joint, and leaves the part it occupied swollen, red, and tender to the touch. The joints most subject to this disease, are the hip, loins, back and shoulder. The pulse is full and hard, the tongue has a slight whiteness, the urine is high colored, the blood, when drawn from a vein, exhibits a light colored crust on its surface; costiveness prevails; and sometimes there is profuse sweating without relief.

Obstructed perspiration, occasioned by wearing wet clothes, lying in damp linen or damp rooms, or by being exposed to cold air, while heated by exercise. Sailors are particularly liable to this complaint, on account of their frequent calls upon deck in rainy weather, and sleeping in wet clothes. Often it attacks sailors on their approach from a warm to a cold climate.

Treatment.—This is to be commenced by bloodletting and purging; the quantity of blood to be taken from an adult may be between one and two pints, according to the strength of his constitution and the violence of the attack, and if the symptoms continue unabated, the operation may be repeated on the following day. As a cathartic, give a dose of Salts, or of Castor Oil, or Flowers of Sulphur and Cream of Tartar, half an ounce of each mixed with molasses. When the bowels have been moved, take Dover's Powders, fifteen grains every four hours, and drink freely of warm herb-tea and toast-water, or barley-water and gruel. Another remedy of great value in acute rheumatism, is Calomel and Opium, two grains of the former to half a grain of the latter, mixed and taken three or four times a day.

When fever has subsided and the pain is confined to one part, blisters will prove useful. Warm fomentations tend rather to aggravate the pain of acute rheumatism. The patient should subsist on a low diet, abstain from stimulating drinks, and preserve an open state of the bowels by occasionally repeating the purgatives before recommended.

When the inflammatory symptoms have subsided, the patient may return to a generous diet, and the use of wine and strengthening medicines.

In approaching a cold climate, the master of a vessel should attend to the clothing of his crew, and see that its warmth increases in proportion to the coldness of the weather; he should also prevent the men's sleeping on damp beds, or in wet apparel. If woolen shirts are best for sailors in all climates, they are more particularly so in approaching from a warm to a cold one.

Chronic Rheumatism —It may be either a consequence and termination of the acute rheumatism, or it may be independent of it. In the first case the parts which were affected with inflammation are left weak, stiff, in some instances swelled, and the pain, before moveable, is now usually confined to particular parts: sometimes however it still shifts from joint to joint, but is unattended by any inflammation or fever. When not the consequence of acute rheumatism, it is most commonly met with in people at the decline of life. The pains are felt in the large joints, which are increased upon motion, and relieved by artificial warmth; the part affected is pale and cold, even when the other parts of the body are warm.

Treatment. — This must differ from that which is recommended in acute rheumatism. General bleeding as well as much purging will be inadmissible. The part affected may be rubbed several times a day with volatile liniment, or with spirits of Camphor, and the part rolled in flannel. In long continued and obstinate rheumatic affections, leeches applied to the part will be serviceable, as also blisters kept constantly running. A valuable application to the part is a plaster of common pitch, spread as thick as a dollar on soft leather, and sprinkled over with Tartar

Emetic, five grains to a surface as large as the hand.

These local applications must be accompanied with such internal medicines as are best adabted to stimulate and warm the system and alleviate pain. Gum Guaiacum is one of the most powerful general stimulants and may be taken in doses of fifteen grains of the powder mixed with sugar, molasses, or gruel, every three hours. Or take the tincture of Guaiacum from two to four tea-spoonsful, in wine or gruel. Mustard and horse-radish may be used freely.

The diet should be rich and stimulating; flannel worn next to the skin: and exposure to cold night-air, wearing damp clothes, and wetting the feet should be carefully avoided.

To relieve pain and promote sleep, take Dover's Powders, fifteen grains on going to bed. Or a powder of Calomel, Ipecac: and Opium, of each one grain.

Measles.—Of the benign.—Cough; —hoarseness;—difficulty of breathing;—sneezing;—sense of weight in the head;—nausea or vomiting; —dullness of the eyes;—drowsiness; epiphora: itching of the face.

On the *fourth* day, small red points or papulæ appear, first on the face and afterwards successively on the lower part of the body. They are generally in clusters, do not rise into visible pimples, but by the touch are found to be a little prominent.

On the *fifth* or *sixth* day, the vivid red is changed to a brownish hue; and in a day or two more the eruption entirely disappears, with a mealy desquammation of the cuticle.

The febrile symptoms are not diminished upon the appearance of the eruption, but rather increase, and become attended with much anxiety and oppression, and symptoms of pneumonia. At the period of desquammation of the papulæ, a diarrhœa frequently comes on, and continues for some time.

Of the malignant.—This form of the disease is accompanied with typhus-fever, and the symptoms of putrescency, that are enumerated under the head of typhus. The eruption appears more early; and all the symptoms above described are in an aggravated form. The fauces often assume the same appearance as in cyanche maligna, probably from a combination of the two diseases.

Cause.—Specific contagion.

The symptoms which distinguish the eruptive fever of measles from variola and other diseases, are the dry cough and hoarseness;—the heaviness of the head and drowsiness;—sneezing;—the appearance of the eyes, which are red, swelled, itchy, very sensible to light, and frequently loaded with tears.

Of the Inflammatory.—To diminish the inflammatory action. To relieve urgent symptoms. The first thing to be attempted:—

1. By abstinence from animal food, and all things that increase blood and inflammation.

2. By placing the patient in a moderately cool atmosphere, the temperature of which should be regulated in a great measure by his own feelings, carefully guarding against any sudden change.

3. By the common diaphoretics and refrigerants; more especially the saline ones.

4. By the occasional exhibition of saline aperients

5. When the febrile symptoms run high, and more especially when symptoms of local inflammation are present, recourse must be had to general and local bleeding.

Practitioners differ much with respect to the time at which blood-letting may be employed with the most advantage. Dr. Morton thinks it requisite as soon as the eruption is completed. Sydenham recommends it after the eruption has disappeared, Dr Mead judiciously observes, that our practice in this respect should be regulated by the degree of the accompanying pneumonic symptoms, without attending to the particular period of the disorder, or the state of the eruption; and this is the generally approved practice in the present day.

Where the inflammatory symptoms become urgent, with much anxiety, pain, and oppression at the chest, general bleeding cannot be dispensed with, unless there be a septic tendency in the system. Topical bleeding, under less urgent symptoms may suffice.

6. By the application of blisters to the chest, in cases where the fever is violent, with delirium or pneumonic inflammation.

1. If the disease be accompanied by inflammation of the lungs, general and topical blood-letting must be enforced; with occasional purges and nauseating diaphoretics, as recommended for the cure of pneumonia.

2. Hoarseness, cough, and inflammation of the throat, will be palliated by barley-water, with gum Arabic; thin arrow-root; orgeat and water; the compound decoction of barley or capillaire and water, taken in very small quantities and frequently, not cold, but with the chill removed. The addition of a little nitre, or of a small quantity of lemon-juice, will render them more palatable.

Inhaling the steam of warm water is also useful.

Mild opiates are occasionally useful against these symptoms, after the febrile action is abated; but when given before, they neither procure rest, nor an abatement of the cough.

Take milk of almonds, five oz.; nitrate of potash, fifteen grains; syrup of white poppies, half oz. Mix. —Let the patient take a moderate spoonful when the cough is urgent.

An opiate, given at bed-time, should always be combined with a saline diaphoretic.

3. When diarrhœa does not take place towards the resolution of the disease, a calomel purge or two should be administered.

4. Where the diarrhœa is excessive, astringents and opium are necessary.

Take chalk mixture, six oz. Let the patient take two large spoonsful after each liquid stool.

Take aromatic confection, one scruple; chalk mixture, twelve drachms; powder of ipecacuanha one grain. Make a draught to be taken every four hours.

Take aromatic confection, one scruple; extract of logwood, ten grains; chalk mixture, twelve drachms. Make a draught to be taken every four hours.

To either of the above five drops of laudanum may be added.

Should the diarrhœa continue, and threaten great exhaustion, recourse must be had to the opiate confection, astringent clysters, and the more powerful astringent remedies recommended against diarrhœa.

5. If the symptoms manifest a tendency to a malignant form of disease, they must be accordingly, as directed in typhus.

Of the malignant.—The treatment of malignant measles is similar to that of typhus fever; it requires the exhibition of mineral acids, cinchona, and red port wine. Delirium, pneumonic symptoms, cough, &c., must be treated as before recommended.

When the eruption of measles disappears before the proper period, and convulsions, or great anxiety, or delirium, take place, the course will be to restore the eruption to the skin. To effect this, recourse must immediately be had to the warm bath, blisters to the chest and feet, the administration of warm dilute wine, camphor and æther, or antimony.

Take of antimonial powder, six grains; Make a powder to be taken every three or four or six hours.

Take nitrous æther, two drachms; water of acetite of ammonia, six drachms; of spearmint, five ounces; syrup of saffron, three drachms. Mix. Let the patient take two large spoonsful frequently.

Low Spirits.—Dyspepsia,—sense of heat and pain in the chest;—languor,—listlessness,—want of resolution and activity,—disposition to seriousness, sadness, and timidity as to future events; an apprehension of the worst, and most unhappy state of them, and therefore upon slight grounds a dread of great evil. Particular attention to health; and, upon any unusual feeling, a fear of emminent danger, and even death itself.—In respect to all these feelings and apprehensions, the most obstinate belief and persuasion.

Treatment.—1. To restore the energy of the brain and nervous system; and to obviate the morbid association of ideas, by which the disease is characterized.

2. To remove the dyspepsia and other concomitant symptoms.

The first indication can alone be accomplished by diverting the attention of the patient from his own feeling by change of scene;—engaging his attention by new and interesting objects; convival society; various amusements and rural sports; moderate and regular exercise;—gaining his confidence; condoling with him rather than ridiculing his foibles; and persuading him of a gradual recovery from his ideal illness, by some innocent medicaments regularly administered.

The second by:

1. The treatment laid down for the cure of dyspepsia.

2. Chalybeate mineral waters.

3. Tonics and antispasmodics; particularly Peruvian bark, assafœtida.

4. Warm and cold bathing.

5. The mineral waters recommended for dyspepsia.

6. Light nutritive diet; as common drink, wine and water, should be substituted for malt liquors.

The violent pain in the head and stomach, to which hypochondriacs are subject, may be relieved by æther, musk, and opium, separately or combined.

The Mumps.—This is a well known specific contagion peculiar to children; it commences with a slight inflammatory fever, pain in the head and ears, and swelling of the head and neck, or the parotid and maxillang glands appearing externally, at which time the patient experiences great dificulty in breathing and swallowing; sometimes a part of the inflammation extends to the breasts of the female and the testes of the male, and in the recessation, delirium will not unfrequently follow. The general treatment recommended in this disease is the same as in that of inflammatory sore throat, the same gargles and plasters are useful; if the disease occurs in cold weather, the head should be kept bound up with a linen bandage, moderately tight, with flannel next to the swollen parts; should violent fever or delirium take place, put blisters to the head, mustard plasters to the feet, and fomentations to the parts affected. The ordinary emetics are very beneficial in the early stages.

Madame Noufer's Cure for Tape worm.—Against the tæniæ or tape worm, most drastis purges have been resorted to. Madame Noufer's remedy is occasionally used with success. She directs as follows:

The day before the patient is to take the remedy, he is to avoid all aliment after dinner, till about seven or eight o'clock at night, when he is to take a soup made thus:

Take a pint and a half of water, two or three ounces of good fresh butter, and two ounces of bread cut in slices; add to this salt enough to season it, and then boil it over the fire to the consistence of panada.

About a quarter of an hour after this, she gives him a biscuit and a glass of white wine, either pure or mixed with water; she even gives water alone to those who have not been accustomed to wine. If the patient has not been to stool that day, or is naturally costive, (which is not usual, however, with patients in this way,) Madame Noufer directs the use of a clyster:

Take a handful of the leaves of mallows, and boil them in a sufficient quantity of water, mixing with it a little salt, and when strained off, add two ounces of oil.

Early the next morning, about eight or nine hours after the supper, the patient takes the following specific:

Take two or three drachms of the male fern, gathered in autumn, and reduced to a very fine powder, in four or six ounces of water distilled from fern, or the flowers of the lime-tree.

It will be right for the patient to drink two or three times of the same water, rinsing his glass with it, so that none of the powder may remain either in the glass or his mouth, in bed; and to avoid the nausea which this medicine sometimes occasions, it will be right for him to chew lemon, or something else that is agreeable to him, or he may wash his mouth with any thing he likes, but he must be careful not to swallow any thing. He may likewise smell vinegar, to check the sickness; but if, notwithstanding all his efforts, the nausea continues, and he is obliged to throw up the specific, it will be right for him to take a fresh dose of it as soon as the sickness is gone off, and then he should try to go to sleep. About two hours after this he must get up, and take a purging bolus.

Take of the panacea of mercury fourteen times sublimed, and select resin of scammony, each ten grains; of fresh and good gamboge six or seven grains; reduce each of these substances separately into a powder, and mix them with some conserve into a bolus.

This is to be taken at one or two different times, washing it down with one or two dishes of weak green tea, the patient walking afterwards about his chamber.

When the bolus begins to operate, the patient is desired to take a dish of the same tea occasionally, until the worm is expelled; then, and not before, Madame Noufer gives him broth or soup, and he is directed to dine as is usual after taking physic. After dinner he may either lie down or walk out, taking care to conduct himself discreetly, to eat little supper, and to avoid every thing that is not of easy digestion.

Nettle Rash.—An eruption resembling that produced by the stinging of nettles; whence its name.—These little elevations often appear instantaneously, especially if the skin be rubbed or scratched, and seldom stay many hours, sometimes not many minutes, in the same place; but vanish, and again make their appearance in another part of the skin.—The parts affected with the eruption are often considerably swelled.—In some persons they last a few days only, in others many months, appearing and disappearing at intervals.—Long weals sometimes are observed, as if the part had been struck with a whip.—The little eminences always appear solid, not having any cavity, or head containing either water, or any other liquor. Intolerable itching is their invariable concomitant. They generally disappear in the day time, and in the evening again break forth, accompanied with slight symptoms of fever. They terminate in a desquammation of the cuticle.

Cause—Mechanical irritation.

Treatment.—Use frequent cooling purges; small doses of calomel; sudorifics; light diet.

Menorrhagia, or Immoderate flow of the Menses. — A flow of the menses is to be considered as immoderate, when it either returns more frequently than what is natural, continues longer than ordinary, or is more abundant than is usual with the same person at other times.

It may be the effect of two different and opposite states of the system; plethora with inordinate arterial vigour; and general relaxation or debility.

Symptoms.—An immoderate flow of the menses, arising from plethora is usually preceded by rigors, acute pains in the head and loins, thirst, turgid flushed countenance, universal heat, and a strong, hard pulse; on the contrary, where the symptoms of debility are prevalent in the system, the pulse is small and feeble, the face pallid, the respiration small and hurried on the slightest effort; the general appearance of the patient indicates a laxity of every muscular fibre; the pains of the back and loins are rather aching than acute.

The causes which predispose to the disease are plethora;—a laxity or debility of the organ, arising from frequent child-bearing;—difficult and tedious labors, or repeated miscarriages;—a sedentary and inactive life, indulging much in grief and despondency;—living upon a poor low diet;—drinking freely of warm enervating liquors, such as tea and coffee; and living in warm chambers.

The exciting causes of menorrhagia are, violent exercise, more especially in dancing; strokes or concussions on the belly; strains;—passions of the mind: violent straining at stool; excess in venery, particularly during menstruation; the pplication of wet and cold to the feet; organic affections of the uterus, such as scirrhus, polypus, &c.

Menorrhagia, when it is the effect of plethora, rarely proves fatal; but when it occurs in habits much reduced by previous disease, or is produced by a laxity of the vessels of the organ, is profuse, long-continued, or of frequent recurrence; if the lips, nails, and other parts, be pale; if the extremities become cold, and with these symptoms the patient fall into syncope, especially if there be any convulsions of the limbs, the danger is very great. When it arises from an organic affection of the part, which is frequently the case after the age of forty-five, it is usually incurable.

The cure of menorrhagia consists in :—

1. Strictly confining the patient to an horizontal posture; especially avoiding every exertion both of body and mind.

2. Keeping the body gently open with laxative medicines that have but little stimulus.

Take tartrite of potash, half oz. best manna, six drachms; boiling water, six oz.; compound tincture of lavender, half oz. Make a mixture, of which let the patient take three spoonsful when necessary.

Take sulphate of magnesia, three drachms; cold water, ten oz. Make an injection.

3. Administering draughts of acidulated cold liquors frequently, as infusion of roses, lemonade, and the like.

4. The internal use of styptics, especially cerussa accetata, as directed against hæmoptysis.

5. When symptoms of debility are present, tonics astringents: cinchona, cascarilla, kino, quercus, and wine.

6. The constant application of astringents to the vagina and hypogastric region; especially ice, very cold water, vinegar and water.

Nervous Fever; or Slow Fever.—It commences slowly and imperceptibly, with general languor, dejection of mind—loss of appetite—alternate chills and flushes—dulness and confusion of thought. In a day or two there is a giddiness and pain in the head, with aching pains over the whole body—nausea; frequent, weak, and often intermitting pulse. At first the tongue is moist, but afterwards becomes dry, brown and tremulous; there is little thirst, and the urine is pale and watery. As the disease advances, the heat and other symptoms of inflammation increase, the urine becomes high colored; sometimes, diarrhœa and immoderate sweating ensue; there is a low, muttering delirium, a starting and twitching of the tendons; sometimes a coldness of the extremities, convulsions and death.

Causes.—Weak and delicate habit of body; poor living; warmth of climate; depressing passions of the mind, as grief, fear, anxiety; excessive venery; intemperance.

It may be known from putrid or malignant fever, by the attack being more gradual and the symptoms milder: from inflammatory fever, by the smallness and weakness of the pulse, and by its more mild accession.

About the 7th, 14th, or 21st day from the attack, the disease usually abates, and the patient from that time slowly recovers.

Treatment.—Commence this by cleansing the stomach and bowels with a mild emetic and cathartic combined as follows:

Take Ipecac, thirty grains, and Calomel five; mix them and give the dose in any convenient vehicle. If this fail to move the bowels once or twice take some other mild purgative, and repeat it as often as there is the least tendency to costiveness.

If the disease be not arrested by this treatment within the first three days, apply blisters to the legs, and poultices to the soles of the feet. If after this there be much stupor, shave and blister head.

The patient may take wine in sago, barley-water, or gruel. He may also take chicken-broth, beef-tea, or other light animal food, but in such quantities only as his stomach craves, and as will be likely to agree with him.

The pulp of an orange, or roasted apples, will be both cooling and agreeable to the stomach.

For common drink, he may take toast-water, lemonade, wine and water, cider, or soda water.

One of the best remedies in the early stage of the disease, after the stomach and bowels have been moved by medicine, is *cold affusions.* The cold water should be dashed on from a pitcher or bucket, wherever the heat of the skin is above the natural standard. If this heat however be confined to particular parts of the body, the cold water may be applied to them alone, with a sponge or wet cloth.

L

The Guinea Mixture has also been found a very good agent for the cure of this fever.

The patient should be kept as quiet as possible, and with a view to promote perspiration and induce sleep, may take every evening a Dover's powder, and have warm poultices renewed to his feet.

During the day time, administer the following drops:—Take spirits of nitre and antimonial wine equal parts, mix them, and give two teaspoonsful every three hours, in toast-water.

Night Mare, or Frightful Dreams.—Although this affection is not noticed in the medical books, it is nevertheless a most distressing malady, which requires medical treatment. A person subject to night mare should be restricted to a very light digestable diet, such as mutton, chicken, &c.; keep the body well open, and eat no gross food or rich pies; eat a very light and early supper, should take plenty of exercise, avoid the reading of or discussion of any horrid or affecting subjects or stories, and should on going to bed keep the neck, chest and limbs entirely free from any legature bandage, or pressure, and on the morning after an attack of night mare, should take a dose of Epsom salts.

Night Sweats.—These are the consequence of some debility of the system, or decline of constitution; they are very prostrating to the powers.—If they do not proceed from decline or consumption, plentiful draughts of cold chamomile tea will cure them, with generous and nourising diet.

Neuralgia Tic-dobureux, or pains in the nerves of the face, head, &c.—This complaint is tolerably well known by peculiar violent and changing pains, which dart from one part to another, accompanied sometimes by a twitching of the muscles; the patient for a time suffers extreme agony. If the affection is in the head, it not unfrequently causes a transcient delirium; the parts are excessively painful from the slightest touch and the patient can scarcely apply his finger or hand near the situation of the pain.

Treatment.—If the pain is situated in the face, attended by more or less swelling, and the patient has any teeth in a far state of decay, the immediate extraction of the teeth will most probably effect a cure; if the teeth be not affected, apply a blister to the cheek: or bind the face up in a flannel, well soaked in sweet oil and laudanum; a leaf of tobacco dipped in water and bound to the part for a short time, has effected a cure; if in the head, leeches and blisters should be used; although cold saline applications have been tried with advantage. Neuralgia is a most obstinate and painful malady, and Mr. Dupie of the French Medical College, has been more fortunate than any other physician in effecting a permanent cure; his principal remedy is as follows:—Take 8 grains of sulphate of Quinine, 2 ounces of Syrup of Rhubarb, 2½ ounces of water of orange flower, and 10 drops of sulpheric Ether.

To relieve the pain from 30 to 80 drops of laudanum may be taken.

On Clysters or Injections.—How to be Administered.—These may be administered with a pipe or tube, inserted into the neck of a bladder. The fluid to be injected being introduced into the bladder, through an opening made in the side, which is to be tied up with a piece of twine, the pipe is to be well oiled, when the patient himself may introduce it into the fundament. He should then hold his breath, while the bladder is gradually pressed from the top to the tube, till all the liquid is injected.

Opening a Tumour, or Abscess.—The opening should be made in the most prominent part, and if it be on a limb, the incision is to be made lengthwise, and not across the limb. The part should be covered with plaster to exclude air.

Pleurisy.—The proper Pleurisy we have noticed under the head of Inflammation of the Lungs, &c. there is a well known complaint which improperly bears the name of Pleurisy, which commences with painful darts or stitches in the side, frequently below the ribs, and often attended with fever; when the latter is the case, immediate bleeding, leeching, the mustard poultice, or a blister, are efficacious. This stitch in the side is frequently occasioned by a portion of wind being confined about that red region, and a patient fancies he has a pleurisy; a dose of castor oil, and a rubbing of the part with a coarse towel, or with spirits of hartshorn and sweet oil, have very frequently cured this.

This description of pleurisy, if pleurisy it may be termed, is very common in cities, in the months of March and November; at which season persons of delicate habit should wear the real flannel about the chest, and avoid exposure to dampness.

Rupture, or Hernia.—This is a portrusion or falling of the intestines or bowels, into the groin, scrotum, and adjoining parts—it is caused by straining, violent exercise, lifting heavy weights, blows in the parts, running, jumping, &c.

When a rupture is produced by bodily exertion, the tumour is formed suddenly, and is generally attended with a sensation of something giving way at the part, and with considerable pain.

Treatment.—Reduce the tumour immediately by the hand; for this purpose the patient should be placed on his back, and the foot of the bed be elevated about twenty inches higher than the head, the thighs should be bent toward the body, and that on the same side with the rupture, inclined inwards. The pressure, which is made on the tumour by the hand of the operator for its reduction should always be directed upwards and outwards for inguinal hernia, and first backwards and then upwards in femoral hernia. If the tumor be not sooner removed, the pressure may be continued half an hour, but no violence is to be used, as it will tend greatly to aggravate the inflammation, and the pressure, when it becomes painful, should for the same reason be discontinued.—Should these efforts fail of success, the patient must be bled, and then another trial be made, and on failure of this also, use the warm bath, and repeat the effort while the patient lies in the water. The next remedies to be employed are the coldest applications to the tumour, as æther or pounded ice, and where these cannot be obtained, a mixture of equal parts of Nitre and Sal Ammoniac, in the proportion of half a pound of the mixture to a pint of water, should be tried by a constant application of it to the tumour. Finally, try an injection of tobacco made by boiling one drachm of tobacco in a pint of water for ten minutes. When all these means fail, if a surgeon can be had competent to perform the operation for strangulated hernia, he should be called, and always within the first twenty-four hours.

With a view of guarding against the dreadful consequences of a strangulated hernia, a ruptured person should immediately procure a well adapted eclastic-spring truss, and wear it night and day, without intermission. These very essential articles can be purchased of any respectable apothecary.

The Painter's Colic.—Pains and spasms in the belly and intestines; eructations or belching, frequent inclinations to go to stool, &c. It very frequently terminates in a palsy in the wrists and extremities, or other parts of the body.

Castor oil in repeated doses is often effectual, in producing stools. Mercury united with opium is very beneficial by exciting salivation. Rub the belly with brandy and Camphor mixed, and relieve the pain by doses of Laudanum of from 40 to 80 drops. Bleeding is recommended in violent stages if the patient is of a full habit. (Blister or Mustard plasters have also proved efficacious.)

The following Prescriptions are recommended by Dr. Hooper.

1st. Take of Calomel, half of a grain; Prepared Sulphurate of Antimony half grain: conserve of roses, five grains; make a pill to be taken three times a day.

2nd. Take sulphate of alum and potash, one half scruple; infusion of roses, twelve drachms; syrup of roses, one drachm. Make a draught to be taken three times a day.

How to prevent the Diseases which arise from the use of lead in certain Trades.—The treatment is extremely simple, requiring the workmen to submit to the following precautions: They are to take two baths of soap and water every week, occasionally adding a little sulphur, and are carefully to wash the uncovered parts of the body with soap and water at every interval between their working hours. They are to drink one or two glasses of lemonade, made with sulphuric acid, every day, according to the greater or lesser quantity of dust, or poisonous vapor with which the surrounding atmosphere may be charged. At the same time they should be more careful than the followers of any other trade to abstain from the use of spirituous liquors. the efficacy of this preventive treatment is easily explained by the fact, that the mineral poison absorbed, is thus converted into a soluble, and therefore, innoxious salts (sulphate of lead,) and the saturnine particles deposited on the surface of the body are taken away.

Scrofula, or King's Evil.—Swelling of the glands of the neck, which after a period break and discharge a white creamy curd, sometimes it manifests itself in the swelling of the eye lids; or in its aggravated form extends all over the system, the throat becomes swollen, the joints become weak and painful, attended with swelling, great emaciation finally takes place, the bones, and the ligaments assume a deadness, and the patient wastes away in death.

Persons of light and smooth skin, of peculiar fullness and rosy appearance of the face, large light eyes and complexions are most apt to be affected with this obstinate disease. The cause may be said to exist in hereditary predispostion, residence in cold climates, bad water, indigestible food, living in low and damp situations, &c. The best remedies are sugar in large quantities, seabathing, residence by the sea side.

The inhalation of oxygen gas, the tincture, or solution of Iodine given 3 times a day and perservered in for a long period. Tonics, especially Peruvian barks, Antimonials, with decoctions of Guarcacum, Sarsaparilla, Sassafras, &c. A strong decoction of the dried leaves of the tusselago, burnt Sponge, light nutritive diet, pure dry air, friction, and moderate exercise.

Small-Pox; or Variola. — The small-pox is distinguished into two species; the *distinct* and *confluent*; implying that in the former the pustules are perfectly distinct and separate from each other, and that in the latter they coalesce, and the eruption is continuous.

Symptoms and Progress of the Distinct Small-Pox.

The eruption of the *variola discreta* or distinct small-pox, is ushered in by a fever of the inflammatory type, characterized by considerable pains in the back and loins, nausea, vomiting, pain in the epigastrium upon pressure, disposition to drowsiness, and in infants often one or more epileptic fits.

Towards the end of the *third* day from its commencement, the eruption makes its appearance on the *face* and *hairy scalp*, in the form of small red points not dissimilar to flea-bites.

During the *fourth*, it extends itself successively to the neck, breast, upper extremities, and at length occupies the whole body.

About the *fifth*, a little vesicle, appearing depressed in the middle, containing a colourless fluid, and surrounded by an inflamed areola or margin, perfectly circular, may be observed on the top of each little point or pustule.—The eruptive fever now disappears.

About the *sixth*, the saliva becomes increased in quantity, and viscid; at the same time that there is a degree of swelling of the throat, difficulty of deglutition, and hoarseness.

On the *eighth* day, the pustules are completely formed and spherical, prominent and appearing almost terminated in a point; and the contained matter has assumed the appearance of pus.—The face swells, and the swelling extending to the eyelids, these often become so much enlarged as to close the eyes.

About the *eleventh*, the pustules have gained their full size (which differs in different epidemics, but is generally that of a pea), the matter has changed from a white to an opake yellow, and a dark spot appears on each.—At this time the tumefaction of the face subsides, and the hands and feet begin to swell.—The secondary fever now also, usually makes its appearance.

After the *eleventh day*, the pustules from being smooth become rough, break, and discharge their contents; which drying on the surface, a small crust is formed over each of them. These in a short time fall off, and leave the part they covered of a dark brown colour, which often remains for many days; and in cases where the pustules have been large, or late in becoming dry, deep indentations of the skin. The swelling of the hands and feet gradually subsides, and about the seventeenth day the secondary fever disappears.

Symptoms and Progress of the Confluent Small-Pox.

Both in its symptoms and progress, the confluent kind differs materially from the distinct or benign. The eruptive fever often early shews a tendency to the typhoid form; and besides possessing the characteristic symptoms above mentioned, which are usually present in a more marked degree, it is frequently attended with coma or delirium; in infants with diarrhoea; in adults, salivation.

The eruption is irregular in its appearance, and in the succession of its stages. It is usually preceded by an erythematic efflorescence upon the face, from which the pustules emerge on the *second day* in the form of small red points; many of which soon coalesse and form clusters greatly resembling the measles. Maturation is more early; but the pustules do not retain their circular form, are of an irregular shape, often flattened, and appear like thin pellicles fixed upon the skin, instead of true pus, containing a brownish ichor; nor are they surrounded by an inflamed margin, the intermediate spaces between the clusters appearing pale and flaccid.—The swelling of the face and salvation appear earlier, and rise to a much greater height, than in the distinct form of the disease.—The fever, though it generally suffers a light remission, does not cease upon the appearance of the eruption, and in some instances all the worst symptoms of typhus supervene; the eruption assumes a livid hue, petchiae and passive haemorrhages make their appearance, and the patient is often carried off on the eleventh day from the commencement of the disease.

TREATMENT.—*Of the Distinct.*— Indications—To moderate the fever when violent.

To support the strength, when deficient.

To obviate all those circumstances that may produce any irregularity in the appearance, or in the progress, of the disease.

In cases of violent action, in full and plethoric habits, bleeding has been resorted to, and is recommended by many; but it is a practice mostly replete with danger, and to be avoided, if possible; for the subsequent debility generally overbalances the temporary advantage that may be gained by this remedy.

Purging is often successful in diminishing the violence of febrile action, without inducing much weakness.

An emetic has been given with advantage at the accession of the disease, except in cases where there is much pain of the stomach.

During the eruptive fever, when this is pure synocha, the febrile symptoms, if considerable, are to be moderated by exposing the body of the patient to a cool atmostphere, by frequently administering cold diluent' fluids, as lemonade, imperial saline draughts, nitre; at the same time administering saline aperients, so as to keep the bowels loose.

If there be great irritability and restlessness, opium in small quantities with a saline draught, will be serviceable, or with a small quantity of antimony.

Take powdered opium half grain Submuriate of mercury half grain Antimonial powder three grains; Make a powder, to be taken every eight hours in a little honey.

Small doses of mercury are often serviceable in moderating the febrile action of variola, even when exhibited so as slightly to affect the gums; no inconvenience is likely therefore to arise from the administration of the above,

If the febrile symptoms indicate a tendency to typhus, the mode of treatment recommended for typhus fever should be resorted to.

When the eyelids swell much, and are inflamed, a blister may be applied behind the ears, or a leech to the temples.

If the throat be much affected, and there is difficulty in swallowing a blister is to be applied to the neck, and gargles of infusion of roses directed.

As debility comes on, recourse must be had to cinchona, wine, and nourishment not so antiphlogistic as in the commencement.

Determination to the head or chest, or other viscera, requires blisters, or mustard poultices to the feet.

Obstinate vomiting, which in this disease often proves both a troublesome and dangerous symptom, is most effectually allayed by saline remedies, in the act of effervescence, with opium.

Take carbonate of potash, one scruple; camphorated mixture, ten drachms; Tincture of opium, four drops; syrup of orange peel, one drachm; make a draught to be taken every four hours, in the act of effervescence, with a large spoonful of lemon juice.

Take camphor, six grains; pulverized opium, half grain; Spanish soap, six grains; make two pills, to be taken every six hours.

In all cases where there is a great propensity to sweating after the eruptive fever has passed by, a cool regimen will be particularly necessary.

Diarrhoea is to be checked only when it is excessive and increases debility.

When the eruption suddenly recedes, or the pocks sink and become very much dimpled and any alarming symptoms supervene as rigors, convulsions, or delirium, recourse must be had to wine, opiates, aether, camphor or musk, blisters and sinapisms.

The general conclusions drawn by Dr. Ritzins, of Stockholm, from his observations of small-pox and the effects of vaccination in Sweden are these:—The protection afforded by vaccination, from the close of the second year of life, against the contagion of the variolous points, usually lasts unimpaired to the end of the thirteenth year or so; after this period it begins to lose its effect, and gradually becomes more and more uncertain to the twentieth or twenty-first year of life. For the next four or five years, the disposition to the small-pox seems almost to have recovered its original integrity; and this state of liability continues unimpaired up to the age of forty years or so. At about this epoch of life it begins to approach nearer and nearer to the limit of its existence—Which it reaches, in the majority of cases, about the fiftieth year—the period when the general revolution of the human body commences to take place."

Tympany or Windy Distention of The Belly.—The wind may collect within the intestines; or without them, in the cavity of the abdomen. In either case the belly, usually in a few hours, becomes greatly distended, tense and elastic, like a drumhead. Sometimes the swelling is gradual in its progress and preceded by rumbling of the bowels. There is diminished appetite, thirst and emaciation. Unless the constitution be much impaired, the disease is generally curable.

Treatment.—The objects are, 1. To evacuate the air; and 2. To prevent its re-accumulation.

The first object is gained by heating medicines, as Ether, Aniseseed, Peppermints, Cayenne Pepper. Ginger, Nutmeg, &c. and by Opium;—thus,

Paregoric, two tea-spoonfuls, Essence of Peppermint twenty drops, Powder of Ginger, half a tea-spoonful, mix in sugar and take every three hours; Or, Powder of Rhubarb and Ginger, of each five grains, Nutmeg, two grains; Opium half a grain, mixed, to be taken every three hours.

To prevent the re-accumulation of air, after it has been once discharged use tonics, as Decoction of Bark, and avoid all food apt to produce wind.

Varicella, or The Chicken-Pox. symptoms After slight symptoms of fever, as lassitude, loss of sleep, wandering pains, loss of appetite, &c. an eruption appears; first on the back, consisting of small reddish pimples, much resembling the first appearance of the small-pox.—On the *second* day the red pimples have become small vesicles, containing a colourless fluid; and sometimes a yellowish transparent liquor.—On the *third*, the pustules arrive at their full maturity, and, in some instances, very much resemble the genuine small-pox.— Soon after, the fluid becomes extravasated by spontaneous, or accidental, rupture of the tender vesecle, and a thin scab is formed at the top of the pock; without pus ever being formed, as in the true variola.—Generally before the *fifth* day the whole eruption disappears, and no cicatrix or mark is left behind.

Aphtha ; or, *The Thrush.*—*Symptoms.*—The mouth becomes redder than usual ;—the tongue swelled and rough ;—small white scars or pustules invade the uvula fauces, palate, tonsils, the inside of the cheeks, the gums, and lips.—They generally commence at the uvula : are sometimes few and distinct, at others numerous and confluent ; sending forth a glutinous mucus, which forms a thick whitish crust, adhering most tenaciously, and which falls off when the pustules have arrived at maturity without inducing an escar on the parts beneath.—The disease sometimes extends to the œsophagus, stomach, and throughout the whole alimentary canal ; when mucus is evacuated, in large quantities, by stool and vomiting ;—at others, to the tracher and bronchiæ, when it is brought up by coughing :—aphthæ sometimes fall off in the space of ten or twelve hours, at others they remain attached for several days, and often a separation and reproduction takes place a great number of times before the final solution of the disease.

CAUSES.—*predisposing.*—Cold and moisture ; debility.

Exciting.—Most frequently a derangement of the intestinal canal.

PROGNOSIS.—*Favourable.*—The aphthæ appearing of a white, pearly colour ; falling off early, and leaving the parts they occupied clean, red, and moist.—Salivation, or moderate diarrhœa, at the period of separation.—When the disease is long protracted, repeated crops are more favourable than the permanence of the original.

Unfavourable.—Then the disease affecting internal parts ; producing violent hiccup, oppression, pain referred to the stomach, vomiting, and sense of suffocation ;—the aphthæ being, from the first, of a brown color, or becoming so in the course of the disease ;—their sudden disappearance ;—the mouth and fauces unusually pallid previous to the eruption ; violent diarrhœa ; coma ; very great prostration of strength ;—any of the symptoms of putridity, accompany cynanche maligna.

TREATMENT.—*Indications.*—1. To remove or moderate the concomitant fever.

11. To produce a separation of the aphthæ,

The first indication must be fulfilled,

By the means laid down for the treatment of synocha, typhus fever, and cynanche maligna.

The second—

1. By emetics, when other means are resisted.

2. Gentle laxatives, as manna, rhubarb, and castor-oil.

Take best manna half ounce ; Aniseed water, one ounce—dissolve. Let the child take a pap-spoonful frequently.

Take oil of almonds, five drachms ; syrup of roses, ten drachms,—mix. Give a teaspoonful when necessary.

Take best manna, six drachms ; powder of rhubarb, half drachm ; infusion of senna, nine drachms; mix. The dose is a pap-spoonful.

3. Copious emollient clysters.

Take oatmeal gruel, three ounces ; olive oil, half ounce—mix. For an injection, to be administered every eight hours.

Veal broth also, with turnips radishes boiled in it.

4. By tonic and stimulant gargles.

Take decoction of cinchona, two ounces ; sulphuric acid diluted, half drachm ; make a gargle.

Take decoction of oak bark, two ounces ; Gum Arabic in powder, one drachm ; Borate of soda, one drachm ; make a gargle.

St. Vitus Dance.—*Symptoms.*—The disease is marked by convulsive motions, somewhat varied in different persons, but generally affecting the leg and arm of one side only.— The lower extremity is mostly first affected ;—there is a kind of lameness and imbecility in one of the legs; and, though the limb be at rest, the foot is often agitated by involuntary motions, turning it alternately outwards and inwards.— In walking, the affected leg is seldom lifted as usual, but dragged along, as if the whole limb were paralytic; and when it is attempted to be lifted, that motion is unsteadily performed, the limb becoming irregularly and ludicrously agitated.—The motions of the arm likewise are variously performed, or it is drawn by convulsive retractions in a direction contrary to that intended.

Cause.—General weakness and irritability of the nervous system; occurring between the tenth and fifteenth years of age.—It is induced by various irritations; as teething, worms, offensive smells, poisons, affections of the mind, fright, horror, anger.

Prognosis.—It is never attended, with danger, unless very violent in degree, when fever supervenes, and it often kills; it passes not unfrequently into epilepsy.

Treatment.—To increase the tone of the muscular system.

After the administration of an emetic and mild aperient,

Tonics; especially zincum vitriolatum,—cuprum ammoniatum,—argentum nitratum, as recommended against epilepsy.

Cold bathing, and electricity.

Terror has sometimes effected a cure.

The antispasmodics, and other remedies enumerated under the head Epilepsy.

Worm Colic.—Worms mostly produce symptoms of colic, and very frequently other symptoms; as variable appetite;—fœtid breath;—picking of the nose;—hardness and fulness of the belly; sensation of heat and itching in the anus; preternaturally red tongue, or alternately clean and covered with a white slimy mucus;—grinding of the teeth during sleep;—short dry cough; frequent slimy stools;—emaciation;—slow fever

with an exacerbation;—irregular pulse;—sometimes convulsion fits.

Worms appear more frequently in those of a relaxed habit;—those whose bowels contain a preternatural quantity of mucus or slimy matter;—in those who live on vegetable food;—in the dyspeptic;—the eating of unripe fruit is a frequent cause of their production.

It may be distinguished from ordinary colic, by the peculiar twisting pain, and retraction of the navel:—by the absence of fever, in the early part of the disease.—by the pain in enteritis being increased, in colic alleviated, by pressure;—by the irregular contraction of the abdominal muscles.

The same characteristic symptoms distinguish it from inflammation of other abdominal viscera.

Symptoms.—Favorable.—The pain remitting or changing its situation;—discharges of wind and fæces, followed by an abatement of symptoms.

Unfavourable.—Violent fixed pain; obstinate costiveness; sudden cessation of the pain, followed by more frequent hiccup, great watchfulness, delirium, syncope, cold sweats, weak tremulous pulse; the pulse becoming peculiarly hard; see *Enteritis*; and the pain before relieved, now much increased, upon pressure;—volvulus:—all the symptoms indicating supervening inflammation and mortification, from the accession of which the chief danger arises.

Treatment.—Indications.—1. To relax the spasm.—

2. To remove the causes, and procure evacuations.

The first indication requires,

1 Bleeding, if the concomitant strength of constitution and fulness of vessels, with strong pulse, are present; but it is seldom neccessary.

2. Carminatives and antispasmodics; opium in large doses, cordial and opiate confection, cardamoms, &c.

Take Aromatic confection, one and half drachms; Rhubarb in powder eighteen grains; peppermint water, twelve drachms.

Tincture of cardamon one and a half drachms;

Syrup of ginger one drachm;

Make a draught.

Take Compound tincture of cardamon three ounces;

Tincture of opium drops twenty;

Syrup of saffron one drachm;

Peppermint water twelve drachms;

Make a draught.

Take Opiate confection one half scruple;

Essential oil of caraway drops two;

Powder of rhubarb sufficient quant.;

Make a bolus.

3. Warm bath and fomentations to the abdomen.

4. Blisters, and warm plasters.

5. Opiate clysters.

6. If there be great irritation of the stomach, with frequent vomiting, the saline medicine in an effervescing state.

7. Colic from the presence of flatus, or wind, is often relieved by some aromatic cordial, or a small portion of brandy.

Evacuations must be produced,

1. By cathartics;—at first by the more mild; as rhubard, magnesia, natrom vitriolatum, castor oil: if these prove ineffectual, calomel united with extractum colocynthidis compositum, especially where there has been bilious vomiting.

A GLOSSARY,

OR

EXPLANATION OF TERMS.

Adynamiæ. A defect of vital power. The second order of the class Neuroses.

Alteratives Medicines which reestablish health without producing any sensible evacuation.

Anasarca. Dropsy of the cellular membrane.

Anomalous. A disease whose symptoms do not appear with regularity; and also a disease with such varied symptoms as not to come under the description of any known affection.

Antiphlogistic. Medicines or diet which oppose inflammation.

Antisceptics. Medicines which prevent and stop the progress of putrefaction.

Antispasmodics. Medicines which allay spasmodic affections.

Aperients. Medicines which gently open the bowels.

Aphthæ. The thrush.

Apoplexia. Apoplexy.

Apyrexia. Without fever.

Ascaris. A genus of intestinal worms.

Ascites. Dropsy of the belly.

Asthma. To breathe with difficulty. A disease so called.

Cachexia. A bad habit of body. Cachexiæ is the name of the third class of diseases in Cullen's nosology.

Carminatives. A term given to those substances which allay pain and dispel flatulency in the primæ viæ.

Catarrhus. A catarrh, or cold.

Cathartics. Medicines which increase the number of alvine evacuations.

Chlorosis. The green sickness.

Cholera. A disease that consists in a purging and vomiting of bile.

Chorea Sancti Viti. St. Vitus's dance, so called from some devotees of St. Vitus having exercised themselves so long in dancing that their intellects were disordered, and could only be restored by dancing again at the anniversary of St. Vitus.

Colica. The colic.

Coma. A propensity to sleep.

Comata. The first order of the class Neuroses.

Coryza. An increased discharge of mucus from the nose.

Crisis. The sudden change of symptoms in acute febrile diseases indicating recovery or death.

Cynanche. Sore throat.

Cystitis. Inflammation of the bladder.

Diabetes. An immoderate flow of urine.

Diagnosis.. The discrimination of diseases.

Diaphoretics. Medicines which promote perspiration.

Diarrhœa. A purging.

Diluents. Remedies which dilute the blood.

Dysenteria. Flux.

Dyspepsia. Bad digestion.

Emetics. Medicines which excite vomiting.

Emmenagogues. Those medicines which promote the discharge of blood from the uterus.

Emollients. Substances which relax the living animal fibre, without producing that effect from any mechanical action.

Emphysema. Air in the cellular membrane.

Emprosthotonos. A clonic spasm, in which the body is drawn forward.

Empyema. A collection of pus in the cavity of the thorax.

Enteritis. Inflammation of the intestines.

Epidemic. A contagious disease is so termed from its attacking many people at the same season and in the same place.

Epilepsia. So called from the suddenness of its attack. Epilepsy.

Epiphora. Involuntary flow of tears.

Epistaxis. Hœmorrhage from the nose.

Errhines. Those medicines, which, when topically applied to the internal membrane of the nose, excite sneezing, and increase secretion, independent of any mechanical irritation.

Erysipelas. St. Anthony's fire.

Exacerbation. An increase of febrile symptome.

Exciting cause. That which, when applied to the body under a state of predisposition, excites a disease.

Exanthemata. The third order of he class Pyrexiæ.

Expectorants. Medicines which increase the discharge of mucus from the lungs.

Gangrene. A mortification.

Gastritis. Inflammation of the stomach.

Hæmorrhagiæ. The fourth order of the class Pyrexiæ.

Hæmoptysis. A spitting of blood.

Hæmatemesis. A vomiting of blood.

Hæmaturia. Bloody urine.

Hepatitis. Inflammation of the liver

Hydrocephalus. Water in the head.

Hydrophobia. Canine madness.

Hydrothorax Dropsy of the chest.

Hypochondriasis. Hypochondriac affections; lowness of spirits

Hysteria. Hysterics.

Icterodes. A species of typhus is so called from the resemblance of the skin to that of jaundice.

Icterus. The Jaundice.

Ileus. The iliac passion; an affection of the small intestines.

Impetigines. The third order in the class Cachexiæ of Cullen.

Indication. That which demonstrates in a disease what ought to be done.

Influenza. An infectious catarrh.

Intumescentiæ. Swellings. The second order of the class Cachexiæ.

Lumbricus. From its slipperiness.

Mania. Raving or furious madness.

Marcores. Universal emaciation. An order in the class Cachexiæ.

Melancholia. Melancholy madness.

Menorrhagia. An immoderate flow of the menses.

Miliaria. Milliary fever.

Narcotics. Medicines which ease pain and procure sleep.

Nephritis. Inflammation of the kidney.

Neuroses. Nervous disease. The second class of Cullen's nosology.

Opithotonos. A tonic spasm of the muscles, in which the body is drawn backwards.

Paralysis The palsy.

Paroxysm. A perodical exacerbation or fit of a disease.

Pathognomic. A term given to those symptoms which are peculiar to a disease.

Pediluvium. A bath for the feet.

Pemphigus. a pubble.

Peripneumonia. Inflammation of the lumgs.

Pertussis. The hooping-cough.

Petechiæ. A flea bite.

Phlegmasiæ Inflammations. The second order in the class Pyrexiæ.

Phrenitis. Inflammation of the brain or its membranes.

Pythisis. Pulmonary consumption.

Pleuritis. Pleurisy, or inflammation of the pleura.

Pneumonia. Inflammation of the lungs.

Podogra. The gout.

Predisposing Cause. That which renders the body susceptible of disease.

Profluvia. Fluxes. The fifth order in the class Pyrexiæ of Cullen's nosology.

Prognosis. The judgment of the event of a disease by particular symptoms.

Pyrexiæ. Febrile diseases. The first class of Cullen's nosology.

Pyrosis. The heart-burn.

Quortan. A fourth day ague.

Quotidian. A daily ague

Rachitis. The rickets.

Refrigerants. Medicines which allay the heat of the body or blood.

Resolution. A termination of febrile and inflammatory affections, in which the diseases disappear without inducing any other disease.

Rheumatismus. Rheumatism.

Rubeola. The measles.

Scarlatina. The scarlet fever.

Stirrhue. An indolent hard tumour.

Scorbutus. Scurvy.

Scrofula. The king's evil.

Sedatives. Those medicines which diminish animal energy, without destroying life.

Spasmi. Spasmodic diseases. The third order of the class Neuroses of Cullen.

Stimulants. Medicines which rouse the animal energy.

Subsultus tendinum. An involuntary movement or leaping of the tendons.

Sincope. A fainting fit.

Synocha. Inflammatory fever.

Synochus. A mixed fever.

Tænia. The tape-worm.

Tertian. A third day's ague.

Tetanus. Spasm with rigidity.

Tinnitus aurium. A ringing in the ear.

Tonics. Medicines which increase the tone of the muscular fibre.

Trichuris. The long hair-worm.

Tympanites. Tympany, or drum-belly.

Typhus. A species of continued fever.

Varicella. The chicken-pox; so called from its being changeable.

Variola. The small-pox.

Vesaniæ. The fourth order of the class Neuroses of Cullen.

Vermicularis. Long and slender like a worm.

Volvulus A twisting of the guts. The iliac passion.

Vomica. An abscess of the lungs.

Urticaria. The nettle-rash.

Urtication. The whipping or stinging with nettles.